SOCIOLOGY

The Key Concepts

Edited by John Scott

Routledge
Taylor & Francis Group

LONDON AND NEW YORK

First published 2006
by Routledge
2 Park Square, Milton Park, Abingdon, Oxon OX14 4RN

Simultaneously published in the USA and Canada
by Routledge
270 Madison Ave, New York, NY 10016

*Routledge is an imprint of the Taylor & Francis Group,
an informa business*

© 2006 John Scott

Typeset in Bembo
by Keystroke, Jacaranda Lodge, Wolverhampton
Printed and bound in Great Britain
by MPG Books Ltd, Bodmin

British Library Cataloguing in Publication Data
A catalogue record for this book is available from the British Library

Library of Congress Cataloging in Publication Data
Sociology : the key concepts / edited by John Scott.
p. cm.
ISBN 0–415–34405–0 (hardback : alk. paper) — ISBN 0–415–34406–9
(pbk : alk. paper) — ISBN 0–203–48832–6 (ebook)
1. Sociology. I. Scott, John, 1949–
HM585.S639 2006
301—dc22

2006012659

ISBN10: 0–415–34405–0 (hbk)
ISBN10: 0–415–34406–9 (pbk)
ISBN10: 0–203–48832–6 (ebk)

ISBN13: 978–0–415–34405–0 (hbk)
ISBN13: 978–0–415–34406–7 (pbk)
ISBN13: 978–0–203–48832–4 (ebk)

SOCIOLOGY

Sociology: The Key Concepts brings together a strong group of well-known experts to review ideas from all areas of this diverse and pluralistic discipline. Exploring the key debates and founding ideas of this exciting field of study, the book is fully cross-referenced and covers such topics as:

- Community
- Childhood
- Emotion
- Discourse
- Race and racialisation
- Modernity
- McDonaldisation
- Gender
- Consumption
- Social capital
- Identity

John Scott is a Professor of Sociology at the University of Essex. His most recent books include *Power* (2001), *Sociology* (with James Fulcher, third edition, 2006) and *Social Theory: Central Issues in Sociology* (2006).

Also available from Routledge

Sociology: The Basics
Martin Albrow
0–415–17264–0

Key Quotations in Sociology
K. Thompson
0–415–05761–2

Cultural Theory: The Key Thinkers
Andrew Edgar and Peter Sedgwick
0–415–23281–3

Cultural Theory: The Key Concepts (Second edition)
Edited by Andrew Edgar and Peter Sedgwick
0–415–28426–0

Habermas: The Key Concepts
Andrew Edgar
0–415–30379–6

The Routledge Companion to Feminism and Postfeminism
Edited by Sarah Gamble
0–415–24310–6

The Routledge Companion to Postmodernism
Edited by Stuart Sim
0–415–33359–8

CONTENTS

LIST OF KEY CONCEPTS

Action and agency
Alienation
Anomie
Bureaucracy
Capitalism
Change and development
Childhood
Citizenship
Civil society
Class
Collective representations
Community
Consumption
Conversation
Cultural capital
Culture
Definition of the situation
Deviance
Discourse
Division of labour
Domestic labour
Elite
Emotion
Ethnicity
Gender
Globalisation
Habitus
Hybridity
Ideology and hegemony
Industrialism

CONTRIBUTORS

Stephen Ackroyd Professor of Organisational Analysis in the University of Lancaster Management School. Specialising in public sector organisations and strategic organisation, his most recent publications include *The Organization of Business: Applying Organizational Theory to Contemporary Change* (Oxford University Press, 2002) and *Critical Realist Applications in Organisation and Management Studies* (with S. Fleetwood, Routledge, 2004).

Alan Aldridge Reader in the Sociology of Culture in the School of Sociology and Social Policy at the University of Nottingham. His publications include *Religion in the Contemporary World* (Polity Press, 2000), *Consumption* (Polity Press, 2003) and *The Market* (Polity Press, 2005).

Meryl Aldridge Reader in the Sociology of News Media in the School of Sociology and Social Policy at the University of Nottingham. Her publications include 'The ties that divide: regional press campaigns, community and populism', *Media, Culture and Society* (2003), 'Rethinking the concept of professionalism: the case of journalism', *British Journal of Sociology* (with J. Evetts, 2003) and 'Teleology on Television? Implicit models of evolution in broadcast wildlife and nature programmes', *European Journal of Communication* (with R. Dingwall, 2003).

Graham Allan Professor of Sociology at the University of Keele, having previously taught at the University of Southampton. His recent publications include *The State of Affairs: Explorations in Infidelity and Commitment* (joint editor with J. Duncombe, K. Harrison and D. Marsden, Erlbaum, 2004), *Social Networks and Social Exclusion* (joint editor with C. Phillipson and D. Morgan, Ashgate, 2004) and *Families, Households and Society* (with Graham Crow, Palgrave, 2001).

Robin Blackburn Professor of Sociology at the University of Essex, having studied and taught at the LSE and Oxford in the 1960s. He has been a member of the editorial committee of *New Left Review* since 1962 and was Editor from 1981 to 1999. He has been consulting editor of Verso since 1970. Research interests include comparative investigations of slavery and of contemporary financial institutions. His publications include *The Making of New World Slavery: From the Baroque to the Modern* (Verso, 1997), *The Overthrow of Colonial Slavery* (Verso, 1988) and *Banking on Death. Or, Investing in Life: The History and Future of Pensions* (Verso, 2002).

Joan Busfield Professor of Sociology at the University of Essex, she trained initially as a clinical psychologist at the Tavistock Clinic. Her research has focused on psychiatry and mental disorder, and her main publications include *Managing Madness: Changing Ideas and Practice* (Hutchinson, 1986), *Men, Women and Madness* (Macmillan, 1996) and *Health and Health Care in Modern Britain* (Oxford University Press, 2000). She is the editor of *Rethinking the Sociology of Mental Health* (Blackwell, 2001).

Eamonn Carrabine Senior Lecturer at the Department of Sociology at the University of Essex. His teaching and research interests lie in the fields of criminology and cultural studies. His books include *Crime in Modern Britain* (with Pamela Cox, Maggy Lee and Nigel South, Oxford University Press, 2002), *Criminology: A Sociological Introduction* (with Paul Iganski, Maggy Lee, Ken Plummer, Nigel South, Routledge, 2004) and *Power, Discourse and Resistance: A Genealogy of the Strangeways Prison Riot* (Ashgate, 2004). He is currently working on a book on *Crime and the Media: Interrogating Representations of Transgression in Popular Culture*.

Nickie Charles Professor and Director of the Centre for the Study of Women and Gender in the Sociology Department at the University of Warwick. She has recently completed a restudy of research into the family and social change carried out in the 1960s in Swansea and is currently working on the book of the project. With colleagues at Swansea she is about to start work on a new, ESRC-funded project, 'Gender and political processes in the context of devolution' which will take devolved government in Wales as a case study. She is the author of *Gender in Modern Britain* (Oxford University Press, 2002).

Amanda Coffey Senior Lecturer at the School of Social Sciences at Cardiff University. Her research interests include young people and transitions to adulthood, education, labour markets and the sociology of gender. Her publications include *Education and Social Change* (Open University Press, 2001) and *Reconceptualizing Social Policy* (Open University Press, 2004).

Robin Cohen Professor of Sociology at the University of Warwick. His notable titles in the field of migration are *Frontiers of Identity: The British and The Others* (1994), *The Cambridge Survey of World Migration* (edited, 1995) and *Global Diasporas: An Introduction* (first published in 1997, with many subsequent editions and translations). His forthcoming book is titled *Migration and its Enemies*.

Graham Crow Professor of Sociology at the University of Southampton, where he has worked since 1983. His research interests include the sociology of families and communities, sociological theory and comparative sociology. His most recent book is *The Art of Sociological Argument* (Palgrave, 2005).

Fiona Devine Professor of Sociology at the University of Manchester, having previously been a Researcher at the Department of Employment and the PSI and taught at the University of Liverpool. She is the author of *Affluent Workers Revisited: Privatism and the Working Class* (Edinburgh University Press, 1992), *Social Class in America and Britain* (Edinburgh University Press, 1997), *Sociological Research Methods in Context* (with Sue Heath, Macmillan, 1999) and *Class Practices: How Parents Help Their Children Get Good Jobs* (Cambridge University Press, 2004).

Jean Duncombe Principal Lecturer at the School of Social Studies at University College Chichester, where she is Head of Childhood Studies and works on issues of family and long-term relationships. She is a member of the editorial board of the journal *Sexualities* and is the joint editor of *The State of Affairs: Explorations in Infidelity and Commitment* (with K. Harrison, G. Allan and D. Marsden, Erlbaum, 2004).

John Field Director of the Division of Academic Innovation and Continuing Education, University of Stirling. His research interests include lifelong learning, vocational education and training and social capital. He is the author of *Social Capital* (Routledge, 2003).

James Fulcher Senior Lecturer in Sociology at the University of Leicester. With John Scott he has recently published *Sociology* (2nd edn, Oxford University Press, 2003) and he is the author of *Capitalism: A Very Short Introduction* (Oxford University Press, 2004).

Miriam Glucksmann Professor of Sociology at the University of Essex, having previously taught at South Bank University, Brunel University and the University of Leicester. Her principal publications include *Structuralist Analysis in Contemporary Social Thought* (Routledge, 1974), *Women on the Line* (as Ruth Cavendish, Routledge, 1982), *Women Assemble: Women Workers and the 'New Industries' in Inter-war Britain* (Routledge, 1990) and *Cottons and Casuals: The Gendered Organisation of Labour in Time and Space* (Sociologypress, 2000).

Chris Harris Emeritus Professor of Sociology at the University of Wales Swansea. His principal publications are *The Family and Social Change* (with Colin Rosser, Routledge and Kegan Paul, 1965), *Family* (Allen and Unwin, 1969), *The Family and Industrial Society* (Allen and Unwin, 1983) and *Kinship* (Open University Press, 1990).

David Howarth Senior Lecturer in Government, University of Essex. He specialises in discourse theory, South African politics and social movements. His publications include *Discourse* (Open University Press, 2000), *South Africa in Transition* (edited with Aletta Norval, Macmillan, 1998) and *Discourse Theory in European Politics: Identity, Policy and Governance* (edited with Jacob Torfing, Palgrave, 2005).

Ian Hutchby Professor of Communication at Brunel University. His work in conversation analysis is widely known and he is the author of, among others, *Confrontation Talk: Arguments, Asymmetries and Power on Talk Radio* (Lawrence Erlbaum Associates, 1996), *Conversation Analysis* (with Robin Wooffitt, Polity, 1998), *Conversation and Technology* (Polity, 2001) and *Media Talk: Conversation Analysis and the Study of Broadcasting* (Open University Press, 2005).

Stevi Jackson Professor and Director of the Centre for Women's Studies, University of York. Her teaching and research interests include feminist theory, theories of gender and sexuality, family relationships and the sociology of childhood. She is the author of *Childhood and Sexuality* (Blackwell, 1982), *Christine Delphy* (Sage, 1996) and *Concerning Heterosexuality* (Sage, 1999), and she is editor of *Contemporary Feminist Theories* (with Jackie Jones, Edinburgh University Press, 1998) and *Gender: A Sociological Reader* (with Sue Scott, Routledge 2002).

Ronald Jacobs Associate Professor of Sociology at the University at Albany, State University of New York. His research explores the relationship between media, public culture and civil society. He is the author of *Race, Media, and the Crisis of Civil Society: From Watts to Rodney King* (Cambridge University Press, 2000).

Ray Kiely Senior Lecturer in Development Studies, SOAS, University of London. His most recent books are *The Clash of Globalizations* (Brill, 2005) and *Empire in the Age of Globalization* (Pluto, 2005).

Jorge Larrain Head of the Department of Social Sciences, Alberto Hurtado University, Santiago, Chile. Former Head of the Department of Cultural Studies and Emeritus Professor of Sociology, University of Birmingham, UK. He is the author of several books on ideology, including *The Concept of Ideology* (Hutchinson, 1979), *Ideology and Cultural Identity: Modernity and the Third World Presence* (Polity Press, 1994) and *Identity and Modernity in Latin America* (Polity Press, 2000).

Maggy Lee Senior Lecturer in the Department of Sociology, University of Essex. Her main areas of research include international migration and trafficking; public and private policing; youth crime and justice. Recent publications include *Youth, Crime and Police Work* (Macmillan, 1998), *Crime in Modern Britain* (with Carrabine *et al.*, Oxford University Press, 2002) and *Criminology: A Sociological Introduction* (with Carrabine *et al.*, Routledge, 2004).

David McCrone Professor of Sociology and Director of the Institute of Governance at Edinburgh University. His early work in urban sociology was followed by research on the sociology of Scotland and the comparative sociology of nationalism and national identity. His books include *The City: Patterns of Domination and Conflict* (with Brian Elliott, Macmillan, 1982), *Property and Power in a City* (with Brian Elliott, Macmillan, 1989), *Scotland the Brand: the Making of Scottish Heritage* (Edinburgh University Press, 1995), *Understanding Scotland: the Sociology of a Nation* (Routledge, 2001; 2nd edn) and *The Sociology of Nationalism: Tomorrow's Ancestors* (Routledge, 1998). With Lindsay Paterson and Frank Bechhofer he has published *Living in Scotland: Social and Economic Changes since 1980* (Edinburgh University Press, 2004).

John MacInnes Reader in Sociology at Edinburgh University and Investigador at the Centre d'Estudis Demogràfics, Universitat Autònoma de Barcelona. When his three-year-old daughter lets him, he researches the gender, national and class dimensions of 'identity', and the relation between demography and sociology. His last book was *The End of Masculinity* (Open University Press, 1998) while his next one, written with with Julio Pérez, is *The Reproductive Revolution* (Routledge, forthcoming).

David Maines Professor of Sociology at Oakland University in Michigan, having previously taught at Wayne State University and Pennsylvania State University. His research interests include urban sociology, stratification, interactionism, narrative. In addition to a number of landmark papers on narrative, including 'Narrative's moment and sociology's phenomena: toward a narrative sociology' (*The Sociological Quarterly* 34, 1993) and 'Writing the self vs writing the other: comparing autobiographical and life history data' (*Symbolic Interaction*, 24, 2001), he is the author of *The Faultline of Consciousness: A View of Interactionism in Sociology* (Aldine de Gruyter, 2001).

Colin Mills University Lecturer in Sociology at the University of Oxford and Fellow of Nuffield College. His interests are in the sociology of work and employment, social stratification, social survey methods and quantitative methods. His most recent book is *Cradle to Grave: Life-Course Change in Modern Sweden* (edited with J. Jonsson, 2001, Sociology press).

Lydia Morris Professor of Sociology at the University of Essex. She is the author of *The Workings of the Household* (Polity Press, 1991), *Dangerous Classes* (Routledge, 1994), *Social Divisions* (UCL Press, 1995) and *Managing Migration* (Routledge, 2002).

Chris Pickvance Professor of Urban Studies at the University of Kent, Canterbury. His books include *State Restructuring and Local Power: Comparative Perspectives* (ed. with E. Preteceille, Pinter, 1990), *Environmental and Housing Movements: Grassroots Experience in Hungary, Estonia and Russia* (ed. with K. Lang-Pickvance and N. Manning, Avebury, 1997) and *Local Environmental Regulation in Post-socialism: A Hungarian Case Study* (Ashgate, 2003).

Lucinda Platt Lecturer in Sociology at the University of Essex. Author of *Parallel Lives? Poverty among Ethnic Minority Groups in Britain* (CPAG, 2002) and *Discovering Child Poverty* (The Policy Press, 2005), her research focuses on ethnic minority disadvantage and on child poverty.

George Ritzer Distinguished University Professor at the University of Maryland. He is best known for his work in social theory and in the application of theory to the social world, especially consumption. His numerous publications include *The McDonaldization of Society* (Pine Forge Press, 1992 and 1996), *The McDonaldization Thesis* (Pine

Forge Press, 1998), *Expressing America* (Pine Forge Press, 1995) and *Enchanting a Disenchanted World: Revolutionizing the Means of Consumption* (Pine Forge Press, 1999). His most recent book is *The Globalization of Nothing* (Pine Forge Press, 2004).

Carlo Ruzza Associate Professor of Sociology at the Università di Trento, having previously taught at Essex University, the University of Surrey and Harvard University. He studies environmentalism, social movements and civil society and is the author of *Europe and Civil Society: Movement Coalitions and European Governance* (Manchester University Press, 2004).

John Scott Professor of Sociology at the University of Essex, having previously been Professor at the University of Leicester. Specialising in social stratification, economic sociology and social theory, his most recent books include *Power* (Polity Press, 2001), *Sociology* (with James Fulcher, second edn, 2003) and *Social Theory: Central Issues in Sociology* (Sage, 2006).

Susie Scott Lecturer in Sociology at the University of Sussex, with research interests in interaction, performance and everyday life. Her publications include various articles on shyness and a forthcoming book, *Shyness and Society* (Palgrave, 2007).

Leslie Sklair Professor of Sociology at the London School of Economics and Political Science. His recent books include *The Transnational Capitalist Class* (Blackwell, 2001) and *Globalization: Capitalism and its Alternatives* (3rd edn, Oxford University Press, 2002). These and other books have been translated into seven languages. He is Vice-President for Sociology of the Global Studies Association.

Stephen Small Associate Professor of African American Studies at University of California, Berkeley. He has previously taught at the University of Massachusetts, Amherst, and at the Universities of Warwick and Leicester. His recent publications include *Representations of Slavery. Race and Ideology in Southern Plantation Museums* (co-written with Jennifer Eichstedt, Smithsonian Institution Press, 2002) and *Race and Power: Global Racism in the Twenty-First Century* (co-written with Gargi Bhattacharyya and John Gabriel, Routledge, 2004).

Rob Stones Senior Lecturer in Sociology at the University of Essex. His research interests include social theory and structuration theory in particular, documentary and fiction films in relation to the public sphere, and the nature of experience in late modernity. He has published *Structuration Theory* (Palgrave, 2004) and *Sociological Reasoning: Towards a Past-modern Sociology* (Macmillan, 1996) and he has edited *Key Sociological Thinkers* (Macmillan, 1998).

Piotr Sztompka Professor of Theoretical Sociology at the Jagiellonian University at Krakow, Poland, and the current President of the International Sociological Association (ISA). He is the author of *Trust: A Sociological Theory* (Cambridge University Press, 1999) and co-author of *Cultural Trauma and Collective Identity* (with Jeffrey C. Alexander, Ron Eyerman, Bernhard Giesen and Neil J. Smelser, University of California Press, 2004).

John Urry Professor of Sociology at Lancaster University. His most recent publications include *Sociology Beyond Societies* (Polity, 2000), *Bodies of Nature* (co-edited with Phil Mcnaghten, Sage, 2001), *The Tourist Gaze. Second Edition* (Sage, 2002), *Global Complexity* (Polity, 2003), *Tourism Mobilities* (co-edited with Mimi Sheller, Routledge, 2004), *Performing Tourist Places* (with Jørgen Ole Bærenholdt, Michael Haldrup, Jonas Larsen 2004) and *Automobilities* (edited with Mike Featherstone and Nigel Thrift, Sage, 2005).

Sylvia Walby Professor in the Department of Sociology, Lancaster University. She has been Professor of Sociology at the Universities of Leeds and Bristol. Her books include: *Gender Transformations* (Routledge, 1997), *Theorizing Patriarchy* (Blackwell, 1990), *Patriarchy at Work* (Polity Press, 1986) and *Complex Social Systems: Theorizations and Comparisons in a Global Era* (Sage, 2006 forthcoming).

Pnina Werbner Professor of Social Anthropology at Keele University. Her authored books include the 'Migration trilogy' (*The Migration Process*, Berg, 1990/2002, *Imagined Diasporas*, James Currey/ SAR, 2002 and *Pilgrims of Love: The Anthropology of a Global Sufi Cult*, Hurst, 2003). She has edited and written extensively on citizenship, multiculturalism and cultural hybridity, and she is currently researching women and the changing public sphere in Botswana.

INTRODUCTION

Sociology is a diverse and pluralistic discipline. There are a variety of
socially located standpoints, each with its own truths and an equal right
to be heard in sociological debates. For this reason, no single and
coherent body of ideas acceptable to all practitioners can be set down.
Many commentators have drawn the conclusion that sociological
concepts are, therefore, 'essentially contested': that there can be no
agreed and binding definition of any of the principal concepts used by
sociologists in their research. This would seem to pose serious problems
for anyone attempting to compile a dictionary or glossary of sociological
concepts: can there be any agreement over what are the 'key' concepts
and how they should be defined?

This is not, however, the counsel of despair that it might seem. The
diversity and plurality of sociology is one of the things that gives it its
attraction as a discipline – there is nothing quite like a good argument
and a gathering of sociologists is guaranteed to provide many. More than
this, however, the range and scope of conceptual disagreement is not as
great as might be feared. Sociology may – like Mao's over-optimistic
view of Chinese intellectual life – 'let a thousand flowers bloom', but the
concepts that bloom in the sociological world are drawn from a relatively
small number of theoretical positions and these are far from being
incommensurable with each other. Sociological theories are not derived
from isolated and hermetically sealed worldviews: they overlap and inter-
penetrate in a whole variety of ways and there are many hybrid and
composite theories that combine elements from a number of approaches.

Our theories are plural standpoints on an independently existing
reality that can never be known as it really is, in all its complexity. We
always select what we are interested in from a particular standpoint, and
the standpoints from which we build our theories are located within the
very social world that we study. Nevertheless, the various views taken
of this reality, taken together, can provide a more comprehensive picture

of the social world than any one can provide on its own. Each perspective has its validity and authenticity within the larger picture. The variety of perspectives that we can take towards a physical landscape are authentic descriptions of the landscape from the particular standpoints adopted, and the same is true of our perspectives on the social world. Just as we attain a wider understanding of the landscape when we recognise the diversity of perspectives from which it can be seen and attempt to understand the limitations of each, so we can move towards a combination of divergent sociological perspectives. This combination of perspectives occurs through dialogue. It is through such dialogue and debate that the limitations of each perspective can be appreciated and more comprehensive understandings can be formulated.

The concepts available for sociological use, therefore, reflect the currently achieved outcome of such dialogues. 'Essentially contested' in principle, sociological concepts are actually contested in the empirically oriented practice of cooperating and communicating professionals. Conceptual innovation occurs not simply within a particular theoretical approach but within a particular state of disciplinary dialogue. The development of sociological knowledge may not be neatly cumulative – indeed, this is not even the case in the natural sciences – but the development of the discipline has seen the building of islands of conceptual agreement that form the vast archipelago of understanding.

It is from this basis that my selection of key concepts has been made. I have attempted to identify concepts from all areas of the discipline and to choose those that are sufficiently broad and general to have a wide application and relevance. Nevertheless, the number of such concepts is immense and some way of selecting the 'key' concepts had to be adopted. My initial long list of concepts was circulated to a number of friends and colleagues, especially those from the large and intellectually diverse department in which I work at the University of Essex. These colleagues were asked to indicate which concepts they would add to my list and which they regarded as of greater and lesser importance. These comments and suggestions helped me to reduce the list to a manageable length for a book in which the various contributors could say something sensible and useful about the various concepts and in which the whole adds up to something greater than the individual parts.

Each contributor to the book was chosen as a leading sociologist in their area, and they have generally sought to indicate the range of agreement and disagreement that surrounds the various concepts. They were, however, encouraged to express their own views and interpretations. The final selection, however, is mine and reflects my view of the current state of the discipline. Many will, no doubt, disagree with my selection, but I am comforted by the assured knowledge that anybody else's selection would raise equally strong objections. As the old saying goes, 'you can't please all of the people all of the time'. I hope, however, that I have managed to please a large number of people for at least some of the time.

No selection can avoid making arbitrary decisions, simply because of the lack of space to include the many more concepts that could have been considered. The book embodies my selection of what I regard as the *key* concepts in sociology today, even though I may, like many other contributors, disagree with some of the conclusions drawn. I have felt uncomfortable about excluding many concepts that others will regard as important or essential. In many cases, however, such concepts appear indirectly within other entries. I have, for example, included an entry on masculinity but not one on femininity. These are closely related concepts and both are alluded to in the general discussions of gender and sexuality. Many of the issues raised in relation to the study of masculinity relate also to femininity, but masculinity is, at the moment, the focus of the most far-reaching debates and seemed the obvious concept to include. I am sure that readers will find other, equally arbitrary, choices, but I hope that it will be realised that such choices are inevitable and that many 'missing' concepts appear in and through related entries. The book provides the tools that are needed to discuss these questions and to problematise the narratives offered. The concepts chosen are among the most important available for sociological work and they must figure in any serious discussion of contemporary societies.

The bulk of the book comprises an A to Z listing of the key concepts, each discussion being followed by a selection of further reading for those who wish to pursue the issue at greater length. I have included cross-references between entries – indicated in bold – to help you to navigate around the text, but I have not attempted to cross-refer all the numerous uses of the concepts in the various entries. Entries generally indicate the main contributors to the debates around each concept. Where their works have not been included in the *Further Reading*, they should be easily identifiable through author searches in library catalogues and online resources. The book ends with a glossary of the key theoretical perspectives current in sociology. The list is not exhaustive but covers the main theories that figure in debates over the concepts explored in the main part of the book. These glossary entries give merely the beginning of an account of theoretical disputes, and interested readers will find the ideas of the key theorists examined in two companion volumes, *50 Key Sociologists: The Formative Theorists* and *50 Key Sociologists: The Contemporary Theorists*.

Further reading

Levine, Donald N. (1995) *Visions of the Sociological Tradition*. Chicago: University of Chicago Press.

Scott, John (1998) 'Relationism, cubism, and reality: beyond relativism' in Tim May and Malcolm Williams (eds) *Knowing the Social World*. Buckingham: Open University Press.

SOCIOLOGY

The Key Concepts

ACTION AND AGENCY

At the most elemental level, action refers simply to the practices of human beings: to what they do. At a more complex level it can refer not just to individuals but also to the practices of collective actors, those sharing characteristics, such as being members of a particular class, age group, gender, or other social categories such as the homeless, the unemployed and so on. Collective actors can, in turn, be distinguished from what Margaret Archer in *Realist Social Theory* calls corporate agents. These are groups of actors who have organised themselves around certain interests in order to pursue strategic interests. They typically articulate shared interests, organise for collective action and can often command serious attentions in decision-making arenas. No matter which category they belong to, actors possess a capacity for action. Agency is the dynamic element within an actor that translates potential capacity into actual practice.

Action and agency are typically contrasted with **social structures** that are seen as the constraining and/or enabling social conditions in which action takes place. Much debate revolves around this relation. From the early days of sociology, however, there has also been a close interest in the constitution of actors and action *per se*. Weber, for example, distinguished between four different types of social action: instrumentally rational action geared towards 'the attainment of the actor's own rationally pursued and calculated ends'; value-rational action pursued for reasons of personally held values, irrespective of the prospects for success of that action; affective action determined by the actor's emotional states and orientations; and traditional action 'determined by ingrained habituation'. Later theorists have elaborated on, connected and developed these different forms of action.

In an influential account of theories of social action, Alan Dawe had noted a theoretical tension between those theories that emphasised social order, and hence the structural or systemic constraints on actors, and those that stressed the elements of creative and dynamic agency. To account for the reproduction of relatively stable social circumstances major theorists such as Talcott Parsons ultimately allowed their concern with action and agency to be drowned out by more structural concerns with the effects of social norms, sanctions and regulations. This was a tendency also associated with French structuralism: structures were presented too much as if they moulded, constrained and determined action. In the late 1960s and 1970s, critiques began to emerge of the excessive emphasis on order as theorists placed more emphasis on how actors played a creative and active part in social life. Dennis Wrong criticised the Parsonian emphasis on the power of structures by labelling it an 'oversocialised conception' of actors that overstated their relative autonomy. This is a theme that has been rigorously elaborated recently by Archer, most extensively in *Being Human* (2000). This argument was pursued in discussions of **roles** and role behaviour.

Two overlapping approaches to action and agency emerged. The first, that of pragmatism and symbolic interactionism, includes George Mead, Herbert Blumer, and Erving Goffman. The second, that of neo-Kantianism and phenomenology includes Weber, Alfred Schütz, Peter Berger and Thomas Luckmann, and Harold Garfinkel. Mead and Blumer emphasised the reflection, reflexivity and creativity inherent in the very process of interaction itself, and in the making of selves. Schutz, and also Berger and Luckmann, drew attention to the store-house of preconceptions, including typifications of objects and people, and the various recipe knowledges of standard types of practices that actors carry around with them and draw upon in appropriate circumstances. Garfinkel highlighted the array of competencies, skills and moral commitments that are intrinsic to the routine accomplishments of actors. Goffman, like Garfinkel, emphasised the part played by tacit knowledge in the production of social practices.

The phenomenological and symbolic interactionist traditions also came under criticism, however, on the grounds that they neglected structural pressures on action. Many theorists sought a middle way of some kind. **Rational action** theorists, for example, although often criticised for paying too much attention to actors' instrumental purposes and intentions, have increasingly stressed the influence on action of structural constraints related to resources and institutional norms. These emergent critiques have since led to an increasingly sophisticated middle way conception of actors, action and agency in the works of Anthony Giddens and Pierre Bourdieu. This emphasis on 'structuration' has further elaborated the internal constitution and dynamics of actors and has focused on the profound but subtle ways in which the external world affects these.

It is most productive to think of these developments, however, within a frame also inhabited by two other emphases that have matured over these years. The first is the emphasis on networks. For network analysts themselves, the focus is on regularities in how people and collectivities behave and on patterns of ties linking the members of social structures together. The essential wider point is that all actors are caught up in a web of relationships that can be facilitating or constraining depending on circumstances. Action takes place in the midst of social relations, practices and structures. The second part of the frame involves the conceptualisation of 'actants', in which individual actors are no longer seen as bounded by the human body. Writers such as Donna Haraway and Bruno Latour have insisted that machines, from automobiles to computer networks, are vital and significant functioning parts of actors, and increasingly so, hence the coining of 'actants' to capture this. Actors, it is said, are parts of human-machine networks of social flows, of communication, money, fluids and so on, that radically challenge what it means to be an actor.

This is the frame within which we should ideally now read the middle way conception of actors that was developed most prominently by Giddens and Bourdieu in the first instance. Both, in turn, are heavily influenced by phenomenology in general, and by Alfred Schütz, Harold Garfinkel and Erving Goffman, in particular. The latter's insightful cameos prefigured their work by drawing attention to the ways in which agential knowledge was permeated by external social norms. All of these writers stress the powerful sense individual agents have that others expect them to behave in manners appropriate to the imme- diate social context. Bourdieu, Giddens, and also Jürgen Habermas, each combine a concern with the stocks of knowledge possessed by agents with an emphasis on the social origins and grounding of agents' knowledgeability and generalised dispositions. The key mediating concepts are **habitus** for Bourdieu, 'practical consciousness' for Giddens and the phenomenological 'lifeworld' for Habermas. Social relations 'out-there' are seen as having entered 'in-here' into the actor. Giddens refers to this as a 'duality' of structure and agency, and a large part of what he means by duality is that the internal constitution of actors themselves already involves the imprint, phenomenologically mediated, of external social structures. Actors are seen as having inter- nalised notions of the **power** relations and normative sanctions that exist in the immediate social context in which they will act. They also possess a set of more generalised practical and ideological dispositions and orientations, inherited from the past, that provide them with the phenomenological frames of meaning that guide their actions in those more specific immediate situations.

Most recently there has been something of a backlash against what was seen as too exclusive an emphasis on the inextricable links between the 'out-there' of social structure and the 'in-here' of actors. Archer and Nicos Mouzelis insisted that one should be able to create a stronger conceptual distinction between external structures, on the one hand, and actors, agency and action, on the other. It is possible, however, to accept this whilst still accepting the essential points about duality. Refinements elsewhere have converged in emphasising the inner temporality and phenomenology of agency and actions, and the significance of the empirical level. In France Luc Boltanski and Laurent Thévenot have shown how actors can switch between different frameworks and principles of justification within the very same social setting depending upon how a given situation is defined. In parallel, Mustafa Emirbayer and Ann Mische's highly influential article 'What is agency?' was a synthesis that drew on a combination of pragmatism, phenomenology and a wide range of empirical studies to distinguish three major constitutive elements of human agency. These were: first, the 'iterational' element of agency, which is very close to Bourdieu's notion of habitus, in which past patterns of thought and action are selectively and tacitly reactivated in relevant circumstances and are routinely incorporated into practical activity; second, the 'projective' element, which encompasses actors' use of creativity and invention to imagine a range of possible future trajectories of action; and third, the 'practical-evaluative' element which involves situationally based judgements about how to act 'in response to emerging demands, dilemmas, and ambiguities of presently evolving situations'. This approach overlapped, in turn, with many of the concepts developed in debates over structuration theory in Europe and the US during the last fifteen years. Whilst the emphasis on imagination, play and the temporal positing of possibilities – extending the work of authors such as Hans Joas and Jeffrey Alexander – is very distinctive, the creative distancing from the routine expectations of habitus that is emphasised in the 'projective element' of agency echoes Mouzelis's explication of a continuum in which actors can have a more or less critical distance from their situation and from the routine dispositions they bring to it. Also, Mouzelis's distinctions between the dispositional (habitus or iterational element), the positional (roles and role-relationships) and the situational-interactional (the practical-evaluative arena), overlap in a mutually enriching way with the concepts presented by Emirbayer and Mische.

Further reading

Archer, Margaret (1995) *Realist Social Theory: A Morphogenetic Approach.* Cambridge: Cambridge University Press.

Boltanski, Luc and Thévenot, Laurent (1999) 'The sociology of critical capacity', *European Journal of Social Theory*, 2, 3: 359–77.

Dawe, Alan (1978) 'Theories of social action', in T. Bottomore and R. Nisbet (eds) *A History of Sociological Analysis.* New York: Basic Books.

Emirbayer, Mustafa and Mische, Ann (1998) 'What is agency?' *American Journal of Sociology*, 103, 4: 962–1023.

Mouzelis, Nicos (1991) *Back to Sociological Theory: The Construction of Social Orders*. London: Macmillan.

Stones, Rob (2005) *Structuration Theory*. London: Palgrave Macmillan.

Rob Stones

ALIENATION

The term alienation entered philosophy with the work of Hegel, and social thought with that of Marx. Marx transformed Hegel's idea into a description of a state and a process whereby men lose themselves and their labour in **capitalism**. Marx takes the term principally from the philosophical debates of the Young Hegelians, though he would certainly have been aware of an echo from legal theory where a similar term describes the transmission of property from one person to another in a legally sanctioned contract of simultaneous loss and gain.

For the Young Hegelians, **religion** was the quintessential expression of alienation because men created and sustained the world of religious belief and authority but then saw it as something external or alien to themselves. Young Hegelians like Ludwig Feuerbach were themselves adding a critical twist to Hegel's own use of the term. For Hegel the development of the 'World Spirit' of mind or **culture** involves successively greater phases of freedom from alienation. Another way of stating this is to say that the given character of the natural world ('creation') is one of alienation, while the growth of human religious awareness is a process of dis-alienation. For Hegel the dialectic of alienation and dis-alienation is intrinsic to the whole of human existence and can be seen in the experience of labour no less than in the progress of civilisation. According to Feuerbach, religion was part of the problem, not the solution, since it is humans who develop religious concepts only to abase themselves before these alienated expressions of their own mental processes.

Marx adopted Feuerbach's critical reversal of Hegel, but extended it to the whole of political and economic life in emerging bourgeois society. For him, the **state** and capitalist private property were alienated social forms just as much as the world of religious belief and organisation. Indeed, he saw the primary alienation as the alienation of the worker. **Class** relations are relations of alienation. The wage worker is deprived of ownership of his or her means of production, and is hence in an unequal bargaining position vis-à-vis the capitalist employer. This allows the capitalist to dominate the process of production and to appropriate the workers' product. While the capitalist pays wages to the worker his command of the working enterprise will enable him to generate a surplus.

It did not escape Marx's attention that human productive labour that is not directly oriented to satisfying the producer's own needs will always involve the producer creating a product over which he loses control. And in a fundamental sense all production involves what might be called 'objectivation', the creation of something new that is relatively autonomous from the producer, without this necessarily being a process of alienation or estrangement. The production and exchange process is alienated when it escapes the control of the direct producer – as happens under capitalism, where the decisive means of production are privately owned. Producing for others' consumption is fine so long as this is the result of a conscious agreement and a consciously chosen scheme of exchange.

For Marx labour was an expression, perhaps the highest expression, of human nature (he called this 'species being'). For the labourer to lose control over this essential human activity was bound to lead to many other expressions of an alienated social order: growing inequality, poverty in the midst of plenty, social antagonism and class struggle, booms and slumps. Indeed even the capitalists were caught up in, and suffered from, this estrangement as they sought to drive one another out of existence.

For Marx, then, alienation is a loss of **self**, which he explains in the 1844 *Economic and Philosophical Manuscripts* as follows:

> the fact that labour is external to the worker, i.e. does not belong to his essential being, that he therefore does not confirm himself in his work, but denies himself, feels miserable and not happy, does not develop free mental and physical energy, but mortifies his flesh and ruins his mind. Hence the worker feels himself only when not working . . . feels that he is acting freely only in his animal functions – eating, drinking, and procreating or at most in his dwelling and adornment . . . It is true that eating, drinking and procreating are genuine human functions. However when abstracted from other aspects of human activity and turned into final and exclusive ends, they are animal.

Hence, for Marx **consumption** as well as production can suffer from alienation.

Marx clearly believed that there were psychological correlates to the state of alienation but it would be wrong to construe the concept itself as one essentially applying to subjective states. Many have, therefore, contrasted it with Durkheim's account of the **anomie** – a sense of normlessness and disorientation – which accompanies increasing division of labour. Notwithstanding the passage quoted above Marx was aware that some alienated social agents could for a time feel happy in their alienation. During an upswing in the trade cycle, the worker might welcome the chance to earn more and to afford little luxuries for the family. But at root such a worker would still be alienated, just as was the satisfied bourgeois or the enraptured religious believer. Herbert Marcuse and other writers in the Frankfurt School were later to chronicle many ways in which there could be an alienated 'happy consciousness'. These critiques are closer to the spirit of Marx's analysis than the attempt by some sociologists to operationalise the concept of alienation as a tool for interrogating worker attitudes, as in Robert Blauner's much cited *Alienation and Freedom*. Since concepts cannot be patented, however, attempts to pin down the psychological dimensions of alienation or estrangement have their place. Blauner separated out four psychological dimensions of alienation – powerlessness, mean-inglessness, isolation and self-estrangement. So far as the workplace is concerned the intensity of alienation starts low with the craft worker, rises with industrialised line work and piece work, and hypothetically declines in the post-industrial world of work.

Marx himself evidently felt the need to pursue his analysis of the world of alienated labour using a more differentiated and institutional language. The term alienation appears more sporadically in Marx's later writings. However his account of the accumulation process and its consequences under capitalism still often echoes idea that he is dealing with a world of estrangement. Marx insisted that the worker sold not a specific labour but rather 'labour power' whose precise articulation would be determined by the employer, enabling the latter to extract surplus value. Once this surplus value had been realised, it returned to renew the dominion of the capitalist over the employees.

Marx has a sharp analysis of alienation and the world of wage labour but he is less clear about what would constitute dis-alienation, though 'self-emancipation of the working class' and 'rule by the associated producers' cover some of the ground. And whereas in his early writings his references to capitalism and the market are almost wholly negative, in the *Communist Manifesto* and subsequent writings he sees an unfolding potential for progress in capitalist development creating sources of productivity and cooperation that will allow the associated producers to suppress the alienation of capitalist private property.

Further reading

Blauner, Robert (1964) *Alienation and Freedom*. Chicago: University of Chicago Press.

Marcuse, Herbert (1941) *Reason and Revolution*. London: Routledge and Kegan Paul.

Marx, Karl (1844) 'Economic and philosophical manuscripts', in *Early Writings*, with an introduction by Lucio Colletti. Harmondsworth: Penguin, 1973.

Meszaros, Istvan (1970) *Karl Marx's Theory of Alienation*. London: Merlin Press.

Robin Blackburn

ANOMIE

Often discussed alongside Marx's concept of **alienation**, anomie in fact describes quite a different social condition. Anomie is the central concept in Durkheim's account of the consequences of a breakdown in cultural regulation and the institutional structure. It was taken up by structural functionalists as the key to understanding some of the key problems of modernity, and in the work of Robert Merton it was seen as the outcome of very specific processes integral to the modern social order.

Although the word has a long history, a sociological concept of anomie was first outlined by Durkheim in his discussion of the **division of labour**. In this book he showed that social differentiation could proceed more rapidly than normative regulation and so leave individual actions uncontrolled by shared norms. He saw this, along with 'egoism', as a factor responsible for economic dislocations and **class** conflict and held that these problems would be eliminated only when full 'organic solidarity' had been achieved. Although he saw individualism as a central characteristic of modern societies, he saw egoism and anomie as 'pathological' forms of individualism. True moral individualism involved the regulation of individuals' desires by social constraints.

It was in his discussion of suicide, however, that Durkheim fully developed this idea in the form that has become a central feature of sociological explanation. His theory of suicide held that variations in suicide rates could be explained by variations in the level of social solidarity. Low levels of solidarity and excessively strong levels of solidarity are equally likely to result in high rates of suicide. Durkheim distinguished between 'integration' and 'regulation' as the two dimensions of social **solidarity**. By integration he meant the strength of the attachment that a person has to social groups, and he measured this on a scale from 'egoism' to 'altruism'. By regulation, on the other hand, he meant the degree to which group norms are able to control the desires and aspirations of people, and he measured this on a scale from 'anomie' to 'fatalism'. His general account of the problems of social solidarity explored all of these and led to his identification of four types of suicide: egoistic suicide and anomic suicide (both resulting from low levels of solidarity) and altruistic suicide and fatalistic suicide (resulting from high levels of solidarity).

Anomic suicide was that form of suicide that resulted from the lack of normative regulation that Durkheim described as anomie, a condition of normlessness or the absence of any regulation by shared norms. His assumption was that human beings could only be content if their needs and passions were regulated and controlled by social norms. Left to themselves, they would have no standards by which to judge their achievements and would be constantly striving to attain more. Only **socialisation** into a normative order would bring their desires and their circumstances into balance with each other. Anomie, then is the breakdown of normative regulation that results in the expansion of unregulated and limitless desires. Irritation, disappointment and frustration are the typical psychological consequences of anomie, and suicide was seen as a likely outcome for many in this condition as they would never be satisfied with their position in life. Their desires and ambitions get out of control and people are easily upset by their inability to achieve them. Further insight into anomie was gained by exploring the polar state of fatalism, where normative regulation is so tight that individuals have no freedom of choice and must subject themselves completely to established social standards of behaviour. In these circumstances, people are characterised by acceptance and resignation and Durkheim saw suicide occurring as an expression of group values – as may be the case with, for example, suicide bombers.

Anomie, then, is that aspect of the breakdown of social solidarity that results from a weakness or absence of shared norms and of socialisation into these norms. Robert Merton explored this further by distinguishing a number of different forms that anomie can take. First is the situation described by Durkheim, where there is an absence of norms and individual behaviour is unregulated and unrestrained. Second, there is the situation in which there are incompatibilities and contradictions between the norms that are promoted in different institutional spheres. In such a situation, individuals are given no clear guidance and must make their own choices between the alternatives. Anthony Giddens has recently argued that this situation is integral to the 'ontological insecurity' and 'existential anxiety' that is experienced by individuals in the pluralistic societies of late modernity.

The third form of anomie identified by Merton, and the one to which he gives the greatest attention, is where there is a cultural disjunction between the *ends* or goals that are promoted and the *means* that people are expected to follow in achieving them. Merton saw this condition of anomie existing wherever there is an imbalance between culturally approved ends and means and, in consequence, an incomplete socialisation of individuals into established normative standards. Conformity is far less likely to occur as individuals lack any strong commitment to cultural standards and are more likely to be swayed by self-interest. This possibility is most likely wherever the actual structure of opportunities that is available to people makes it difficult or impossible for them to achieve the approved ends through legitimate means. They may desire what other members of their society hold out to them as goals to pursue, but their lack of resources precludes them from achieving these goals by conforming with social norms to which they have no strong commitment. Merton, like Durkheim, saw this latter condition of anomie as particularly characteristic of modern societies such as the United States. The individualism of modern culture places great stress on the need to maximise income through diligence and application in a chosen occupation. A high salary is seen as the means for securing high levels of personal and family consumption. Individuals are, however, rather weakly socialised into the accepted ways of achieving these goals and many may find that their position in the distribution of resources is such that they cannot compete on an equal basis in this race for financial success. They may, for example, be disadvantaged by their **class**, **gender**, or **ethnicity**, which set limits on the life chances that they are able to enjoy.

Merton identified four possible responses to this form of anomie, as shown in the diagram opposite.

Innovation occurs where a person's response to these cultural strains involves rejecting the legitimate means and turning to illegitimate ones. Merton saw this as typical of those situations in which financial gain is pursued through criminal activities rather than through employment and promotion in a conventional organisation. He saw this as the most likely response of those who are poor and have few opportunities for legitimate gain. It is also, however, the response of those who are relatively successful, but who engage in fraud and embezzlement to increase their income. *Ritualism* occurs where there is little possibility

	Commitment to	
	ends	means
Innovation	+	−
Ritualism	−	+
Retreatism	−	−
Rebellion	±	±

+ acceptance
− rejection
± rejection of dominant values and acceptance of alternative values

that any significant success can be achieved and people simply abandon the attempt. It is distinguished by the fact that they nevertheless follow the conventional means in a purely ritualistic way. His example is the time-serving bureaucrat or 'jobsworth' who rigidly follows rules and procedures with no regard for their consequences. *Retreatism* is a response involving a rejection of both the prescribed means and the ends. Merton sees this as marking the hobo or vagrant who has 'dropped out' of conventional society. The final response, *rebellion*, occurs where people reject the legitimate ends and means but replace them with alternatives that pose a challenge to conventional ideas. His example is radical political action that aims at transforming the distribution of resources or the political system.

Durkheim saw high levels of anomie associated with high levels of suicide and class conflict. Merton saw it as also associated with high levels of innovation, ritualism, retreatism and rebellion. Both writers, therefore, saw deviance and class conflict as consequences of the anomie of modern society, of a failure to build an integrated cultural system and to socialise individuals into it.

Further reading

Clinard, Marshall (ed.) (1968) *Anomie and Deviant Behaviour*. New York: Free Press.

Durkheim, Émile (1897) *Suicide: A Study in Sociology*. London: Routledge and Kegan Paul, 1952.

Merton, Robert (1938) 'Social structure and anomie', in R. Merton, *Social Theory and Social Structure*. New York: Free Press, 1968.

John Scott

BUREAUCRACY

Bureaucracy is a developed form of large-scale administrative **organisation** that is present in advanced capitalism, and is sometimes taken to be characteristic of it. However, as Weber showed, bureaucracy is not restricted to capitalism. Bureaucracy develops in and reinforces a monopoly of provision. Thus, bureaucracy developed in the Catholic Church and in association with the state in various places (such as pre-modern China). It was only in the early twentieth century that bureaucracy developed in capitalist society in the form of large-scale industrial enterprises and the welfare state.

Many people have written about bureaucracy, but none, before or since, have made a contribution comparable to Weber's. His work delineated a perceptive model of bureaucracy and also analysed its impact on economy and society. For Weber, bureaucracy has some distinctive structural characteristics and also some internal features that interlock with these. The structural characteristics of bureaucracy include its centralised and unambiguous pattern of authority with many hierarchical levels, an elaborate division of labour between officials and extensive specialisation of their activities. Underpinning such structures is the central feature of bureaucracy: an elaborate system of rules, usually backed by law. These rules dictate the conduct of officials and the procedures they must follow, and they make the bureaucracy machine-like and predictable in operation. Elaborate rules ensure that the bureaucracy is marked by impersonality, and this makes it unlike other social regimes, such as patrimonialism or patriarchalism (see **tradition and traditionalism**). Bureaucrats are selected and promoted because of their qualifications and knowledge of official rules and case files (and strictly not because of any personal connections). For this reason, bureaucracy also entails high levels of education for the administrative elite, and at least literacy for other participants. Weber saw bureaucracy as being machine like and highly effective. He thought it would take over more and more areas of social organisation with fateful consequences.

The examples of bureaucracy mentioned above include the most enduring **institutions** in history. The Chinese state existed in broadly the same way for millennia, whilst the Catholic Church is probably the most enduring of all Western organisations. Clearly, bureaucracy can provide order and stability. By the same token, bureaucracy is not adaptable and it was not long after the establishment of societies dominated by bureaucratic organisations in the West that sociologists took note of its damaging effects. At the same time as Weber delineated the features of bureaucracy, Roberto Michels identified its tendency to concentrate power in the hands of a ruling oligarchy, and argued that such forms always drive out elements of democracy. Robert Merton, like Weber, formed a very unfavourable view of the effects of bureaucracy on the personalities of its personnel. Empirical studies such as those of Alvin Gouldner and Michel Crozier, however, showed that, in practice, bureaucracies were not totally unresponsive to internal movements and external pressures. Indeed, as Weber asserted, bureaucracy can be efficient, as large-scale and bureaucratically organised industry allowed mass production (sometimes called Fordism) to develop and this, in turn, contributed greatly to the prosperity of the developed world. In the long run, bureaucracy did not lead to bureaucratic gridlock, as Weber feared. One reason for this was that mass production also created consumers who want high quality and differentiated products that bureaucratised industry is too inflexible to supply. Thus, production had to become less bureaucratic. In this way, despite its superior efficiency compared with traditional patterns, industrial bureaucracy undermined the conditions for its own long-term dominance.

Today it is widely suggested that bureaucracy is being dismantled. However critics have not identified new principles of organisation. Charles Heckscher and Anne Donnelon's influential work on 'post-bureaucracy', for example, suggests that bureaucracy has been transcended, but their proposed new organisational configuration merely amends or negates the attributes of bureaucracy without proposing new organisational principles. It is true that organisations (but not firms) are becoming smaller, and thus some bureaucratic features (such as large scale, numerous levels of hierarchy and extended division of labour) are less evident. Yet it is still plausible to think that bureaucracy is not so much being removed as supplemented by additional control processes including surveillance. The result is recognisably a version of bureaucracy, and this form of organisation has not so much been dismantled as partially reconfigured.

Further reading

Clawson, Dan (1980) *Bureaucracy and the Labour Process*. New York: Monthly Review Press.

Crozier, Michel (1964) *The Bureaucratic Phenomenon*. Chicago: University of Chicago Press.

Gouldner, Alvin (1954) *Patterns of Industrial Bureaucracy*. New York: Collier Macmillan.

Heckscher, Charles and Donnellon, Anne (eds) (1993) *The Post-Bureaucratic Organisation*. London: Sage Publications.

Stephen Ackroyd

CAPITALISM

Capitalism is a system of economy, and form of **society**, characterised by generalised commodity production, in which all economic relations are monetised and the boundary of the economic itself expands to include all aspects of life. Capitalism as a system of economy can be distinguished from earlier economic forms where buying and selling – and long distance trade – might have been quite important but in which most of the labour of direct production of goods and services required for everyday life was not itself a commodity, that is to say the labourer received no wage or salary. Typically both slaves and serfs were forced to work for their master or lord, delivering surplus product, or sometimes rent in the case of the serf, to the former and receiving no remuneration for this. Prior to the sixteenth century wage labour, as now understood, was quite rare. Signs of an incipiently capitalist management of trading or manufacturing enterprises are not unknown – some argue that medieval European monasteries played this role or that the merchants of South China were beginning to behave in capitalist ways, but the early shoots of capitalist development were always vulnerable to the predatory claims of the **state** with its thirst for revenue. However, in some parts of North Western Europe – notably the Low Countries and England – capitalist social relations spread in the sixteenth and seventeenth centuries, based, especially in the English case, on capitalist agriculture as well as trade and manufacture and leading to what some have called a capitalist **world system**.

Robert Brenner has argued that it was the characteristic structure of social relations in the English countryside that permitted capitalist growth to acquire a critical mass sufficient to begin to dominate a whole social formation. Tenant farmers owed rent to landlords, a circumstance that impelled them to produce goods for sale (wheat, wool, etc.). Lacking sufficient dependants to expand production they hired labourers and had an incentive to adopt methods of farming and processing that raised labour productivity. By contrast, those with an available pool of dependent labour have often opted to squeeze their dependants harder as the main route to expanding output and revenue. A further feature of wage labour is that – together with the growth of rent, fees and salaries – it creates a wider internal market. While this way of organising economic relations proved to be very dynamic, it is not particularly 'natural'.

The classical political economy of Adam Smith and other writers achieved considerable insight into the characteristics of capitalism as a system of competitive production whose results could be different from the motivation of the particular agents present within it. But they did not rigorously explore either the social pre-conditions, or the mentalities, that conduced to the rise of 'commercial society' (as they called it). This aspect of matters was most thoroughly addressed by Karl Marx and Max Weber using the words capitalist and capitalism in characteristically modern ways. Marx stressed the process of primitive accumulation which separated direct producers from means of production, creating **class** relations that rendered them available as labourers obliged and willing to work for money. (By contrast peasants or farmers who still had possession of land would work it rather than hire themselves out.) Marx also pointed to the revolutionary role of the small master and employer, engaged in rivalry to raise productivity, in promoting an industrial revolution. For his part Weber pointed out that the early capitalist needed to have a peculiar combination of characteristics, to pursue economic gain while being personally ascetic, to achieve a new intensity of personal discipline, methodically economising on time and labour in the interests of profit and so forth. In Weber's view Puritanism helped foster such attitudes and therefore promoted the rise of capitalism. The approaches of Marx and Weber to the understanding of the rise of capitalism have inspired research agendas and led to protracted and illuminating debate; it is possible that they are complementary rather than rival accounts.

In capitalism the decisive means of production are privately owned and the mass of employees need to work to cover the living costs of themselves and their families. Competition spurs each capitalist enterprise to search for lower unit costs, for wider markets and for the product innovation that will give it a temporary monopoly. Recurrent episodes of crisis and restructuring winnow out the less profitable, and see the latter's remaining assets parcelled out to the more profitable. The 'capital' owned by capitalists comprises machinery, buildings, land, patents and franchises, means of transport, contracts relating to supply and distribution and last but not least the power to raise credit. The value of capital relates essentially to its ability to generate future profit not to its cost of acquisition, though there will not be profit unless the former is greater than the latter. The entrepreneur who spots profitable new ways of combining means of production and market outlets plays a key role in capitalism and helps to explain its dynamism.

From the perspective of the first decade of the twenty-first century it is clear that capitalism is by far the most dynamic system of economic organisation that has yet appeared in human history. In siege conditions the Soviet command economy was capable of successfully meeting a specified but quite narrow range of targets, but it eventually buckled under the strain of competing with the capitalist world. The Soviet economy produced vast quantities of coal, steel, cement and electricity but was bad at matching consumer needs. Communist China has achieved an extraordinary rate of economic growth, supplying a wide range of consumer good to the entire world, but seemingly only because it has adopted many aspects of capitalist organisation.

While generalised commodity production is defined by its commodification of labour power, it has also always had a tendency to expose every aspect of life to commercial exchange and arbitrage. The growth of the Atlantic slave trade and of slavery in the Americas was based on commodification of human beings themselves. This ultra-commodification proved politically unsustainable and economically limited, but it was followed by labour regimes and colonial orders that repeated this pattern. The growth of capitalism has also turned out to be highly unequal and uneven, as some areas lack the resources or dispositions required for capitalist success. While some parts of the former 'third world' have found a path to capitalist success, many have not – ironically those states still equipped with some of the instruments of Communist rule tend to be in the former category (North Korea excepted). In many parts of the world where capitalism is stalled the result is urbanisation without development, leading to a rising global population of desperate populations of shanty-town dwellers, deprived of minimum services.

Marx pointed out that capitalism needed, for its own sake, to be embedded in regulatory institutions and that this gave openings to movements such as that calling for a limit to the length of the working day. The development of capitalism has witnessed successive attempts to constrain, direct or supplement capitalist principles by 'de-commodifying' institutions of public welfare (i.e. free public education, health, old age pensions, etc.). 'De-commodification' enables sections of the population to live without entering paid employment – or at least to reduce their dependence on pay. Since the 1970s the institutions of 'welfare capitalism' have been subject to attack and erosion but remain significant, accounting for between a fifth and a third of GDP in most advanced capitalist states. More generally, the postwar period exhibited a sustained attempt to organise capitalism at both national and international level, with Keynesian policies to sustain employment and with a 'Fordist' model of mass consumption matching this full employment. But the oil-shock and 'stagflation' of the 1970s witnessed the abandonment of these models and the assertion of a 'neo-liberal' free market model of capitalism, accompanied by privatisation of public assets and attempts to curb social budgets.

Prior to the era of 'neo-liberal' **globalisation**, important aspects of the general reproduction of society still occur outside the sphere of commodity exchange. Family relations are pervasively influenced by a consumerism that reflects the rewards and pressures of commodification but it would be wrong and reductivist to suppose that they can be wholly understood in these terms. However the advance of fast food and **McDonaldisation** certainly bear witness to the way in which commodification can supplant the non-wage labour of household production. (Note that in doing so the purchaser as well as the provider will be spurred to extra wage labour.) **Culture** and communication have also been subjected to pervasive commodification leading to influential work on the culture industries and on knowledge-based capitalism.

Historically capitalism has encountered bitter and persistent opposition from both organised workers and peasant-based movements. While it has so far always succeeded in defeating or containing these movements, capitalism in the era of globalisation remains as controversial as it is dynamic.

The growth of capitalism has involved the rise of some tens of thousands of multinational corporations, which typically enjoy the rights of personhood but with special immunities not afforded to persons. Consumer and corporate capitalism has entailed a huge growth in personal indebtedness while fuelling the profits of the banks and finance houses. The finance houses also control most of the deferred wages or savings that stem from the commercialisation of social insurance and the growth of pension funds. About a quarter of the shares on the London and New York stock exchange are owned by pension funds. Attempts to dismantle or commodify social security in its various forms still prompt major acts of resistance in the leading capitalist states.

The runaway success of capitalism at the close of the twentieth century poses a major challenge to the twenty-first. In some areas the problem is overdevelopment as capitalist growth and consumerism threaten the habitability of the globe. In others it is the absence of capitalist development and the inability of the major regulatory institutions – the IMF, World Bank and WTO – to accept, respect and protect non-capitalist ways of life. Instead these institutions seek to enforce an ever more intrusive commodification – for example of 'intellectual property' – and to prevent or inhibit attempts to constrain or regulate corporate activity. This has prompted calls for an alternative globalisation but as yet its shape is not clear. But Marx's prediction that the post-capitalist order might well redeploy forms of cooperation and financial control developed by capitalism itself could still prove to be correct. To prevail, an alternative globalisation would certainly need to rally and reconcile a wide and various range of constituencies.

Further reading

Blackburn, Robin (ed.) (1992) *After the Fall*. London: Verso.

Harvey, David (1999) *The Limits to Capital*, 2nd edn. London: Verso.

Hilton, Rodney (ed.) (1976) *The Transition From Feudalism to Capitalism*. London: New Left Books.

Lash, Scott and Urry, John (1986) *Disorganised Capitalism*. Cambridge: Polity Press.

Marx, Karl (1967) *Capital*, Volume 1, with an introduction by Ernest Mandel. Harmondsworth: Penguin, 1974.

Scott, John (1997) *Corporate Business and Capitalist Classes*. Oxford: Oxford University Press.

Weber, Max (1904–5) *The Protestant Ethic and the Spirit of Capitalism*. Harmondsworth: Penguin, 2002.

Robin Blackburn

CHANGE AND DEVELOPMENT

Change is a fundamental property of **society**. This is well rendered by the metaphor of 'social life'. Like life itself, social life consists of incessant changes: when they stop, life ends. Any distinction between 'social statics' and 'social dynamics', or the 'anatomy' and 'physiology' of society is misleading. If we assume, with most contemporary theorists, that the ultimate components of society are the actions of its members, we cannot see society as anything but a dynamic entity, because actions by definition involve some change. Whereas change is ubiquitous, the speed, scope, depth and tempo of changes differ among societies. Change is particularly pervasive, rapid and salient in modern societies

The most general notion of change indicates some shift in the state of a certain entity occurring in time. In order to emphasise the dynamic quality of that particular entity referred to as society, contemporary sociology often applies the concept of a social field, by which is meant the fluid networks of actions, interactions, social relations and social **institutions**. All seemingly solid entities, like groups, associations, **organisations**, nation-states, are conceived as temporary outcomes of specific configurations of actions. Needless to say, the concept of a social field is general enough to embrace all levels of social complexity, from micro through meso to macro. A family is a social field, but so equally is a local **community**, voluntary association, political party, industrial corporation, nation-state, and in an increasingly obvious sense, the global society. Thus we may define social change as the shift in the state of the social field occurring in time.

The state of the social field is determined by a set of variables: (a) the number and type of actors and their actions; (b) the character of interactions and more lasting relationships among actors; (c) the role of actors and their actions for the field as a whole; (d) the boundary delimiting the field from other fields, i.e. criteria of inclusion and exclusion of actors and their actions; (e) the relations in which it remains with other fields, e.g. dependence or domination, cooperation or conflict; and (f) the environment of social and extra-social character impinging upon the social field, e.g. geo-political position and access to natural resources.

Accordingly, it is possible to distinguish various types of social change: (a) a change in composition (e.g. recruitment to the group, migration, demographic growth); (b) a change of structure (e.g. crystal-lisation of friendship ties, emergence of leadership, proclaiming a constitution); (c) a change of functions (e.g. occupational mobility, decay in the economic role of the family, decline of the welfare state); (d) a change of boundaries with other fields (e.g. linking families by marriage, fusion of corporations, imperial conquest); and (e) a change of environment (e.g. collapse of a dominating empire, discovery of oil fields, a major earthquake).

The shifts in all these variables may differ in their scale, their sig-nificance for the whole field and their tempo. Some changes are internal to the field: they are repeatable and sustain or reproduce the field intact. Examples would be changes in the daily routines of a family, the fluctuations of traffic from morning till evening, or the seasonal sequence of labour in farming communities. Other changes bring qualitative shifts, modifying the nature of the whole field. Most often, this is brought about by changes in structures and in functions, such as the emergence of capitalism, democratisation of the political system and secularisation of modern societies. Social change of this sort that is comprehensive, that embraces most aspects of the field, and that is also relatively rapid is a social revolution.

Social changes are usually linked in temporal and causally linked sequences. A sequence of interlinked changes, whether reproductive or transformative, is called a social process. Such social processes include urbanisation (see **urbanism**), industrialisation (see **industrialism**), economic growth and **globalisation**. Important differences among social processes have to do with their form or shape. A process is linear, when no state of the field repeats itself, or in other words when each later state is unique (e.g. the growth of technology). A process is cyclical, on the other hand, when the field returns to its earlier state from time to time, as occurs with price fluctuations in a market. An important variety of linear process is the directional process, where each later state of the system brings the field consistently closer to some final, optimal, or preferred state. Examples of directional processes are economic growth, scientific progress and modernisation.

Another criterion for classifying social processes has to do with their driving forces. We speak of endogenous processes, when their causes are located within the field, as, for example, when political reforms are enforced by grievances and citizen unrest. Exogenous processes, on the other hand, have their causes outside the field, as when changes in political regime are imposed by military intervention.

Yet another typology of social processes takes into account their rhythm. Some are gradual or incremental, proceeding step by step, and are referred to as evolutionary. Other processes show a periodic speeding up in which changes generate radical and qualitatively new forms after passing some threshold of slower, quantitative change. These can be described as revolutionary or dialectical patterns of change.

Social development is a more complex concept, referring to a process that has three combined characteristics: it is directional, endogenous and proceeds through discernible stages. Thus it implies some image of the end state of the social field towards which the process is moving. Examples of such end states include Comte's positive society, Spencer's industrial society, Marx's communist society and Durkheim's state of organic solidarity. In development, the movement itself is treated as unfolding and realising the inherent potentialities present in the field from the beginning. Proceeding towards the fulfilment of their potentialities, societies follow certain pre-set trajectories of typical phases. The outcome of such development has often been conceived as the increasing structural and functional differentiation of the field. The concept of development has been intimately related to ideas of social progress that transposes it from the descriptive to the evaluative level and regards the end-state as morally good or just and the road towards it as betterment, improvement, liberation, or self-fulfilment.

The weakness of the concept of development is its often deterministic, finalistic and fatalistic flavour, when it is conceived as necessary and irreversible, as following a predetermined, single and universal path towards the inevitable goal, and thus pre-empting human choices or preferences. Recognising these faults, recent social theory has tended to abandon the concept of development and to replace it by the idea of social becoming, where the state of the social field is conceived as the unique outcome or achievement of human actors, whether acting individually or collectively, and depending on their choices, decisions, programmes and policies. Creativeness of human agency, constrained to some extent by the encountered state of the social field (structural conditions), is nevertheless not entirely determined and leaves space for contingency, with the outcomes of the process always open-ended. Social fields, from families to states, are such as the people make them. From this point of view, progress comes to mean the creation of greater opportunities for the free realisation of human **action and agency**, as might be the case in democratic as opposed to autocratic regimes, or in unconstrained and pluralistic human communication as opposed to fields characterised by censorship.

Further reading

Boudon, Raymond (1986) *Theories of Social Change; A Critical Appraisal.* Cambridge: Polity Press.

Nisbet, Robert (1969) *Social Change and History.* New York: Basic Books.

Strasser, Hermann and Randall, Susan. C. (1981) *An Introduction to Theories of Social Change.* London: Routledge.

Sztompka, Piotr (1991) *Society in Action: The Theory of Social Becoming.* Cambridge: Polity Press.

Sztompka, Piotr (1993) *The Sociology of Social Change.* Oxford: Blackwell.

Tilly, Charles (1984) *Big Structures, Large Processes, Huge Comparisons.* New York: Russell Sage Foundation.

Piotr Sztompka

CHILDHOOD

In 1962 the French historian, Philip Ariès, argued that it is only since the sixteenth century that a distinct gap has emerged between adulthood and 'childhood'. There remain, however, disagreements over how far childhood is a universal biological 'journey towards adulthood', or whether it is a social **institution**, that is, the variable outcome of socio-historical, political and economic processes.

Traditionally, developmental psychologists have viewed children as 'human *becomings*', whose 'natural' needs and capacities mature through age-linked stages of **socialisation**, via the passive absorption of the influences from adults who provide care and protection (a universal model that pays little attention to differences of social class, gender and ethnicity). Adopting a similar perspective, earlier sociologists neglected to research children except in relation to socialisation or women's domestic oppression.

Recently, some have advocated a more 'active' sociological perspective in 'childhood studies'. In addition, both the UN Convention on the Rights of the Child and the British 1989 Children Act now require the views of the child to be taken into account in matters affecting children's welfare, such as divorce. These changes in perspective entail a new definition of childhood, where children are to be viewed as social actors in their own right, with 'competences' that are not restricted by biological age, with worthwhile views and contributions to make, and with rights over consent and confidentiality. However, the attempt to grant children more of the autonomy and respect accorded to adults, while continuing to protect them against harm and exploitation, has brought some confusions and ethical dilemmas.

Somewhat problematically, 'childhood' is now officially defined in Britain and many other countries with an upper limit of eighteen years. This appears to signal a need to extend legal protection beyond some existing definitions of maturity, e.g. beyond the age of sixteen for sexual consent or school leaving in Britain, and beyond the age for entry to the labour market in developing countries. Ambiguously, writers and policy makers alternate between talking about 'children', 'older children' and 'young people', and there are difficulties in framing policies to cover the full age range.

Researchers have often found it difficult to discuss research ethics and findings outside the framework of biological age. Nevertheless, ingenious methods have helped to explore the views and behaviour of younger children, their contributions to housework, care and finance, and their participation in the formal and informal labour market. Middle-class parents tend to see children's contributions as 'moral' socialisation, whereas in poorer families they can be vital to the household economy. There is growing appreciation that quite young children may be caring for adults, and more is now known about children's involvement in domestic violence and family breakdown. There is also more recognition that symptoms of depression, anorexia and self-harm are emerging in younger children.

Contradictions in our changing views of childhood currently appear in controversies over what has been called 'paranoid' or over-protective parenting, and about the 'death' or 'theft' of childhood by the media and commerce. However, amid current panics over paedophilia, discussion of children's control over their sexuality has gone underground.

Further reading

James, Allison and Prout, Alan (eds) (2004) *Constructing Childhood: Theory, Policy and Social Practice*. Basingstoke: Palgrave Macmillan.
James, Allison, Jenks, Chris and Prout, Alan (1998) *Theorizing Childhood*. Cambridge: Polity Press.
Lee, Nick (2001) *Childhood and Society: Growing Up in an Age of Uncertainty*. Buckingham: Open University Press.
Mayall, Berry (2002) *Towards a Sociology for Childhood*. Buckingham: Open University Press.
Wyness, Michael (2000) *Contesting Childhood*. London: Falmer Press.

Jean Duncombe

CITIZENSHIP

In strict legal terms, the idea of citizenship refers to the rules for conferring national belonging, which are variously based on lineage (jus sanguinis) or territory (jus soli), or some combination of the two. Most scholarship in this field, however, refers back to a more specific agenda established in T. H. Marshall's classic work 'Citzenship and Social Class', itself rooted in Leonard Hobhouse's earlier account. A key feature of this essay was its implicitly evolutionary account of the development of civil, political and social rights in Britain from the eighteenth to the twentieth century. Marshall's main interest, however, was the role of social rights in accommodating the tension between capital and citizenship, and the possibility that equality of **status** (via citizenship) might override the material inequalities of social **class**. Duties, as a necessary counterpart to rights, received a brief mention, including notably the duty to work, though it was Marshall's belief that the general direction of change had been away from duties and towards rights. He also recognised that the ideals of citizenship had been only imperfectly achieved, and that the associated rights themselves functioned as a basis for inequalities of various kinds. Among the interesting questions he posed was whether there are 'limits beyond which the modern drive towards equality cannot pass'.

Marshall's argument has been much criticised on a variety of points: its evolutionary assumptions and neglect of process and struggle, its reliance on the British experience, its neglect of the particularisms of gender, culture, race and sexuality, and the taken-for-granted status of the national community and corresponding neglect of trans-national forces. There have also been a number of concrete developments since Marshall's essay, which to some extent reflect these criticisms. Most notable is the entry into force of the European Convention on Human Rights (ECHR) in 1950, and the two key international covenants on Civil and Political Rights and on Economic, Social and Cultural Rights (both in 1966), along with a wealth of other trans-national conventions. There has also been a growth in the long-term presence on national territory of varied groups of non-citizens, many of them laying claim to the rights embodied in such conventions, though there has been a recent intensification of immigration controls in all European countries, and we have witnessed some notable contractions of those rights. Yasemin Soysal argues that citizenship has been superseded by the position of long-term residence and an emergent model of post-national membership, while Rogers Brubaker and Lydia Morris have rather emphasised the expansion of positions of partial membership based on differentiated statuses and stratified rights.

The latter work draws on David Lockwood's concept of 'civic stratification', a system of inequality based on the rights that may be granted or denied by the state. This work reverses the traditional question of how class formation affects social integration and asks how institutions of social integration affect class formation. It offers a development of Marshall's recognition that the institutions of citizenship may themselves be the foundation for certain legitimate inequalities, not fully developed in the original essay. Lockwood identifies two paired oppositions with respect to rights: civic expansion and exclusion, which refer to formal entitlement, and civic gain and deficit, which refer to stigma and prestige factors and may enhance or impede access to rights in practice. Although this work is mainly focused on the inequalities generated by the functioning of citizenship rights, it contains the basis for a much broader sociological treatment of rights.

Further reading

Brubaker, W. Rogers (1989) *Immigration and the Politics of Citizenship in Europe and America*. Lanham MD: University Press of America.

Lister, Ruth (1997) *Citizenship: Feminist Perspectives*. London, Macmillan.

Lockwood, David (1996) 'Civic integration and class formation', *British Journal of Sociology*, 47, 3: 531–50.

Marshall, T. H. (1950) *Citizenship and Social Class*. Cambridge: Cambridge University Press.

Morris, Lydia D. (2002) *Managing Migration: Civic Stratification and Migrants Rights*. London: Routledge.
Soysal, Yasemin (1994) *Limits of Citizenship*. Chicago: University of Chicago Press.

Lydia Morris

CIVIL SOCIETY

Civil society refers to all of the places where individuals gather together to have conversations, pursue common interests and, occasionally, try to influence public opinion or public policy. In many respects, civil society is where people spend their time when they are not at work or at home. For example, a group of people gather at a local park every Thursday afternoon for a game of football. Most of them arrive well before the game begins and stay for some time after it ends. Some of them go out for dinner or a drink after the game. In the course of their meetings they talk about a wide range of topics, including football but also extending to include issues such as work, family, relationships, community events, racial issues and politics. Most of the regulars look forward to their weekly get-together, and feel a sense of attachment to the other players they see at the park. This kind of **solidarity** can be found in a variety of other places in civil society – such as pubs, bowling leagues, reading groups and **social movements** – where individuals get together to associate on the basis of some shared interest.

The kinds of associations that take place in civil society are important because of the way they help to foster more effective forms of **citizenship**. Even though people may come together on the basis of an interest they all share in common, they eventually have to develop productive strategies for dealing with conflicts and differences that emerge within the association. Members of a reading group, for example, do not always agree what book they are going to read. Team mates in a bowling league discover that, on certain issues, they have significant differences of opinion. And yet, because they value the association and look forward to participating in its activities, they do not respond to these differences by exiting the scene. Instead, they search for compromise decisions that everybody can accept, and ways of interacting that will not threaten the solidarity of the group. In the process, they learn to appreciate and to tolerate social differences, which is a valuable skill to have in an increasingly multicultural **nation**. They also develop a general sense of social trust and mutual obligation, which makes society function more efficiently (this is what political scientists and sociologists are talking about when they refer to the importance of **social capital**).

For political theorists such as Jean Cohen, Jürgen Habermas, Charles Taylor and Iris Marion Young, civil society is also important because of the way it provides private citizens with an effective way to influence public policy. When people gather together in an association, they begin to think about their shared private interest as a collective public interest, and they try to make sure that this public interest is represented in policy debates. For example, the group that gets together for a weekly football game begins to talk about the park as an important community resource; if they feel that the park is being mistreated or mismanaged, they will organise a 'save the park' campaign to try to influence their local politicians and the other residents of the **community**. The members of a reading group all agree that reading is a crucial civic skill and not just a private pleasure, and they try to support causes that promote literacy in the community. Environmental groups organise 'bike to work' campaigns, to try to raise public awareness about the negative consequences of automobile dependence. Those who lack the time or the inclination to volunteer to help with these kinds of campaigns can still help the cause by lending their name and their commitment to the association and its leadership. This has the effect of increasing the political power of the association, since there is legitimacy in the simple fact of being able to claim a large base of supporters. In this way, as the American sociological theorist Talcott Parsons argued, associations add to the total amount of political influence circulating in society.

Recently, there has been growing concern that civil society is weaker than it used to be, because people are losing interest in joining associations. The loudest warning call has come from Robert Putnam, a political scientist from Harvard University. Drawing on national survey data from the United States, Putnam showed that voluntary association membership has decreased dramatically since the 1950s and 1960s – in all age groups, at all levels of education and in every type of association. As compared to the 1950s, individuals today are much more likely to donate money to an organisation than to offer their time or involvement. For those who do offer their time, they are more likely than ever to treat their volunteer work as a one-time event rather than an ongoing commitment. And many of the largest, most important civic groups of the past have experienced dramatic declines in membership, with some disappearing altogether. As citizens become increasingly disconnected from voluntary associations, Putnam worries that they will experience less trust and less social connection, and as a result political institutions will function less efficiently.

Not all scholars agree with Putnam's dire warnings about the future of civil society, pointing out that many people are simply choosing to participate in different kinds of associations than they used to. For example, it is likely that people are joining more informal associations (for example, a weekly football game in the local park), and fewer formal associations such as social movements or bowling leagues. They may be participating in fewer face-to-face meetings, but they are supplementing those meetings with 'virtual' interactions facilitated through email, internet bulletin boards, or video conferencing. They may be donating money instead of volunteering their time, but they are doing this because they recognise that their interests can be defended more effectively by political professionals. And for those people who do get involved in social movements and other formal associations, the amount of time they volunteer has actually tended to increase. According to these scholars, the way that people participate in civil society has changed, but it has not necessarily declined.

Further reading

Keane, John (2003) *Global Civil Society*. Cambridge: Cambridge University Press.

Putnam, Robert D. (2001) *Bowling Alone: The Collapse and Revival of American Community*. New York: Simon and Schuster.

Tester, Keith (1993) *Civil Society*. London: Routledge.

Ronald Jacobs

CLASS

The claim of Marx and Engels that 'The history of all hitherto existing society is the history of class struggles' provides the starting point for class analysis. Their claim was that certain economic divisions – to which they gave the label 'class' – could be seen as the basis of people's life chances, interests, and forms of consciousness and so drive all social conflict. The influence of this point of view is such that sociologists have often been criticised for 'reducing everything to class'. Recently, however, these strong claims for the relevance of class have weakened, and some have even alleged the 'death of class', holding that new forms of social division are now far more important than class. Properly understood, however, class remains an significant factor in social life and it is important to understand both its potential and its limits.

Marx's view was that the basic classes in a society were defined by the possession or non-possession of the means of production and that these property relations were the basis of class relations in the capital and labour markets. Class relations, therefore, are relations of property and employment. Classes exist in all societies where there is a legal framework of property relations that differentiates possessors from non-possessors, and where there is also a division of labour that allows the producers to produce more than is needed for their own sub-sistence. He saw a division between a class of possessors and a class of non-possessors as fundamental to any society's mode of production. Weber also saw 'class situations' as resulting from economic divisions rooted in property and market relations. Property and market divisions together constitute a person's 'market situation': the kinds of goods and labour services that they possess, that comprise their opportunities for the exercise of power in the labour, commodity and capital markets, and that they can use to generate an income. People occupy similar class situations when they can be regarded as having a similar ability to secure market-mediated life chances. These class situations are 'causal components' in their life chances, shaping their conditions of living and life experiences.

These arguments point to the constitution of class situations at the economic level and numerous issues arise concerning their number and boundaries, the particular property and employment relations that define them, and their continuing relevance as causal components in the lives of their members. Although Marx adopted a broadly dichotomous view of class relations, he recognised a number of 'inter-mediate' classes. Weber took an even more differentiated view of the nature of class divisions. Contemporary analysts vary considerably in terms of the number of classes that they recognise at the economic level, but a fairly simple account, drawing on the work of John Goldthorpe, might distinguish eleven economic classes: large property owners, small employers, farmers, self-employed, higher service, lower service, routine non-manual, supervisory manual, skilled manual, non-skilled manual, and agricultural workers. These categories and their boundaries are neither sharp nor universal, and it is often useful to aggregate or disaggregate class situations according to particular research needs.

There is, however, a further question concerning the extent to which these economic categories of class situations – economic classes for short – are formed into what Weber called 'social classes'. A social class is an actual collectivity rather than a mere statistical aggregate, and Marx looked at this question in terms of the transformation of an economic 'class-in-itself' into a social 'class-for-itself'. This process was described by Anthony Giddens as a process of 'structuration', a process of social closure through which the individuals who occupy specific class situations are tied into broad social aggregates that are more or less clearly bounded from other aggregates. Such social classes are demographically formed wherever patterns of **mobility**, interaction and association tie the occupants of class situations together. They exist to the extent that the individuals who occupy class situations are linked, through their occupational mobility, into relatively stable social groupings. Goldthorpe has argued that 'it is the rate and pattern of mobility that will determine the extent to which classes may be recognised as collectivities of individuals or families occupying similar locations within the social division of labour over time'. Class situations are a part of the same social class if there is easy and frequent movement and interaction among them. They form a cluster of property and employment positions around which movement is possible as the lifetime mobility of individuals (*intra*-generational mobility) or movement between generations (*inter*-generational mobility) and among which there is easy and frequent interaction. This interaction might involve links of family and household formation, bonds of marriage, partnership, and parenting, **kinship**, friendship and similar forms of intimate interaction, such as leisure-time socialising and club membership. In all of these ways individuals may be tied into the larger and more cohesive structures that are layered on top of each other to form a system of social stratification in which the members of a particular social class share crucial experiences and life chances in common.

The distinction between class situations and social classes helps to resolve a fundamental issue in studies of social stratification. Feminist critics rightly pointed to the inadequacies of an approach to class that simply subsumed women into their family of origin or marriage, arguing that individuals, not families, are the units of stratification. It is now clear that the allocation of women and men separately, as individuals, is the appropriate strategy for investigations into class situation, but that the fundamental units of social class are the family households that women and men form together.

There is a further issue in class analysis that comes to the heart of the argument over the death of class. This is the question of class consciousness and class identity: the extent to which class situations are associated with forms of class awareness that involve specific class identities and images of societies as divided into classes. It may be possible to demonstrate that economically defined class situations are the bases of crucial life chances and that people tend to be formed into social classes through their patterns of mobility and association, yet they may not develop a class consciousness and may not engage in collective class-based action. Critics of class analysis have pointed to the fact that fewer people today are willing to identify themselves in class terms and that **gender**, **ethnicity**, and **consumption** lifestyles have become far more important in social identity. Post-industrial and post-modern forms of social life, it is held, have involved a long-term erosion in the marks of inferiority and superiority and the forms of consciousness that previously made class relations visible and distinct. From this they draw the conclusion that classes no longer exist. Proponents of class analysis, however, point to the continuing importance of class in terms of life chances and social relationships, and see current trends as highlighting simply a non-correspondence between the structural reality of class and its forms of consciousness and action. Class continues to exist and to exercise an influence in people's lives, but it is no longer experienced as such a fundamental reality as in the past. Class relations have not disappeared, but they have become less visible and less tangible.

Class, therefore, remains an important part of the research agenda in sociology. Among those who recognise the need for class analysis, there has been a growing consensus that the so-called 'Goldthorpe scheme' offers the most useful measure of social class. Versions of this have been used in a number of comparative investigations of social **mobility** and it has received wide international support. A slightly modified version of the Goldthorpe scheme has been developed for use in the census and official government statistics (the so-called NS-SEC, developed at Essex University), and this, too, is beginning to be used in sociological investigations.

Further reading

Crompton, Rosemary (1998) *Class and Stratification*, 2nd edn. Cambridge: Polity Press.

Devine, Fiona (1996) *Social Class in America and Britain*. Edinburgh: Edinburgh University Press.

Savage, Mike (2000) *Class Analysis and Social Transformation*. Buckingham: Open University Press.

Scott, John (1996) *Stratification and Power*. Cambridge: Polity Press.

Scott, John (ed.) (1996) *Class*, Four Volumes, London: Routledge.

John Scott

COLLECTIVE REPRESENTATIONS

Collective representations are the shared mental phenomena through which people organise their lives and are the fundamental constituents of any **culture**. The term was introduced by Durkheim to refer to one of the principal types of 'social facts' with which sociology is concerned: they are the beliefs, ideas, values, symbols and expectations that form the ways of thinking and feeling that are general and enduring within a particular society or a social group and that are shared as its collective property.

Durkheim held that people, including sociologists and other scientists, can only ever understand their world through the use of concepts that allow them to grasp and organise the chaotic experiences received through their senses. Before they can act upon the world, they must imagine it in some way and try to anticipate the consequences of their actions. Collective representations are the socially shared concepts through which people are able to operate in relation to the natural world and to the other people they encounter. Reality is, therefore, always a socially constructed reality. In symbolic interactionism, this same idea was formulated in relation to the employment of symbols and meanings to construct a **definition of the situation**. This point has also been recognised in the work of Jean Baudrillard, who prefers the term 'simulacra', in order to emphasise that collective representations should not be seen as direct mental reflections of an independent external reality. They must always be seen as constitutive of that reality.

Durkheim saw collective representations as comprising a 'collective conscience' or 'social consciousness' that is 'external' to the individuals of a society: it pre-exists them and it persists after they have died. Individuals are born into a pre-existing world of collective representations and, through their **socialisation**, they learn these collective representations and develop a sense of moral commitment towards them. This moral commitment means that representations are experienced as having an obligatory character and so are able to constrain the actions of individuals and the relationships that they build with others.

This idea of the externality of the collective conscience and collective representations does not mean, however, that they exist separately from the minds of the individuals who are the members of the social group. There is no 'group mind' or 'collective mind' over and above the minds of the individuals. Collective representations can exist only in the minds of individuals. It is the fact that they are shared and, therefore, general throughout a society that gives them their collective and external character. Durkheim did, nevertheless, try to make a distinction between collective representations and the purely 'individual representations' that are the direct products of an individual brain and its sensory apparatus. He found it difficult to sustain this distinction, however, and saw all the principal contents of minds as social in origin and character.

The communication of collective representations from one individual to another is the means through which individuals are socialised into the representations shared within their society or social group. The interaction and association of individuals depends upon their communication with each other, and so there is a constant circulation of representations around a society. It is through this circulation that representations pass from one individual to another and so can be reproduced. In acting on representations and communicating them to others, however, individuals are will always deviate, modify and creatively innovate. As a result, particular representations and the total stock of representations are transformed over time.

Social **institutions**, and hence whole societies, are built from collective representations. As the sets of related representations that individuals learn, institutions are the means through which people's social relations crystallise into distinct and recurrent patterns. As such, they may become established as customs or, more formally, as legally sanctioned practices. Solid as they are, societies comprise individuals socially related to one another through their shared representations.

Collective representations have what Giddens has called a 'virtual' existence outside the minds of individuals and they can become visible or tangible only if given some external, material form. This might be, for example, in letters, books, newspapers, official documents, tapes, or disks. These documentary forms are merely the material indicators of the actual collective representations that they express or codify, but they are the principal channels through which collective representations can be communicated within a society in which face-to-face interaction has been supplemented by written-language communications and systems of mass communications that make possible interaction at a distance.

Many writers on those phenomena that Durkheim described as collective representations were concerned with the ways in which social groups are able to influence the behaviour of their individual members. Contemporaries such as Gustave Le Bon stressed the importance of collective behaviour and the influences generated within crowds, while Gabriel Tarde stressed the diffusion of representations through networks of social relations. The foundations of these processes of group pressure have been explored in the social psychology of Serge Moscovici, who shows that the attitudes and opinions that are organised into cognitive structures are 'social representations' (the term that he prefers). He contrasts the communal representations of pre-modern traditions with the more diverse and fluid representations found in modern societies, and he sees the mass media playing a key role in the dissemination and transformation of these representations. This argument parallels the controversial claim of Baudrillard that collective representations in contemporary societies must be seen as 'simulations'. People are no longer constrained by the idea of external things standing behind the mental representations: in everyday consciousness, representations of things have come to replace the things being represented. This defines the media-induced state of hyperreality that now defines contemporary existence.

Further reading

Durkheim, Émile (1898) 'Individual and Collective Representations', in D. F. Pocock and J. G. Peristiany (eds) *Sociology and Philosophy*. London: Cohen and West, 1965.

Durkheim, Émile (1895) *The Rules of the Sociological Method*. London: Macmillan, 1982.

Farr, Robert M. and Moscovici, Serge (eds) (1984) *Social Representations*. Cambridge: Cambridge University Press.

Pickering, W. S. F. (ed.) (2000) *Durkheim and Representations*. London: Routledge.

John Scott

COMMUNITY

The concept of community has a long and contested history within sociology. At an everyday level, it is used to express ideas of common experience and shared interests. Its popular meaning(s) now not only convey traditional notions of shared locality and neighbourhood, but also ideas of solidarity and connection between people who share similar social characteristics or identities. For example, ideas about the 'black community' or the 'gay community' are now common in popular discourse. Within sociology, however, the usefulness of the concept of community for analytical purposes is much more contentious. In particular, important concerns have developed about the extent to which the concept is adequate for exploring the nature of people's involvement with one another. In many ways the concept is seen as too encompassing and too evaluative to be particularly useful for examining the ways in which individuals are connected or tied to others.

The initial use of the concept of community within sociology is associated with the concerns of the discipline's founding fathers who sought to understand and explain the social and economic transformations of industrialised capitalism in the nineteenth century. In particular, Ferdinand Tönnies, echoing commonly held fears, argued that **modernisation** resulted in a loss of community and local **solidarity**. In the developing industrial economies of northern Europe, the mutual knowledge and social control generated through living in comparatively small-scale rural locations was no longer possible in the emerging large-scale, anonymous and socially diverse urban centres. This theme of loss of community in turn became central within the development of the highly influential Chicago School's studies of **urbanism** of the 1920s and 1930s, particularly through the work of writers like Louis Wirth, Robert Redfield and Ernest Burgess. Many empirical studies were conducted in North America and Europe in the mid-twentieth century to test the extent to which community solidarity existed in different localities within urban, industrial society. Most argued that elements of community continued to characterise certain parts of modern cities, especially established working-class neighbourhoods and those with clear ethnic identities, despite the evident changes urbanisation generated in wider patterns of social organisation.

By the end of this period, however, various sociologists became increasingly concerned with the analytical and methodological dilemmas associated with the concept of community. To begin with, it appeared impossible to reach agreement over what the term actually meant, as, significantly, the concept seemed to be imbued with normative connotations reflecting assumed patterns of social integration drawn from rather idealised images of small-scale societies in the past. Analytically, the very notion of community appeared to encourage researchers to take an 'inward gaze', focusing on relationships within a bounded geographical area (or other bounded entity) rather than examining the structuring of relationships at other than a 'local' level. Moreover a number of celebrated community re-studies appeared to highlight the lack of methodological rigour in traditional community studies methodologies by coming to quite different conclusions from the original studies. This may, of course, have reflected the changed circumstances of these communities with the passage of time, but the disparity of results led to significant questions being raised about the validity and reliability of the methods used in such studies.

As a result of these various factors, different approaches which were not so reliant on the concept of community were suggested for studying patterns of social integration. In particular, ideas from social network analysis appeared to offer a possible means of resolving the difficulties seen as inherent in the idea of community. An advantage of the network analysis approach was that it did not focus 'inwards'; it was not bound by geography in the way 'community' was. Nor did it carry the normative 'baggage' associated with community; analytically it was neutral, allowing a wide range of relationships of different types to be mapped. It also promised the possibility of a structural analysis based on network configuration. While detailed network analyses have not proved as influential as some thought they might become, the network perspective has certainly been important in shaping sociologists' understandings of how best to capture individuals' incorporation and commitment to localities and other social fields to which the term community is applied.

If questions about the existence or otherwise of communities are now understood as too simplistic for analysing contemporary patterns of social participation, this does not mean that concerns over the significance of 'the local' in people's lives are no longer of interest. With globalisation, the development of new forms of electronic communication and increasing levels of mobility across the life course, people's lives are less geographically bounded than they were. Nonetheless local relationships remain salient for many, albeit to differing degrees. The question then is not whether a community exists, but more what types of local relationships do different people sustain and what dependence do they have on local institutions. To put this a little differently, to what extent are people's lives *embedded* in the localities in which they live? Within this, to what degree are their informal networks based in the locality? How much do they rely on local services? And how important is the local economy for their well-being and lifestyle? While the answers to such questions will vary significantly in any locality – and in a sense this is the point – this type of approach allows for a much more subtle investigation of the significance and strength of locality than global terms like community afford.

Importantly, answers to questions like these are inherently dynamic. The processes of late **modernity** are such as to ensure that people's embeddedness in local social and economic structures shifts over time. Thus globalisation has an impact on local labour and housing markets; migration patterns are influenced by the 'push' and 'pull' of economic opportunity; new technologies and cheaper travel allow personal relationships to be sustained across spatial divides. Moreover, some individuals have the resources necessary to render locality of little consequence. For them, the local simply becomes the place they have chosen to live, at least for now. For others, geography remains highly constraining, with much of their lives being lived within a particular locale. For still others, relationships may be concentrated, but in more than one location. For example, those who migrate for work often manage to sustain strong connections with 'home', even while living elsewhere for significant periods. While the concept of community may itself no longer serve well for analysing the varied patterns of personal association and commitment evident with late modernity, the issues that first made it attractive for understanding the transformations of industrial urbanisation continue to be important, albeit in the different social and economic environment characterising the twenty-first century.

Further reading

Bauman, Zygmunt (2001) *Community: Seeking Safety in an Insecure World.* Cambridge: Polity Press.

Bell, Colin and Newby, Howard (1971) *Community Studies.* London: George Allen and Unwin.

Crow, Graham and Allan, Graham (1994) *Community Life. An Introduction to Local Social Relations.* Hemel Hempstead: Harvester Wheatsheaf.

Delanty, Gerard (2003) *Community.* London: Routledge.

Graham Allan

CONSUMPTION

The sociology of consumption has risen to spectacular prominence over the last couple of decades and has radically challenged the basic premises of the discipline. In nearly all of its early English uses, consumption had negative connotations, meaning to destroy, to waste, to exhaust. By the nineteenth century it had come to be contrasted with the positive (and masculine) virtues of production as socially useful work, while consumption was denigrated as women's work. The polemical advocates of a new approach to consumption insisted that an understanding of the character of contemporary social life required an abandonment of the old concerns of the nineteenth-century theorists who had identified industrial production and **class** location as the prime source of meaning and antagonism in society. It is no accident that many key studies of consumption were published in the 1980s when many countries experienced consumer spending booms that fuelled economic growth, states adopted neo-liberal market policies, and the rhetoric of freedom of choice had come to pervade political, economic and social life. The new sociological definitions of consumption, however, do not restrict themselves to the individual purchases and uses of goods and services that were so apparent at this time. Rather, they reveal the social relations structuring the apparent individuality of such choices, desires and meanings.

Yet the explosion of academic interest in consumption is not simply a reflection of this recent historical context, nor is it entirely fair to claim that the classic tradition ignored the topic. Consumption was understood in different ways by the classical theorists, but usually on the margins of a more general social theory. Marx, for instance, regarded the desire to consume as an instance of the 'commodity fetishism' induced by **capitalism**, while Weber's analysis of **status** groups and Veblen's account of 'conspicuous consumption' addressed social stratification in terms of instrumental displays of wealth and prestige. Durkheim gave dire warnings that modern **industrialism** produces pathologically insatiable consumer desires that corrode the moral basis of social order. Simmel was the first in the classic tradition to recognise the seductive qualities of such apparently trivial matters as fashion and to explore the tensions between social dependency and individual freedom encountered in the desire to be different but also to fit in. These treatments of consumption meant that subsequent sociologists have tended to treat consumption with some disdain and in highly gendered ways. Consumption was seen as something that goes on within families and in which the 'consumers' are women. This is the orthodoxy that began to be challenged from a number of different directions.

One such challenge came from the revival of urban sociology in the 1970s as Manuel Castells made the neo-Marxist argument that 'collective consumption' is the primary process that shapes the city and ensures the survival of capitalism. He drew attention to the role of the state in providing goods and services – such as education, housing, transport and medical facilities – that at other times and other places were provided by the market. The ensuing privatisation programmes of many Western governments have not diluted these arguments. In fact, they underline the way that the distinction between privately and collectively provided goods was not a result of any intrinsic qualities they possess, but occurs through specific struggles between private economic interests and social justice movements. Although critics soon complained that the 'urban' could not be purely defined in terms of collective consumption (see **urbanism**), other approaches appeared that challenged this political economy perspective.

A more cultural form of analysis became influential through the Frankfurt School's critique of mass culture, which they regarded as a cause of **alienation**, as exploitative and dehumanising. However, this argument did not engage with the realities of everyday life and it was the emerging discipline of cultural studies, during the 1970s and 1980s, that produced a range of ethnographic studies on the ways ordinary people creatively consumed the materials produced by the mass media.

A third challenge came from feminists, who took issue with many of the gendered assumptions behind the concept of consumption. These arguments began from an emphasis on women's exploitation in the consumption process, but have moved on to consider the pleasure gained from consumption and have questioned the extent to which consumption is an oppressive chore rather than an empowering pleasure. This work has given rise to studies of fashion, the body, shopping and advertising.

New approaches to consumption have come from the debates surrounding postmodernism and the work of Jean Baudrillard in the 1980s. This has seen a proliferation of studies on the fragmentation of culture, the aestheticisation of everyday life, and the reorganisation of capitalist production along post-Fordist lines conspiring to give birth to a new consumer culture. What unites a diverse set of authors is a concern with consumption as a communicative rather than an instrumental activity. This focus on the images, signs and symbols of consumption has also led to a renewed interest in personal identity over collective practice.

Finally, the work of Pierre Bourdieu has cast a major spell over the discipline, partly because there are clear links back to the classic tradition but also because of the detailed empirical support contained in his arguments. For Bourdieu consumption is motivated by the need for social groups to achieve status through forms of 'distinction' that reinforce class position. Taste judgements, rooted in the **habitus**, are a marker of social class and are deeply tied to hierarchical access to economic capital, **cultural capital** and **social capital**.

From these sources there has emerged a vast literature on consumption with much emphasis on consumer culture and personal identity. Largely ignored, however, are accounts of what Elizabeth Shove and Alan Warde have termed 'inconspicuous consumption' – the more mundane and unglamorous dimensions of practice that nonetheless pose major problems of waste and destruction of scarce resources. For instance, petrol for the car, electricity for the fridge and water for the washing machine are just some of the environmentally significant energy supplies that make consumption possible. It is also significant that cars, fridges and washing machines themselves have moved from extra-ordinary, luxury commodities to being almost universal, unremarkable features of many Western homes. Furthermore, First World consumption patterns contribute not only to Third World suffering but as a new form of colonialism that some critics argue erodes **tradition and traditionalism**. It is through a return to the political economy of consumption that sociology will find its critical bite in this area.

Further reading

Baudrillard, Jean (1998) *The Consumer Society: Myths and Structures*. London: Sage.

Clarke, David, Doel, Marcus and Housiaux, Kate (eds) (2003) *The Consumption Reader*. London: Routledge.

Corrigan, Peter (1997) *The Sociology of Consumption*. London: Sage.

Gronnow, Jukka and Warde, Alan (eds) (2001) *Ordinary Consumption*. London: Routledge.

Miller, Daniel (ed.) (1995) *Acknowledging Consumption: A Review of New Studies*. London: Routledge.

Eamonn Carrabine

CONVERSATION

Although sociologists have often observed that our capacity to use language is a major factor distinguishing humans and human society from the animal world, paradoxically that capacity does not tend to be treated as a topic of analysis in its own right. Rather, sociologists have *relied* on language as a resource which provides them with access to the other phenomena they are interested in – whether these are 'external' phenomena such as class, gender, power, ethnicity, deviance, etc., or 'internal' phenomena such as people's beliefs and attitudes about such factors. Sociologists have therefore tended to see talk – especially ordinary conversation – as essentially trivial, except in so far as it is a tool for finding out about larger-scale social phenomena such as class, gender or deviance, through responses to interview questions for example.

During the 1960s an alternative perspective developed, arguing that sociology should instead treat talk and its interactional organisation as a *topic* of analysis, rather than a resource for the pursuit of other questions. This approach became known as *conversation analysis* (CA), and it has since been applied to a wide range of different forms of talk. While some conversation analysts have focused mainly on the investigation of ordinary conversation, examining talk as a social **institution** in its own right with its own structures, others have concerned themselves with the analysis of 'institutional' interaction, applying the findings of CA to the study of how talk plays a role in the management of other social institutions.

CA contributes, alongside work in related fields such as pragmatics, sociolinguistics and discourse analysis, to the development of a naturalistic, observation-based empirical science of human communication. Its procedure is to gather recordings of naturally occurring interactions which are analysed in order to discover how participants understand and respond to one another in their turns at talk, with a principal focus on how sequences of activities are generated. The main objective of research is to uncover the socio-linguistic competencies underlying the production and interpretation of talk in sequences of social interaction (talk-in-interaction). CA thereby represents a major bridge between more formally linguistic analysis in fields such as pragmatics, and the sociological investigation of human sociality.

CA emerged in the pioneering researches of Harvey Sacks into the structural organisation of everyday language use, at the University of California in the 1960s. Sacks was partly influenced by Harold Garfinkel's programme of research into everyday methods of practical reasoning, known as ethnomethodology, and by Erving Goffman's explorations of the structural properties of face-to-face interaction. Building on these influences, Sacks initiated a radical research programme designed to investigate the levels of social order which could be revealed in the everyday practice of talking.

CA's main tenet is that ordinary conversation is not a trivial, random, unorganised phenomenon of little interest to sociologists, but a deeply ordered, structurally organised social practice. Its second tenet is that this order can best be explored through the use of audio and video recordings of naturally occurring data which can be looked at repeatedly, transcribed and analysed in depth. Through engaging with what is observable in their transcripts of recorded talk, conversation analysts take a unique approach to the study of ordinary language. This begins from what Sacks, Schegloff and Jefferson described as the 'economy' of conversational turn-taking: the methods by which persons are able to manage the routine exchange of turns while at the same time minimising gap and overlap between their individual contributions.

Beginning from this standpoint, CA's aim is to reveal how the technical aspects of speech exchange represent structured, socially organised resources by which participants perform and coordinate activities through talk-in-interaction. Talk is treated as a vehicle for social action; but it is also seen as the principal means by which social organisation is mutually constructed and sustained within interaction. Hence it is a strategic site in which social agents' orientation to and evocation of the social contexts of their interaction can be empirically investigated.

Although CA began with an interest in the organisation of ordinary conversation, it has also been applied within a broader framework to analyse the distinctive methods of turn-taking and activity organisation found in specialised settings such as courts of law, classrooms, radio and television talk shows, doctors' surgeries, public speeches and many others. In studies of such 'institutional' settings, CA has developed a distinctive perspective on how participants themselves play a central role in establishing and reproducing the 'context-specific' nature of their interaction. At root, this is based on the idea that different forms of talk should be viewed as a continuum ranging from the relatively unconstrained turn-taking of mundane conversation, through various levels of formality, to ceremonial occasions in which not only who speaks and in what sequential order, but also what they will say, are pre-arranged – for instance, in wedding ceremonies. By selectively reducing or otherwise transforming the full scope of conversational practices, concentrating on some and withholding others, participants can be seen to display an orientation to particular institutional norms as relevant for their current state of interaction.

Using this approach, CA has distinguished two basic types of institutional discourse, referred to as *formal* and *non-formal*. The formal types are represented by courts of law, many kinds of interview, certain kinds of classroom environment and various ceremonial occasions. In such settings there is a close relationship between the social identities adopted by participants and the types of turn that they produce in interaction. The distinctiveness of the interaction is embodied mainly in its formal turn-taking system, where activities are conducted by means of question–answer sequences in which it is the institutional representative or professional incumbent (e.g. attorney/interviewer) who produces the questions, while the other (e.g. witness/interviewee) is restricted to the activity of answering those questions.

However, the question–answer pre-allocation format is only a minimal characterisation of the role played by talk in these settings. Any of a range of actions may be done in a given turn, provided that they are done in the *form* of a question or answer. In short, CA recognises that formal institutional interactions are not sterile occasions in which, purely and simply, questions get asked and answers given. Through the medium of questions and answers certain figures – institutional representatives such as attorneys or journalists, for instance – may seek to challenge other participants (witnesses, interviewees) while those others may, in turn, seek to resist such challenges. In short they are domains of contestation in which the contest is played out through the exchange of turns which are at least minimally recognisable as questions and answers.

The category of formal institutional interaction incorporates only a small number of institutional settings. Far more widespread are the 'non-formal' types which occur in medical, psychiatric, social service, business and other similar environments. In such settings, much less uniformity in the patterning of conduct is evident. But the interaction may be more or less explicitly directed towards carrying out 'official' tasks such as diagnosing illness or assessing a client's financial or welfare needs. As a result there may emerge noticeable asymmetries between role incumbents. For instance doctors may be seen to ask far more questions than patients, even though there is no normative constraint restricting patients from questioning doctors.

For this reason, non-formal types of institutional interaction can be said to have a 'quasi-conversational' character. Any observable asymmetries in turn-taking are not provided for on the basis of normative constraints on participation opportunities for speakers in given institutional roles (as in formal systems), but rather seem to emerge out of patterns of interaction that participants 'settle into' on the basis of a tacit mutual orientation to specific activities associated with the situation's task-oriented work. Nevertheless, as in studies of other types of talk-in-interaction, the aim of analysis is not simply to describe distinctive turn-taking patterns. Rather CA typically begins from such structural descriptions to reveal complex patterns and connections between interaction practices, social relations and social order, while always keeping in view the fact that talk-in-interaction is central to the achieved organisation of such phenomena.

Beginning from an interest in the orderly features of everyday conversation, therefore, CA has developed a distinctive approach to the relevance of social context which emphasises the participants' displayed orientations to context. This illustrates a central methodological policy that distinguishes CA from many other perspectives within sociology: an insistence that is it is more important to explicate the ways that the participants in any interaction display their understanding of what they are doing than to begin from theoretically driven assumptions about what might be going on.

Further reading

Atkinson, J. Maxwell and Heritage, John (eds) (1984) *Structures of Social Action: Studies in Conversation Analysis*. Cambridge: Cambridge University Press.

Drew, Paul and Heritage, John (eds) (1992) *Talk At Work: Interaction in Institutional Settings*. Cambridge: Cambridge University Press.

Hutchby, Ian and Wooffitt, Robin (1998) *Conversation Analysis*. Cambridge: Polity Press.

Sacks, Harvey (1992) *Lectures on Conversation*. Oxford: Blackwell.

Sacks, Harvey, Schegloff, Emanuel A. and Jefferson, Gail (1974) 'A simplest systematics for the organisation of turn-taking for conversation', *Language*, 50: 696–735.

Ian Hutchby

CULTURAL CAPITAL

Pierre Bourdieu coined the concept of cultural capital, along with that of **social capital**, as a way of theorising the role of cultural knowledge and tastes in relation to the processes of **class** formation. During the 1960s he became interested in the ways that members of the bourgeoisie – that is, the middle and upper strata of French society – were able to call on material and non-material resources to maintain their power and privileges, and to transmit them to their children. In a key theoretical statement, Pierre Bourdieu and Jean-Claude Passeron argued that as **capitalism** became more corporate, and thus 'de-personalised', direct property inheritance declined in importance as a means of passing economic wealth and social **status** on to one's offspring; among the other mechanisms that elite groups started to deploy, the most important was the capacity to negotiate the education system successfully. Parental cultural capital, according to Bourdieu, meant that children both valued school (and university), and were in a position to understand the unwritten 'rules of the game', enabling them to leave with credentials that would win them good jobs.

Initially, then, Bourdieu saw cultural capital as largely important in the transmission of **power** and privileges between generations. However, he also used the concept as a way of explaining the distribution of power and status within the middle and upper classes. As with educational achievement, moreover, cultural capital worked precisely because it appeared neutral, simply the manifestation of natural abilities and taste. Enjoyment of Bach, post-Impressionism or skiing, for example, was not a sign of intrinsic superiority but formed part of a set of signals used by members of a particular social group in order to strengthen its internal bonds and maintain its superiority over others. This operated within social classes, and not just between them. In music, for example, Bourdieu showed that upper-class people who had been educated in the elite *Grandes Écoles* had a marked preference for Bach, while workers with no qualifications had an equally strong liking for Petula Clark.

As these names suggest, Bourdieu's fieldwork was largely conducted in the 1960s, and he has been accused of assuming that the superiority of a particular high bourgeois culture was more enduring than it has turned out to be. The highly pluralistic cultural industries of the early twenty-first century compete in a relatively open marketplace, and taste is often intentionally socially ambiguous, allowing people – particularly the young – to play and experiment with a variety of cultural identities. Bourdieu also tended to portray workers as somewhat passive, in their cultural dispositions as in their educational orientations, leading to the accusation of determinism. He is also accused of ignoring gender, though equally a sizeable body of feminist analysis draws heavily on his work to help explain the role of cultural capital in the reproduction of **patriarchy**. For some contemporary sociologists, Bourdieu's entire project is tied to a dated neo-Marxist conception of class as the basis of social order. Yet he will certainly be remembered as a major influence on the sociology of education in the 1970s and 1980s, and many critical sociologists still acknowledge his lasting contribution to the analysis of culture as a material force.

Further reading

Bourdieu, Pierre (1986) *Distinction: A Social Critique of the Judgement of Taste*. London: Routledge.

Bourdieu, Pierre and Passeron, Jean-Claude (1973) *Reproduction in Education, Society and Culture*. London: Sage.

Lane, Jeremy F. (2000) *Pierre Bourdieu: A Critical Introduction*. London: Pluto Press.

Robbins, Derek (2000) *Bourdieu and Culture*. London: Sage.

John Field

CULTURE

'Culture' is a term that, like '**community**', is much used but for which it is impossible to point to a single definition beyond general formulations like 'the social realm in which shared meanings are produced'.

Even this is potentially controversial: one of the areas of disagreement about 'culture' is whether a given society (however defined) has one or many. If many, is it defensible to claim that some are more valuable that others? Or are these kinds of claims simply a weapon in the struggle for societal power and influence? Contemporary definitions of 'culture', in other words, are always based in an implicit theory of society.

Historically, however, culture was defined in opposition to nature. Just as skills in cultivation have been applied to make the plant and animal world more productive so, metaphorically, human intellect and creativity has cultivated a 'civilisation' in the realm of ideas. This narrow concept of 'culture' as high-status symbolic production in areas like painting, sculpture and literature meant that, from the mid-nineteenth century to the mid-twentieth century, there was little interchange between scholars in the humanities and the rapidly developing social sciences. In *Culture and Anarchy* (1869) Matthew Arnold, English educationalist and writer, argued that pursuing and disseminating the highest forms of aesthetic culture was vital to countering the social turmoil of rapid industrialisation and urbanisation, and the consequent demands from ordinary people for greater citizenship rights. This 'civilising' mission, of social improvement and benign pacification, would axiomatically be the responsibility of an **elite** of the most educated.

By contrast, Marx's account of the same social world does not recognise 'culture' as a separate sphere because, in his analysis, the central dynamic of capitalism is the inevitable conflict between those who live by selling their labour power and those who exploit that labour power for profit. This 'base' generates both individual consciousness and shared ideas. Together with social institutions (for example the family and the law), these form the 'superstructure', which can be understood only through its function of sustaining the base.

The period between the 1890s and 1930s was as turbulent in the symbolic realm as the previous sixty years had been demographically and politically. New printing and distribution technologies made newspapers, magazines and novels widely available and affordable, and this was followed by radio and then cinema. In response, the literary critics and controversialists Frank and Queenie Leavis argued that schooling should include explicit instruction aimed at making people more critical of this profit-driven mass production of entertainment for mass consumption. An educated public, they believed, would grasp the debased nature of this supposedly 'popular' culture and understand the value of authentic 'organic' culture ranging from skilled country crafts to sophisticated drama.

The Leavises' desire to reinstate what they believed to be the proper, pre-industrial, cultural order was not deliberately inegalitarian. Their Romantic vision, however, certainly had no place for the emancipation of the working class. It is ironic that, contemporaneously, much of the same distaste for and despair about the impact of mass-consumed culture was being expressed by key figures in the 'Frankfurt School' of social critique. In the 1940s this multidisciplinary group of social scientists was based in the United States, having fled from Germany in the 1930s because of Nazi persecution of the Jews. Their explicit purpose was to pursue *praxis* in the Marxian tradition: that is, to use intellectual work to bring about real change in social conditions for working people. Theodor Adorno and Max Horkheimer argued that, as with all industrialised products, commercial entertainments such as the cinema, recorded music and radio were bound to work to standardised formulae. (At this time television was not widely available.) Not only would this bring economies in the production process, but predictable film plots and musical structures were more likely to satisfy a passive audience lacking the background knowledge, time, or energy to enjoy more challenging cultural forms. This was not, however, merely a response to audience demand. It was the culture industries acting as an active means of social control; providing emotional catharsis and relief from boredom to tranquillise the masses. Or worse: Adorno suggested that the rhythms of popular music could induce the same obedience as military marches.

The Frankfurt School's pessimism about the public response to mass culture can be understood as following logically from their Marxian position, particularly in the context of a still-continuing world war fuelled by political mass movements. By the early 1950s the United States' prosperity and position in the world provided a compelling context for social theories that put the mechanisms that deliver and sustain social order, rather than endemic conflict, in the foreground. In this optimistic intellectual world, Talcott Parsons, pre-eminent American sociologist of the era, embarked with colleagues on the project of integrating the social sciences, incorporating psychology, sociology, economics, politics and insights from anthropology.

In his writings Parsons assigns 'culture' a pivotal role as the domain of shared symbolic meanings. Such meanings enable us to move from the particular to the general, which makes communication – and thus society itself – possible. Parsons clearly did not regard culture as a residual category: his triadic model of social action gave it the same status as 'personality' and 'the social system'. In his writings, however, culture is discussed only in relation to the social formations in which the shared meanings operate, for example religion, the family or the doctor/patient relationship. Given his theoretical emphasis on **society** existing in a moving equilibrium, culture becomes, paradoxically, impossible to isolate for separate analysis. As Parsons put it 'A cultural system does not "function" except as part of a concrete action system, it just "is".'

Thus during the rapid expansion of sociology in the United States and Europe in the 1950s and 1960s 'the cultural level' was regarded as not capable of fruitful study in its own right either by conservative or radical thinkers. Consequently little scholarly attention was paid to the production and consumption of mass popular culture. The impetus for this came (again) from the humanities: from historians and literary critics, though this time from an explicitly socialist perspective. Raymond Williams, Welsh educator and social commentator, took the famously anti-elitist stance that 'culture is ordinary', meaning that the everyday experiences, ideas and customs of the mass of the population should not be dismissed as worthless beside 'high' culture. Even so, Williams was worried about mass-consumed culture because it is 'produced for conscious political and commercial advantage'. Understanding how this 'advantage' works was the impetus, at last, for the methods of sociology (for example, ethnography and content analysis) and the objects of study of the humanities (texts, both print and visual) to converge in 'cultural studies'. Much of the early work was carried out at the University of Birmingham (UK) Centre for Contemporary Cultural Studies. Stuart Hall, Jamaican-born sociologist and one of the key figures in the development of cultural studies, has written of the importance of the Marxist scholar Gramsci's concept of 'hegemony' (see **ideology and hegemony**) for the work of the Centre. Gramsci argued that in the modern world ideas are as much a force of repression as crude economic domination. This defence of culture as 'semi-autonomous' – that is, capable of generating social effects in its own right – stimulated the study of many dimensions of cultural production (for example, Hall *et al.*'s *Policing the Crisis* on the naming and reporting of the new crime of 'mugging', and the emphasis on romance as the most important thing in life in comics for teenage girls in Angela McRobbie's *Jackie: Ideology of Adolescent Femininity*) and cultural reproduction (Paul Willis's *Learning to Labour* on the complex relationship between the economy, masculinity and the official values of schooling).

The same question – how does culture sustain the existing power structure? – was at the same time being addressed in France by Pierre Bourdieu, using a classic technique of sociology: the large-scale social survey. Despite the avowedly meritocratic values of the republic, Bourdieu argued that those with an already privileged home background are best placed to take advantage of the education system. From the interplay of both they acquire the set of tastes and preferences bound up in 'legitimate culture' (as opposed to 'middle-brow' or 'working-class' culture). Crucially, this **cultural capital** can be converted into economic advantage and transmitted from one generation to another. But the mechanisms of the class system are obscured: having high status aesthetic tastes is socially constructed as being 'naturally cultivated'.

The importance of Bourdieu's work is his demonstration that judgements over aesthetics are not self-evident absolutes, as Arnold and the Leavises believed and many still believe, but are a direct expression of class struggle. He does, though, presuppose that the hierarchy of taste is widely, if resentfully, recognised and accepted. Similarly, early cultural studies work on texts took their meaning, and thus their ideological impact, as self-evident. Since the early 1980s the text/audience relationship has been radically questioned. Both in the humanities and the social sciences the concept of 'polysemy' has taken hold: a text, whether a novel, TV programme, or item of clothing, can be given several meanings – even an infinite number. In some senses this 'semiotic democracy' is indeed a challenge to the assumed authority of the producer (and the institutional order that produces producers) over the reader/consumer. On this basis many scholars have celebrated 'cultural populism', arguing that 'readings' of mass-produced popular culture can be 'oppositional', for instance that standardised items of clothing can be customised or popular newspapers treated as a joke.

Just as the real democratic significance of consumerism is increasingly in question, however, some writers on culture, particularly those from a sociological background, are restating the long-standing questions about the relationship between the hierarchies of value in the symbolic realm and their actual impact on people's life chances. If mass culture is commercially produced, is it not bound to reflect the interests of the producers? Can those who argue for 'oppositional readings' of mass culture demonstrate that these practices make any difference to the distribution of life chances? Even if the boundaries of what is seen as 'legitimate' taste have been flexed to include, for example, soccer and some popular music, is there not still an elite that polices that boundary? And, not least, there is the intractable political and methodological problem: are we, the audience, restricted to cultural preferences that have already been provided for us?

Further reading

During, Simon (ed.) (1999) *The Cultural Studies Reader*, 2nd edn. London: Routledge.

Storey, John (ed.) (1998) *Cultural Theory and Popular Culture: A Reader*, 2nd edn. Harlow, Essex: Pearson Education/Prentice Hall Europe.

Storey, John (2000) *Cultural Theory and Popular Culture: An Introduction*, 3rd edn. Harlow, Essex: Pearson Education/Prentice Hall Europe.

Tudor, Andrew (1999) *Decoding Culture: Theory and Method in Cultural Studies*. London: Sage.

Meryl Aldridge

DEFINITION OF THE SITUATION

The term derives from symbolic interactionism and the Chicago School of sociology, with its focus on the way people make sense of their encounters with others in everyday life, and how these interactions between knowledgeable social actors can be built up into more stable routines that give the appearance of social order. From this perspective, society is an ongoing, dynamic process of individuals interacting and giving meaning to their actions, albeit in an *ad hoc*, provisional manner.

William Thomas coined the definition of the situation in *The Unadjusted Girl* by claiming that, 'if men [sic] define situations as real, they are real in their consequences'. By this he meant that regardless of any claims we might try to make about the 'objective' conditions under which people live, it is also important to consider how the individuals themselves perceive their situation subjectively. An example of this would be Townsend's discussion of the difference between absolute and relative **poverty**, the latter being a subjective interpretation of the objective state. In the longer term, Thomas argued, moral codes and norms are established through successive definitions of the situation. He pointed to the significance of local communities as 'defining agencies' that established codes of socially desirable behaviour that could be enforced informally through practices like gossip, which served to deter people from deviant behaviour through the fear of social judgement. It was through collective mechanisms like this that social order was maintained.

At the level of face-to-face interaction, Thomas suggested that people always go through an initial stage of examination and deliberation, which allows them to take stock of who else is present, what they are doing and how we might best align our own action with theirs. This was not merely a psychological process but, rather, a collective activity, involving teams of actors all striving to 'take the role of the other', as Mead put it, and to establish a shared understanding of what is going on and how the situation ought to proceed. A clear example of this comes from Fred Davis's study of interactions between disabled and able-bodied people. He demonstrated how these teams of actors would work together to overcome any potential awkwardness and embarrassment: for example, the disabled people would show that they could participate in various 'normal' activities, and the able-bodied people might make jokes or affect a light-hearted attitude that served to 'disavow' any deviant or unusual behaviours. Pairs of actors thus created a definition of the situation as one in which the disability would not be a barrier to interaction, and in which they could rely upon each other to play their respective roles.

As American sociology developed over the twentieth century, Thomas's ideas were incorporated into more general theories of how social order was created and sustained through routine interaction. Herbert Blumer's account of symbolic interactionism emphasised that people act on the basis of meanings that are produced in social inter-action, and that the definition of the situation is always open to revision: people can make alternative interpretations or behave unexpectedly, and this requires those around them to adapt accordingly. Erving Goffman's dramaturgical theory also identified the strategies actors use to control the impressions that they make upon others, and how these 'team-mates' respond to embarrassing mistakes and blunders. These arguments also echoed Alfred Schütz's suggestion that actors rely upon common stocks of background knowledge and 'typifications' that lend order and predictability to social encounters, and that actors trust that everyone will follow these unspoken rules.

Anselm Strauss introduced the related idea of the 'negotiated order'. This is a social condition that has to be constantly accomplished, and that involves a precarious balance between the interests of various actors and the normative demands of the situation. As a medical sociologist, Strauss was particularly interested in the negotiation of social order in hospitals, where a strict hierarchical division of labour demands that medical staff and their patients interact in a smooth and predictable way. In a study conducted with his colleague Barney Glaser he described how nurses attended to the 'awareness contexts' of dying patients, adjusting what they said and did according to how much they thought the patients knew about their prognoses. While focusing on small-scale, face-to-face interaction, Strauss maintained that structural conditions would constrain individual action: in this case, the power held by various hospital staff gave them more or less freedom in the way that they carried out their roles. He also identified certain properties of the 'negotiation context', such as the number of views being represented and the visibility of transactions, which could shape the outcome of an interaction. Thus Strauss's work, like that of Thomas and others in the interactionist tradition, helps us to see the order that lies in even the most spontaneous of social encounters.

Further reading

Blumer, Herbert (1969) *Symbolic Interactionism: Perspective and Method.* Englewood Cliffs, NJ: Prentice-Hall.
Goffman, Erving (1959) *The Presentation of Self in Everyday Life.* Penguin: Harmondsworth.
Strauss, Anselm L. (1978) *Negotiations: Varieties, Contexts, Processes and Social Order.* San Francisco: Jossey-Bass.
Thomas, William I. (1923) *The Unadjusted Girl.* Boston: Little, Brown & Co.

Susie Scott

DEVIANCE

Deviance refers to behaviour, demeanours, attitudes, beliefs and styles which break the norms, rules, ethics and expectations of a society. In contrast to biological, psychological and individual positivist accounts that view deviance as something inherent in a certain type of conduct or person, sociologists have challenged a simple distinction between the normal and the pathological, considered deviance as a feature of social situations and social structures, and highlighted not just the processes of rule-breaking but also rule-making, rule-enforcing and rule-transmitting. There is no fixed agreement on the substance of deviance. Indeed, sociologists of deviance suggest that the determination of deviance, its meaning and societal reaction to it depends on the context, biography and purpose.

The study of deviance has been central to the concerns of sociological theory. For Durkheim, crime (and, by extension, deviance in general) is 'normal' and functional for the social order; it serves to heighten collective sentiments and solidarity and to clarify and reinforce the values and norms of the group. His original notion of **anomie** (or a state of normlessness) as a source of deviant behaviour has been taken up, expanded upon and reworked by others. Robert Merton stressed socially induced strains (i.e. a lack of symmetry between the culture and the social structure) and deviant adaptations. Chicago sociologists in their ecological theories and ethnographies of crime and delinquency stressed the socially disorganised zones in a city. Subcultural theorists such as Albert Cohen, David Matza and Richard Cloward and Lloyd Ohlin stressed deviant **subcultures** as learned problem solutions and group processes of status frustration and drift.

By the 1960s and 1970s, structural-functionalist and early sub-culturalist approaches to deviance had been challenged by more radicalising approaches in sociology and criminology. Symbolic interactionists emphasised the significance of the social audience, social reactions and public meanings in shaping and transforming deviant phenomena. Critical criminologists were concerned with mapping the structures of power, their interconnections with the state and its control apparatus, and with synthesising neo-Marxist and conflict theories. Members of the Birmingham Centre for Cultural Studies in their substantial work on youth **culture** stressed resistance to sub-ordination through rituals and symbols, and processes of control – especially the policing of black youth – within the context of class conflict and hegemonic crises. Feminist criminologists were critical of malestream accounts of deviance and their sex-linked biases and argued for the analytical centrality of the relations between gender, crime and both formal and informal social controls.

During the heyday of the sociology of deviance, critical conceptual-isation of deviance went hand in hand with a restructuring of empirical concerns. Sociologists turned their attention to the social construction of the deviant **role** and identity in diverse areas of everyday life (for example, dwarfs, giants, stutterers, strippers, drug takers, nudists, the blind, the dying, the physically and mentally ill). For theorists in the labelling tradition, the process of 'becoming deviant' becomes apparent when someone perceives another person as departing from accepted norms (which may be legal, religious, cultural, sexual or political in nature), interprets the person to be some kind of deviant (for example, mad, bad, perverted, heretic, subversive), and influences others also to regard the person as deviant and to act on the basis of that interpretation (for example, with suspicion, avoidance, censure, vengeance). Edwin Lemert argued that rule-breaking is commonplace in everyday life and that many episodes of norm violation provoke little reaction from others or have marginal effect on a person's self-concept (i.e. 'primary deviance'). In most cases, rule-breaking becomes normalised and accommodated into the fabric of accepted life. It is when negative societal reaction to initial deviance takes place (as stigma) and sets in motion an individual's repeated rule-breaking behaviour and adoption of a deviant identity as a means of adjustment that the deviation arguably becomes 'secondary'.

This pattern of labelling and discrediting certain classes of behaviour at certain times has been noted by Harold Garfinkel in his discussion of the degradation of officially recognised criminals. In the study of mental illness, sociologists such as Thomas Scheff and Erving Goffman and anti-psychiatrists such as Thomas Szasz and Ronald Laing have argued that mental disorder is a social role (the role of the mentally disturbed patient), and that the societal reaction is the most important determinant of entry into the role and status of the mentally ill. Mental disorder involves labelled violations of taken-for-granted social norms (so-called 'residual' rule-breaking), lay and professional responses to such infractions, and application of labels of madness (rather than, say, labels of wrongdoing or as 'problems of living'). Physicians play a key part in the social processes leading to mental disorder, making evaluative judgements of what counts as sanity and insanity and acting as agents of regulation. Seen in this light, the concept of mental disorder is inextricably linked to issues of control and power and to pressures to maintain conformity.

The concept of deviance amplification has been most commonly used to explain escalations in expressive forms of deviancy, notably Becker's work on marijuana use and the creation of deviant careers. Studies of police and judicial reaction (for example, William Chambliss on the Saints and the Roughnecks) have been taken to suggest the discriminatory and amplificatory implications of formal intervention, though the concept's applicability to other less publicised forms of rule-breaking is less clear (it could be argued that it is a lack of negative social reaction in some instances, such as domestic violence, which promotes its continuation). Others have gone beyond the labelling processes (stigmatisation) and explicitly brought political analysis (criminalisation) into deviancy study. From this, sociologists examined the rhetorics and the power struggle behind the construction of deviance and produced a series of empirical studies concerning the origins of deviancy definitions through political actions that identify certain social problems as crime problems whilst ignoring other dangers to society. Examples are Joseph Gusfield's analysis of temperance legislation and his 'symbolic crusades' during the Prohibition era, Anthony Platt's discussion of delinquency definitions and the 'child saving movement', and Stan Cohen's discussion of the role of the media in producing folk devils and moral panics.

Critical insights of deviancy theory also dovetailed into penal reform movements in the 1970s. If, as labelling theorists suggested, social reaction does not reduce offending but confirms deviant careers, then the reach of social reaction and penal censure should be minimised.

Decriminalisation, decarceration and radical social work movements grew out of an abolitionist critique of penal and institutional responses to deviance and other criminalised problems. Abolitionists such as Tom Mathiesen pointed to the top-down, repressive character of penal control, the appropriation of conflicts from their owners and the fundamental shortcomings of the law in realising social justice, and argued that legal sanction should be replaced by dispute settlement and redress. Total institutions in general and the prison system in particular were seen as brutalising, ineffective in terms of their stated goals (they neither deter nor rehabilitate), perpetuating class relations and widening the net of social control (more, rather than fewer, deviants are drawn into the correctional continuum), though critics such as Andrew Scull have argued that the state-sponsored closing down of hospitals for the mentally ill and the rhetoric of treatment in the community often amounted to benign neglect in practice.

Whilst deviance remains an important sensitising concept in the sociological canon, many have argued that the sociology of deviance has lost its cutting edge and become yet another sociological orthodoxy. Critical criminology has gone beyond the symbolic interactionist paradigm to embrace a much more diverse agenda, including analyses of discipline, state power, human rights as well as the left realist idea that crime has to be 'taken seriously' as it tends to hit the most vulnerable parts of society.

Further reading

Becker, Howard (1963) *Outsiders*. New York: Free Press.
Downes, David and Rock, Paul (2003) *Understanding Deviance: A Guide to the Sociology of Crime and Rule Breaking*, 4th edn. Oxford: Oxford University Press.
Matza, David (1969) *Becoming Deviant*. Englewood Cliffs, NJ: Prentice-Hall.
Sumner, Colin (1994) *The Sociology of Deviance: An Obituary*. Buckingham: Open University Press.

Maggy Lee

DISCOURSE

A growing interest in the concept of discourse has resulted in many new theoretical approaches in the social sciences, as well as a widening of its scope and sophistication. In traditional linguistics, discourse refers to 'talk and text in context', i.e. any connected sequence of writing or speaking, and discourses are usually understood as the products of a single speaker or writer, or by a set of subjects engaging in **conversation** or written communication. In this narrow sense, discourse analysis investigates the structures of discourse by analysing the way its grammatical concepts and terms organise a speech or text.

One particular variant of this restricted concern with spoken and written discourse in the social sciences, but which rejects a purely grammatical approach, is evident in conversation analysis. Here efforts are made to discern *what* speakers and receivers do when conversing – and *how* they do it – purely by observing their interactive behaviour. This approach holds that sociology ought to be concerned with ways in which subjects make sense of, and exhibit, their understandings of the social world by ordering their experiences in specific contexts.

Another more narrowly conceived approach to discourse analysis is found in speech act theory, which was developed by the English philosopher J. L. Austin. Austin directed attention in philosophy away from 'assertoric' utterances – statements that assert something about the world – to 'performative' utterances, in which to *say* something is also to *do* something. To say 'I promise' is to *act* in the here and now, while committing yourself to future actions. And to assess such an utterance is not to inquire into whether or not it is true or false, but whether it is carried out. Speech act theory thus brings out the performative character of language. This has been used by theorists such as Judith Butler to analyse rhetoric – the art of persuasive speaking and writing – and controversial political discourses and speeches.

More expansive versions of discourse are evident in approaches that stress the way speaking and writing are connected to *social contexts*. Michel Foucault is important here in his attempt to develop an 'archaeology of knowledge', which centred on analysing the conditions under which statements of knowledge are deemed acceptable and truthful. This involves describing the rules informing particular discursive formations, and the way these rules are connected to wider social and political practices. Foucault's later genealogical approach to discourse analysis focused on the emergence of 'power/knowledge' complexes. Here he was concerned with the intermeshing of discourses and **power** strategies, such as the coupling of criminological discourse and the modern penal system, and on the critique of such articulations through a focus on their historical elaboration, which involved political exclusions and foreclosures.

'Critical discourse analysts' like Norman Fairclough build on Foucault's endeavour to connect discourse to its wider social and political context, while retaining an emphasis on the careful grammatical and linguistic analysis of texts and speeches. This enables them to ask critical questions about the discourses they analyse. How and why was a particular text articulated? To whom is it addressed, and for what purpose? What are the assumptions or surmises that are concealed in a text? How do texts 'organise in' and 'organise out' certain interests and values? In what ways, if any, are texts complicit with dominant and oppressive power structures? For example, Fairclough draws attention to a process of 'nominalisation' in which a word such as 'change' is used as a noun instead of a verb. He shows how in the speeches of Tony Blair the result of this nominalisation is a simplifying abstraction of complex social processes, the concealment of who or what is changing, the 'backgrounding' of change itself, and a 'foregrounding' of the outcomes of change. The result of such 'backgrounding/foregrounding' is to render questions about agency and causality less visible, thus presenting social processes as inevitable and possessing a life of their own.

Within the domain of moral and political philosophy, Jürgen Habermas has developed a further aspect of the concept by elaborating a notion of 'discourse ethics' in his critical theory. Locating the latter within his overall social theory, especially his account of language, in which linguistic meaning depends on the presence of other language users – a state of 'intersubjectivity' – Habermas proposes an 'ideal speech situation' in order to determine the validity, and thus accept-ability, of utterances. The procedure requires each participant to be sincere in reasoning towards the best argument, and that the procedure include all those affected. If this is approximated, then agreement or consensus on 'the force of the better argument' can be expected. In this context, discourse ethics is a form of normative ethics, comprising the argumentative rules that social actors must accept if they are to argue reasonably for the claims they propose to validate. So conceived, discourse becomes central in resolving conflicts and disagreements that emerge between asymmetrically positioned actors in the modern social world. For Habermas, conflicts arise because different systems of instrumental **action** (such as the bureaucratic capitalist state) clash with and dominate – or 'colonize' – the social lifeworld, where agents interact and relate to each on the basis of communicative (rather than 'instrumental') action. Discourse ethics enables a legitimate and democratic resolution of such contestation. Habermas's political theory then arises from his account of ethics, and comprises a commitment to the ideals of inclusiveness, equality, and universal solidarity, each of which he argues is implicit in discourse and language-use.

Finally, one of the most extensive and elaborate versions of discourse theory is found in the work of Ernesto Laclau, together with Chantal Mouffe and those associated with his research programme. Synthesising aspects of post-structuralism, psychoanalysis, Marxism, and aspects of the work of Ludwig Wittgenstein, Laclau endeavours to account for the political structuring of social orders, and the constitution of subjective identities. This model draws upon Ferdinand de Saussure's structural linguistics to conceptualise social orders as systems of differential elements, and to account for their political structuring through the logics of equivalence (substitution) and difference (combination).

In making discourse co-extensive with society, and a constitutive dimension of all social relations, Laclau greatly extends the scope of the concept. This means that systems of social relations are understood as *symbolic* orders; that all objects and practices in the social world are meaningful entities; and that *all* **social systems** are essentially incomplete, as they are constituted by political exclusions and conflicts. The role of social antagonisms, which mark the limit points of any social order, are thus crucial for constructing and contesting particular discursive formations. In turn, antagonistic constructions presuppose the idea that social orders are marked by absences or lacks – they are, in short, 'dislocated' – and constant efforts have to be made to 'cover-over' such gaps by articulating new discourses. In this model, the identities of social agents are constituted within discourses, and novel political subjects arise when the dislocated character of social relations is made visible and agents arc 'compelled' to identify with newly available objects.

Further reading

Butler, Judith (1997) *Excitable Speech*. London: Routledge.

Fairclough, Norman (1992) *Discourse and Social Change*. Cambridge: Polity Press.

Finlayson, Gordon (2005) *Habermas: A Very Short Introduction*. Oxford: Oxford University Press.

Howarth, David (2000) *Discourse*. Buckingham: Open University.

Torfing, Jacob (1999) *New Theories of Discourse*. Oxford: Blackwell.

David Howarth

DIVISION OF LABOUR

This classic and almost foundational concept of sociology has endured over time, being extended and reformulated with changing historical circumstances and new analytical perspectives. The central focus of the division of labour is the socio-economic organisation of production, and its relation to more general societal modes of cohesion or integration. Although it has a long pre-history, the division of labour came into its own as a sociological concept with attempts to understand the rapid and momentous social transformations of nineteenth-century Europe, **industrialism** and **urbanism**.

Both Aristotle and Plato had linked the formation of societies with the need for a division of labour. It was also an important concept for classical political economy. In *The Wealth of Nations*, Adam Smith argued that the division of labour increases the productive powers of labour and hence the capacity for wealth creation. Using the celebrated example of a pin factory, he showed that 'division and combination of different operations' into successive tasks resulted in a minimum 240-fold increase in manufacture. While sociological appropriations of the concept by Durkheim and Marx also highlight specialisation, individuation and consequent interdependence, they do not link these in the same way or so positively as Smith with the free market and competition. Their concern is rather with the socio-economic-political underpinnings of the division of labour and with its accompanying forms of cohesion, **solidarity**, inequality, **power** and morality or **ideology**.

In *The Division of Labour in Society*, Durkheim's primary interest was the effect on social solidarity of different kinds of division of labour. He counterposed 'organic' to 'mechanical' solidarity, seeing the former as characteristic of 'advanced' and 'technical' societies and the latter of clan or kinship-based 'primitive' societies. In the latter, he argued (on the basis of incorrect anthropological data), people are relatively undifferentiated from each other. All engage in the same activities and adhere to a set of common values and norms (the 'conscience collective') which binds them together. Where the division of labour is undeveloped, as in such mechanical societies, **solidarity** and individuality are incompatible. In modern industrial societies, by contrast, organic solidarity derives from complementary difference and interdependence that results from functional differentiation and specialisation. Individuation and difference produced by the division of labour here become the basis of social solidarity, rather than undermining it, and cohesion is a result of enhanced social ties. Individualism is a collective value shared by the whole society.

Durkheim's theory of the division of labour differs from many others, including that of Marx, in attaching greater significance to its beneficial effects for social solidarity than to its economic advantages. In his interpretation, social conflict is evidence of pathological, incomplete or abnormal development of the division of labour, rather than being seen as arising from or endemic in societies with complex divisions of labour. Class conflict results from the **anomie** of the unregulated division of labour, when industrialisation proceeds too quickly for social mechanisms to be developed for controlling competition and regulating markets. Where a mismatch occurs between peoples' abilities and talents and their occupations and jobs, a 'forced' division of labour results.

Unlike Durkheim, Marx, and the later Marxist tradition, understood the division of labour as inherently contradictory. Subdivision and fragmentation of tasks carry the potential for asymmetric relations of power, skill, knowledge and economic reward. **Power** and **class** are central to their politically critical analysis. Writing in the period when factory manufacture superseded handicraft production, Marx drew attention to the demise of the all-round craft worker, the repetition of fragmented and simplified tasks, reduction of the value of labour power and vast expansion in the proportion of unskilled workers, who share common conditions and hence the potential for forming a class. New forms of inequality were inevitable when the division of labour was enmeshed with the private property and commodity relations of capitalist production. A hierarchy of labour powers emerged with a corresponding scale of wages, and there was an ever-expanding divide between rewards to labour and capital. However, since the effects of the division of labour are closely shaped by the exchange relations of the mode of production of which it is part, they may differ in non-capitalist social formations where it is implemented differently. In some earlier writings, Marx argued for total abolition of the division of labour, suggesting that in a future communist society it would be possible 'to hunt in the morning, fish in the afternoon, rear cattle in the evening, criticise after dinner'. This aim continued to characterise certain utopian strands of twentieth-century Marxism. However, in *Capital* and his later work, Marx narrowed this concern to overcoming the division between mental and manual labour. This too remained a target for socialist theory and practice, notably in Chinese and Indian communisms and in Western academic commentary.

Extensions of the concept, attempting to account for new realities, tend to take as given the detailed division of occupations in economic life that had prompted classical thinking. Attention has shifted to the ways this is underpinned by, produces or connects with, other social or economic divisions in mutually determining relations which exist at a variety of levels and scales. Uneven economic development between countries, highlighted in Marx's analyses of colonialism and Lenin's of imperialism, became a major focus, widening the scope of the concept to the global plane. Attention is drawn to the complex relations of unequal power and wealth linking different regions and countries by studies of the dense spatial and international divisions of labour where different places specialise in different fields of work (for example agricultural versus high-tech production or the transfer offshore of routine information processing jobs from Western to developing countries). Initiated by Harry Braverman, 'labour process' approaches pursue in-depth analysis of the forms of managerialism and organisational power relations associated with new technologies of production, distribution and sale of goods and services, including information and knowledge. Particular emphasis is attached to processes of deskilling.

A significant and fruitful development of the concept, stimulated by the insights of the women's and anti-racist movements of the 1970s, focuses on the intertwining of the technical division of labour with ethnic, gender or other principles of social division. Ethnicised or racialised divisions of labour are characteristic of many countries, with migrant workers or their descendants concentrated in lower-paid and skilled jobs, resulting in a hierarchically segmented labour market. Long-standing gendered divisions of labour underlie the concentration of women in particular occupations and men in others. Cultural, educational and life-stage factors are clearly implicated in perpetuating the distribution of work and the detailed way that the division of labour enmeshes with gender, sexuality, ethnicity and so on. Recent reformulations of the concept, in contrast to those confined to formal paid employment, extend its reach across socio-economic modes. This facilitates analysis not only of unpaid and non-market work but also of the connection and intersection between and across divisions of labour undertaken within differing socio-economic relations. The concept is renewed with enhanced power to cope with ongoing historical change and social divisions unknown or ignored by its classical proponents.

Further reading

Bradley, Harriett (1989) *Men's Work, Women's Work.* Cambridge: Polity Press.

Braverman, Harry (1974) *Labor and Monopoly Capital: The Degradation of Work in the Twentieth Century.* New York: Monthly Review Press.

Cohen, Robin (1987) *The New Helots: Migrants in the International Division of Labour.* Aldershot: Avebury.

Durkheim, Émile (1893) *The Division of Labour in Society.* New York: Free Press, 1964.

Glucksmann, Miriam (2000) *Cottons and Casuals: The Gendered Organisation of Labour in Time and Space*. Durham: Sociologypress
Marx, Karl (1867) *Capital, Volume 1*. Harmondsworth: Penguin, 1976. Chapter 14: The division of labour and manufacture.

Miriam Glucksmann

DOMESTIC LABOUR

Originally developed in the women's movement, this concept was absorbed into sociology from the 1970s, initially through Ann Oakley's study of housework as low-status job with long hours and poor pay. Taken-for-granted assumptions, naturalising women's association with the home and femininity with domestic work, were effectively disrupted. The recognition that housework was a worthy topic of study and that cooking, cleaning, washing and the other tasks involved in running a household involved *work* had far-reaching long-term repercussions, signalling the beginnings of major change in sociological thinking not only about work and employment, but also about gender and social division.

Much feminist analysis had focused on determining who were the main beneficiaries of the unpaid work of women in the home. In what became known as 'the domestic labour debate', radical feminists centred on men and husbands as appropriating women's unpaid labour. Socialist feminists initially focused on the 'free' transfer of value to capitalist employers made possible by employing male workers whose costs of daily reproduction they did not bear, shifting later to a broader interpretation of the role of domestic labour in reproducing **capitalism** as a mode of production, including its ideological conditions. Marx's theory of surplus value, revolving around the cost of reproducing labour power in terms of the value of 'necessary' commodities (food, shelter, clothing) was underpinned by his important distinction between production and reproduction. However, no consideration was accorded to the additional and unpaid domestic labour required to reproduce labour power, thus presenting a fundamental challenge to the theory. In the 1980s, arcane disputes notwithstanding, there was widespread agreement that unpaid household labour contributed to the perpetuation of both **gender** and **class** relations since men's availability for formal paid employment was normally predicated on the unpaid domestic labour of women. Then dominant stratification theories, which took occupation as the indicator of class, were seriously undermined by growing awareness that paid employment could not be understood in isolation from other forms of work that underpinned it.

Approaches to domestic labour have matured and diversified, but gender and inequality remain structuring principles of analysis. Influenced by Arlie Hochschild, domestic labour was extended to non-material emotion and caring work. Studies of transformations in domestic technology stimulated vigorous debate as to whether 'labour saving' devices, such as the microwave oven, actually save time or merely raise standards of household perfection. Much empirical research has been devoted to the impact on the domestic division of labour of increasing levels of women's paid employment. Figures suggesting increasing domestic gender equality amongst professional groups, however, may be an effect of buying in technologies or labour rather than of internal redistribution. Contemporary concerns centre on the re-emergence of domestic service, the rapid growth of paid domestic work, notably by migrants recruited from less developed countries, and the resultant complex intersections of gender, ethnic and class inequality. Domestic labour is acknowledged as integral to the global **division of labour**. International awareness of the contribution of domestic labour has generated attempts to measure its value, usually time-based given the absence of monetary transaction. The consequent 'satellite' accounts, which parallel and complement standard national financial accounting, provide a novel means for comparing previously incommensurable forms of work and the potential for official economic recognition of domestic labour.

Further reading

Anderson, Bridget (2000) *Doing the Dirty Work. The Global Politics of Domestic Labour*. London: Zed Books.

Ehrenreich, Barbara and Hochschild, Arlie R. (eds) (2003) *Global Woman: Nannies, Maids and Sex Workers in the New Economy*. London: Granta.

Cowan, Ruth Schwartz (1989) *More Work for Mother*. London: Free Association Books.

Kaluzynska, Eva (1980) 'Wiping the floor with theory: a survey of writings on housework', *Feminist Review*, 6: 27–54.

Oakley, Ann (1974) *Housewife*. Harmonsdsworth: Penguin.

Miriam Glucksmann

ELITE

The word 'elite' has been one of the most general terms to be used in descriptive studies, and almost any powerful, advantaged, qualified, privileged, or superior group or category has been called an elite: politicians, bishops, intelligent people and successful criminals, to name just a few. A more useful approach is to narrow it down and see elites distinguished from other kinds of social group by the fact that they are groups with a particular kind of **power**. Following Gaetano Mosca, an elite should be seen as comprising those who occupy the top positions in a hierarchy of command.

Any hierarchy of command is headed by an elite. The leading positions of command within a ministry, an established church, or a business enterprise, for example, each comprise an elite. The boundaries of elites are identified from their inter-organisational relations. Political elites formed within ministries and departments of a state – government, judiciary, military, etc., – have various formal connections with each other that link them as branches of a **state**. It is possible, therefore, to talk of a state elite. Similarly, the economic elites within particular business enterprises – their directors and top executives – may be inter-organisationally linked through common ownership, membership in employers' federations and sales cartels, and interlocking directorships in such ways that it may be possible to talk of an overall economic or corporate elite rather than simply a collection of separate company elites. Members of such an elite will have powers of command that connect and coordinate the activities of large numbers of enterprises and they may be able to bring about a degree of coordination across the economy as a whole

Since Mosca, particular attention has been given to the extent to which the members of the various elites in a society overlap or circulate from one elite position to another. Where the overlap and circulation is great, it is possible to speak of the elites of a society forming a single, overarching elite to which Mosca gave the name 'ruling class' or 'ruling elite' and Mills the name 'power elite'. Such a ruling elite has a merely formal existence unless it can be shown that its members actually associate with each other and share a particular outlook on power. Explorations into the social background and recruitment of elites have investigated the networks of interaction and association – of social mobility, leisure time interaction, education, intermarriage and friendship – through which elite members may be connected into a cohesive group. Elites are not always unified or cohesive. Political and business elites may be internally divided along ideological, religious, ethnic, or other lines, and these divisions may prevent the formation of a larger ruling elite and preclude them achieving any overall solidarity. An important issue is the extent to which elites recruit from particular **class** or **status** backgrounds. Wealthy classes and honoured status groups are, in analytical terms, quite distinct from commanding elites, even though they may be closely associated in actual situations.

Elites should be seen as related to the distribution and exercise of power in structures of command. The attempt to extend the term beyond this should be resisted. People in highly paid occupational groups and those with high IQs, for example, are not usefully seen as elites. To call them elites, as that term has been defined here, makes it more difficult to study either group with any precision.

Further reading

Bottomore, Tom (1993) *Elites and Society*, 2nd edn. London: Routledge.
Scott, John (ed.) (1990) *The Sociology of Elites*, three volumes. Cheltenham: Edward Elgar Publishing.

John Scott

EMOTION

Although 'the sociology of the emotions' is now a rapidly expanding area of study, it first emerged in the United States as recently as the mid-1970s, to be taken up in Britain only from the 1980s. Why was there such a delay in developing sociological ways of thinking about and researching emotion? How have changes in sociology made it easier to accommodate emotion, and what new areas of discussion are being opened up?

The first major problem is what precisely are emotions? Historically, there have been a number of contrasting perspectives in the analysis of emotion. The evolutionary theorist Charles Darwin regarded the physical expression or display of emotion as a 'natural' part of our human evolution and biological inheritance, while the psychoanalyst Sigmund Freud viewed emotion in terms of the tension or anxiety caused by dammed up 'libido' (sexual drive). Neither perspective, at least initially, appeared to point to any need for further sociological analysis. Indeed, and following the Western philosophical tradition of splitting mind from body, and reason from emotion, classical sociologists were seen as having viewed emotions as individual, private, irrational and 'feminine' – and therefore not important topics for theorisation. Some feminists have criticised mainstream sociology for being 'malestream', formulating a sociology where emotion was omitted or rendered invisible through the discussion of disembodied 'rational men' rather than 'sentient persons'.

Recent re-reading, however, has underlined that while classical sociological texts do not explicitly focus on the analysis of emotions, they do contain important ideas about them. Marx, for example, wrote of **alienation** as involving feelings of anger, bitterness and resentment provoked in workers by the way that **capitalism** organises work relationships. Durkheim described how collective rituals could heighten feelings of group solidarity, while Weber saw the development of **bureaucracy** involving the elimination of love, hatred and all personal, 'irrational' and emotional elements. Weber contemplated a future society gripped in the 'iron cage' of rationality.

In 1939 the German sociologist, Norbert Elias, analysed the 'civilizing process' in European society. This was a process through which the unpredictable, highly emotional and self-indulgent life of the Middle Ages gradually came under the control of social codes of emotional and bodily self-restraint. Elias noted how the expression of emotion combines biologically 'programmed' and socially learnt processes: the human smile is an *innate* reflex in young babies, but older individuals learn to 'steer' or manage their facial muscles to simulate a range of real or false emotions.

From the late 1950s the American sociologist, Erving Goffman, developed the study of interpersonal relationships in ways which would open up further possibilities for the sociological study of emotion. He distinguished between 'backstage' behaviour (emotionally uncontrolled when out of sight) and the way that individuals manage their presentation of **self** in their daily relationships with others in order to arouse favourable feelings and avoid embarrassment. Since the 1970s, many other sociologists have tended to discount the 'objective' biological and psychic bases of emotion in favour of exploring how emotional experiences are socially patterned and even 'socially constructed': that is, how emotions are evoked, enacted, heightened or downplayed through shared language, rituals and conventions. Indeed, Norman Denzin argues that all persons are joined to society through their subjective experiences of emotion − their 'self-feelings' − without which everyday life would become an empty repetitive round, devoid of moral significance.

Arlie Hochschild carried out research into the ways in which individuals 'manage' their emotions, but she stresses that those emotions have important bodily and psychic roots. What she calls 'real' (i.e. unmanaged) feelings provide individuals with valuable understanding of their relationships with the world and expectations of it, and also indicate how they should act. But individuals are also subject to pressures from society, through sets of 'feeling rules' that prescribe how they 'ought' to feel in particular situations ('It's my wedding day, so I *should* feel happy'). Individuals may try to act in conformity with these rules by doing 'emotion work' (involving psychic and/or physical energy) on 'managing' their real feelings to bring them into line. Such emotion work may be done by individuals on themselves or on others, or by others on the individual, and it is expressed through different levels of acting. 'Surface acting' involves merely a shallow pretence of emotion for the benefit of others, but in 'deep acting' individuals work on their 'real emotions' in order to try to change them.

Hochschild highlights the importance of gender in what she calls the 'commercialization of human feeling', where (mostly) women are paid to do 'emotional *labour*' in service sector jobs. In such labour, they must, for example, smile and say 'have a nice day' to McDonalds' customers or airline passengers, in order to make them feel good. (Men, on the other hand, tend to be paid to look tough, and to act as if they are in control.) Such emotional labour, however, has its costs. Actors may 'feel phoney' and experience emotional 'burnout', and they may come to question the 'authenticity' of their own feelings: 'Am I acting now? How do I know?'

Today, the sociology of emotion is rapidly expanding to explore a range of new areas. For example, concepts from the sociology of emotion are being used to explore such things as gender differences in the outcomes of early **socialisation**, contrasting attitudes to 'love' and 'intimacy' in couple relationships, 'anger management' courses for the perpetrators of domestic violence, the role of nurses in managing illness, the ways in which emotion links bodily health and bodily images, and the teaching of 'emotional literacy' in management training and in education more generally. On a broader scale, the sociology of emotion is now an element in sociological studies of shopping, the entertainment, sport and leisure industries, **community** relations, the internet, war and 'ethnic cleansing'.

Indeed, such large efforts are now being exerted in arousing and manipulating emotions – through **McDonaldisation** or 'Disneyfication' – that people are increasingly turning to therapists and counsellors to help them to get in touch with their 'real' feelings. Some theorists, however, argue that we now live in a 'post-emotional' society, where individuals are no longer capable of experiencing 'authentic' emotions.

Further reading

Bendelow, Gillian and Williams, Simon J. (eds) (1998) *Emotions in Social Life: Critical Themes and Contemporary Issues*. London: Routledge.

Hochschild, Arlie R. (1983) *The Managed Heart: The Commercialisation of Human Feelings*. Berkeley, CA: University of California Press.
Lupton, Deborah (1998) *The Emotional Self*. London: Sage.
Mestrovic, Stjepan (1996) *Postemotional Society*. London: Sage.
Williams, Simon J. (2001) *Emotion and Social Theory*. London: Sage.

Jean Duncombe

ETHNICITY

Ethnicity is a self-conscious and claimed identity that is shared with others on the basis of belief in common descent, and may be linked to country of origin, language, religion, or customs, and may also be shaped by contact with others and experiences of colonisation or migration. The concept is, however, a slippery one that, as Weber pointed out, is not easily susceptible to rigorous sociological analysis, as it is hard to be precise about either its definition or its stability across different contexts. It is often also, either conceptually or in usage, merged with particular understandings of **race**. In Britain and Europe the language of ethnicity has generally replaced that of race as it is not, like race, explicitly tied to the erroneous belief in the existence of distinct racial groups. However, the two terms continue to be tied together to allow a discussion of racism in relation to ethnic difference. Moreover, the primordialist conception of ethnicity essentialises ethnic groups and differences in such a way as to make it very close to theories of race. In addition, ethnicity is not universally held to be a less problematic term than race. For example, in South Africa, the language of ethnicity was associated with the apartheid era government's attempts to foster divisions within the Black majority and to justify its 'homelands' policy. And in North America, the term race is regularly used in sociological discussion with the assumption that race is already known and accepted to be a social construction.

In so far as ethnicity is self-consciously claimed, it is part of an individual's identity. However, its salience as an aspect of identity will tend to vary with context as will the particular ethnicity stressed. A person might feel their dominant ethnicity as Welsh or British or white in different situations. The notion of layering of identities has been used to explore these different levels of ethnicity and of how they interact with other aspects of identity. Identification with a particular ethnicity may also not be stable over time. Research has drawn attention to how in particular contexts people 'become' white or begin to recognise Native American ancestry as an element of their identity.

Identification with a particular ethnicity will also be affected by the perceptions of others and their use of ethnic categories to situate an individual. Such processes of own and others' identification, along with a sense of shared ethnicity, result in conceptions of distinct ethnic groups which can then be the focus of exploration of differences between them. Fredrik Barth argued that it is a focus on the limits or boundaries of groups, rather than their 'ethnic' content, that both forms and maintains discrete categories with clear parameters for inclusion and exclusion. Such ethnic groups are, in sociological analysis, often assumed to be both stable and to be self-evidently meaningful categories. However, they are subject to the processes of shifting identification noted above. Moreover, there is a danger that by distinguishing ethnic groups, explanations for differences between them will be sought in their ethnicity, however vaguely that is defined, rather than in other characteristics which also happen to be associated with particular groups. For example, as James Nazroo has discussed, differences in morbidity between ethnic groups may predominantly represent differences in **class** profiles across groups, rather than any specifically 'ethnic' practices or susceptibilities.

The categories available for defining particular ethnicities and thus allocating individuals to ethnic groups operate at a number of levels. For example, they may be associated with particular nationalities, such as (British) Pakistanis or (Kosovan) Albanians. They may distinguish at sub-national or supra-national levels, identifying tribes or distinct language groups. They may refer to the prior settlement in a colonised country, for example, Native Americans or Australian Aborigines; and they may draw on racialised perceptions of divisions between peoples, for example Black or Asian. Some may combine elements from more than one of these; and, as indicated above, different levels may come into operation in different contexts: one person may be Sylheti, Bangladeshi, British, and Asian at different times and places, and sociological investigation may also treat their ethnicity in these different ways depending on the focus of the investigation.

Sociological interest in ethnicity can take a number of forms. The primary focus can be the conceptualisation or realisation of ethnicity itself. Ethnicity can be explored as part of wider interests in identity and identification. A body of sociological research is concerned with the relations between different social groups, and ethnic relations are thus a major focus of inquiry. Examining whether particular groups are disadvantaged and whether and how societies discriminate against minorities requires analysis of different ethnic groups' experiences and life chances. However, when attempting to identify processes of discrimination, sociologists may be employing different conceptions of ethnic groups to those who are assumed to be doing the discriminating. For example, there has been recent discussion in Britain as to whether discrimination is particularly directed at Muslims – or those thought to be Muslim – rather than at minority ethnic groups as a whole or as defined in relation to their nation of origin (e.g. Pakistanis). Indeed, this area of sociological inquiry is one where sociological definitions have a particular tendency to be impinged upon by popular terminology and conceptions. The continued merging of the language of **race** with that of ethnicity, noted above, is one example of this. How the world is viewed – and therefore experienced – by society and by different social groups is of course highly relevant, in this area as in others. But taking on popular conceptions of ethnicity and race can risk losing all clarity about what is being investigated and why. Some would go further and argue that a real rejection of racial theory must involve ceasing to make such categorical distinctions between groups at all.

There is a tendency to regard ethnicity as a property only of minority groups, thus normalising the experience of the (white) majority. Moreover there has been a relatively recent popular diffusion of the term 'ethnic' to refer to clothing, consumption and practices that are regarded as exotic or deriving from abroad. Conceptually, however, all individuals belong to an ethnic group, regardless of whether the personal identification with that particular ethnicity is weakly felt. And majority practices, dress and consumption patterns can be investigated as ethnically differentiated to the same extent as those of minorities.

Further reading

Barth, Fredrik (1969) *Ethnic Groups and Boundaries: The Social Organisation of Culture Difference*. London: Allen & Unwin.

Cornell, Stephen and Hartmann, Douglas (1998) *Ethnicity and Race: Making Identities in a Changing World*. Thousand Oaks: Pine Forge Press.

Fenton, Steve (1999) *Ethnicity: Racism, Class and Culture*. Basingstoke: Macmillan.

Mason, David (2005) 'Ethnicity', in G. Payne, (ed.) *Social Divisions*, Basingstoke: Macmillan.

Nazroo, James (2001) *Ethnicity, Class and Health*. London: Policy Studies Institute.

Ratcliffe, Peter (2004) *Race, Ethnicity and Difference: Imagining the Inclusive Society*. Maidenhead: Open University Press.

Lucinda Platt

GENDER

Gender refers to those behaviours which define individuals as male or female in particular social and cultural contexts. Within Western culture it is generally assumed that differences in behaviour correspond with bodily differences which provide the material substratum for the elaboration of gender; this correspondence, however, is not necessarily present. It is also assumed that there are only two genders, an assumption that is not universally valid and which poses problems for those who are born with genitals that are not easily categorised as female or male or for those whose bodies are experienced as contradicting their gender.

Sandra Harding suggests that the study of gender involves three dimensions, gender symbolism (**culture**), the socio-sexual division of labour (**social structure**) and gender identities (**action and agency**). Within sociology different theoretical traditions conceptualise gender in different ways, usually emphasising one or another of these dimensions. In classical social theory women's and men's different places in the social division of labour were assumed to be 'natural' and based on their different roles in biological reproduction. Similar assumptions are present in the structural functionalism of Talcott Parsons. He developed a theory of sex roles which were rooted in the differentiation between expressive and instrumental action within the conjugal family. According to Parsons, women adopted expressive while men adopted instrumental roles. Social **roles** are associated with particular positions in the social division of labour and provide scripts of femininity and **masculinity** that are learnt through the process of socialisation; these scripts are differently gendered for girls and boys. Socialisation is gender specific and corresponds to biological sex; culture elaborates on a foundation provided by nature. This elaboration is not predetermined, however, and socialisation can be 'faulty'. This may lead to the acquisition of 'inappropriate' sex roles. 'Faulty' socialisation can, therefore, be used to explain homosexuality or other 'deviations' from normative sex roles. The idea of sex roles and gender socialisation are important in debates about gender equality and how young people can be encouraged to take up non-traditional jobs.

The idea of gender as role is also present in the work of symbolic interactionists. Erving Goffman, for instance, defines role as performance, akin to acting on stage. This suggests that roles are subject to change and can be taken on and off by individual social actors. This opens the door to conceptualising gender as performance which is an influential strand in current debates about gender and sexuality.

Feminist sociologists took sex-role theory to its logical conclusion, arguing that the almost infinite variety of sex roles cross-culturally suggest that they are not based on biological differences but are socially and culturally constructed. Ann Oakley made a conceptual distinction between biological sex, which relates to women's and men's different reproductive capabilities, and gender, which varies cross-culturally and is socially constructed. This conceptualisation of gender sees it as an ascribed position with associated sex-specific roles which vary within and between cultures. The conceptual separation of gender (cultural) from sex (natural) made it possible to understand that social relations based on sexual difference were social rather than natural.

This development, although important, did not take account of the relation between **power** and gender. Feminist sociologists who were influenced by Marxism and who took a political economy approach to understanding gender focused on gender/sexual divisions and the inequalities in access to power and resources which underpinned them. Gender was therefore seen as describing specific forms of social inequality and attempts were made to explain gender inequalities in terms of **capitalism** and/or **patriarchy**. Gender relations were conceptualised as rooted in the way production and reproduction were organised in society with women being associated with reproduction and men with production. Gender ideology as well as material differences in women's and men's reproductive roles was offered as a way of explaining why capitalist societies were marked by gender inequalities. Patriarchy was also advanced as a concept to define the 'sex-gender' system, separate from but interacting with capitalism, which advantaged men and disadvantaged women; or advantaged some groups of men over other men and all women.

With the advent of postmodernism attempts to explain apparently universal gender inequalities of power were abandoned and the focus returned to gender as an attribute of individuals constructed through cultural practice. Instead of analysing gender in terms of social structures and social systems the construction of gendered subjectivities of **self and identity** became important. This can be seen as part of the 'cultural turn' within sociology whereby **culture** displaced society and the economy as a focus of theoretical concern. This shift can be understood as a move from studying socio-sexual divisions of labour to studying gender symbolism and gender identities.

Michel Foucault's theorisations of discourse and power have been very influential in the way gender is conceptualised. The process of construction of subjectivities within gendered discourses and the ways that individuals engage with this construction have become an important focus for studies of gender; especially for studies of boys and men. Judith Butler has developed this approach and, in common with Goffman, sees gender as performance but, unlike Goffman, as performance supported by institutional structures. She sees gender not as an essential or ascribed attribute, but as something that we all 'do' in the course of our daily lives and it is this 'doing' which constructs our 'being' as gendered. Butler conceptualises gender as a system of signs that is infused with power. Gender, **sexuality** and identity are all elements of the discourse of heterosexuality and it is within discourses that power is constituted. The only way of challenging or resisting this power is to disrupt the elements of the discourse by doing gender in a way which challenges the assumed link between biological bodies and social gender. This can be done by cross-dressing for example which sets bodies and sartorial style at odds with each other. Such performances disrupt the supposedly natural association of gender, sexuality and identity which is thereby shown to be arbitrary. This way of theorising gender has given rise to queer theory which argues that playing with gender not only disrupts the association between gender, sexuality and identity but also the binary definition of gender (masculine/ feminine), thereby facilitating the end of gender as a meaningful social category. There is an ongoing debate about the effectiveness of this strategy in disrupting the power relations underpinning gender and heterosexuality with some arguing that such transgression serves to reinforce the power relations of heterosexuality rather than disrupting them.

Conceptualisations of gender as performance or as part of the discursive construction of subjectivities has been criticised for its lack of attention to systemic power relations which, it is argued, derives from Foucault's apparent denial of an extra-discursive, material reality in which power is based. Many feminist sociologists continue to assert the importance of a materialist analysis of gender and sexuality. This new materialism sees gender as a constitutive part of the material basis of society and, like Judith Butler, argues that sex, as well as gender, is fundamentally social and that sexed bodies are socially constructed. This position has been most consistently adopted by French materialist feminists such as Christine Delphy who argues that sex is a sign which marks the dominant and dominated; indeed sex refers to the way in which 'a given society represents biology to itself'. Delphy asks us to imagine a society without gender, arguing that gender is constituted by hierarchy and if the gender hierarchy is eliminated then gender will also disappear.

Gender has also been conceptualised in terms of social practice and here the theories of Pierre Bourdieu, particularly his concepts of **habitus** and disposition have been influential. Bourdieu's theory provides a materialist alternative to the idealism of Michel Foucault and post-structuralism. For him social reality exists, notwithstanding its social constructedness. This sets him apart from the idealist formulations of those who argue that social reality has no existence outside discourse. His concepts of disposition and habitus can be used to understand how it is that gendered social actors come into being and are predisposed to maintain (or to challenge) social relations as they have become familiar to them. These concepts can also be used to understand how gender differences are embodied through the acquisition of a gendered (and classed and 'raced') habitus. Thus a gendered habitus is reproduced through daily social practices such as sharing food and learning how to sit, move, dress and talk; gender is thereby conceptualised as embodied practice. And it is through social practice that gender relations are reproduced and/or transformed. This sort of approach can be found in the work of Cynthia Cockburn who explores the way in which gender identities, as well as having cultural meaning, are dependent on the continued existence of particular material social relations, and shows how gendered social actors reinforce or challenge gender relations through the social practices of their daily lives.

Sociological theorisations of gender are therefore marked by a tension between idealist and materialist theories and between those which see gender as difference and those which take gendered power as fundamental to gender relations. For all, however, sex, sexuality and the body as well as gender have come to be seen as socially constructed.

Further reading

Bourdieu, Pierre (1977) *Outline of a Theory of Practice*. Cambridge: Cambridge University Press.

Butler, Judith (1990) *Gender Trouble: Feminism and the Subversion of Identity*. Routledge: New York.

Charles, Nickie (2002) *Gender in Modern Britain*. Oxford: Oxford University Press.

Connell, Bob (2005) *Gender*. Cambridge: Polity Press.

Delphy, Christine (1996) 'Rethinking sex and gender', in D. Leonard and L. Adkins (eds) *Sex in Question: French Materialist Feminism*. London: Taylor & Francis.

Jackson, Stevi and Scott, Sue (eds) (2003) *Gender: A Sociological Reader*. London: Routledge.

Nickie Charles

GLOBALISATION

Globalisation has been analysed in many ways. The central feature of all current approaches is the view that many important contemporary problems cannot be adequately studied at the level of nation **states**, that is, in terms of national **society** or inter-national relations. Rather, they need to be theorised in terms of globalising (transnational) processes beyond the level of the nation state. It is useful to distinguish globalisation in general (generic globalisation) from its dominant form in the world today (capitalist globalisation) and from alternative forms.

Generic globalisation can be defined by four phenomena that have emerged or intensified since the middle of the twentieth century:

(a) the electronic revolution that has transformed the technological base and global scope of the mass media and much of the material infrastructure of the world today;
(b) the decolonisation of most of Africa, Asia, and the Caribbean with its major impacts on cross-border economic and cultural activities and migration and post-colonial forms;
(c) the creation of transnational social spaces; and
(d) qualitatively new forms of cosmopolitanism that enable people and groups to construct multiple identities.

These characteristics of generic globalisation manifest themselves most clearly in the dominance of capitalist globalisation, and this global-isation of **capitalism** has been studied in four main ways, through competing conceptions. These are the world-systems approach, the global culture approach, the global politics and society approach, and the global capitalism approach.

The **world systems** approach, inspired by the work of Immanuel Wallerstein, draws a distinction between core, semi-peripheral and peripheral countries in terms of their changing roles in the international **division of labour** dominated by the capitalist world system. There is no distinctively global dimension in the world systems model, as it remains locked into an inter-national focus. Many critics also hold that the world systems model is economistic (that is, reduces all questions to economic factors) and are not convinced that it can adequately deal with cultural issues.

The global culture approach sees globalisation as driven by a homogenising mass media-based **culture** that threatens national and local cultures and identities. The inspiration for this is the emergence of what media theorist Marshall McLuhan famously called the global village, the very rapid growth that has taken place in the scope and scale of the mass media. The basic idea is that the spread of the mass media, especially television and now the internet, means that everyone in the world can be exposed to the same images, almost instantaneously. The anthropologist Arjun Appadurai has seen this in terms of the development of mediascapes (flows of images) that are complemented by ethnoscapes (flows of people), technoscapes (flows of machinery), finanscapes (flows of money) and ideoscapes (flows of ideas). Similarly, the 'informational society' idea of Manuel Castells develops ideas on the space of flows. These dynamic approaches problematise the existence of global culture, as a reality, a possibility or a fantasy. The debate has been enlivened by studies of the cultures of globalisation in the plural, and ongoing attempts to connect globalisation, **modernity** and post-colonialism. Global culture theorists have been particularly interested in what happens to territorial identities (within and across countries) in a globalising world.

The inspiration for the global politics and society conception is the pictures of earth sent back by space explorers. A classic statement was the report of Apollo 14 astronaut Edgar Mitchell in 1971: 'It was a beautiful, harmonious, peaceful-looking planet, blue with white clouds, and one that gave you a deep sense . . . of home, of being, of identity. It is what I prefer to call instant global consciousness.' This individualistic conception of global consciousness, derived from simply being in or gazing at the world (usually via the media) can be contrasted with a collective conception derived from being with and mobilising fellow human beings to solve global problems. Global politics and society theorists argue that the concept of the global has become a believable idea only in the modern age when science, technology, industry and universal values are increasingly creating a world that is different from any past age. The globalisation literature is full of discussions of the decreasing power and significance of the nation-state and the increasing significance (if not actual power) of supra-national and global institutions and systems of belief. For these theorists, globalisation can have many causes, but the most desirable driver for the future will be the organisation of global governance through such institutions as a global civil society. Echoes of this view can be found in writers such as Anthony Giddens and David Harvey, who connect social and political globalisation with modernity through ideas of space-time distanciation and time-space compression.

The global capitalism approach proposes a more explicit model of capitalist globalisation. To distinguish between state-centred and transnational conceptions of globalisation, Leslie Sklair has introduced the concept of the 'transnational practices' that originate with non-state actors and cross state borders. The research agenda of this theory focuses on the characteristic institutional forms associated with three constellations of transnational practices: transnational corporations in the global economy (the economic sphere), the transnational capitalist class in global politics and society (the political sphere) and the culture-ideology of consumerism (the culture-ideology sphere). These are seen as transforming the world in terms of a global capitalist project.

Each of the four conceptions of globalisation has its own distinctive strengths and weaknesses. The world-system approach tends to be economistic (minimising the importance of political and cultural factors), but as globalisation is often interpreted in terms of economic actors and economic institutions, this approach cannot be entirely ignored. The globalisation of culture model, on the other hand, tends to be culturalist (minimising economic factors), but as much of the criticism of globalisation comes from those who focus on the negative effects of homogenising mass media and marketing on local and indige-nous cultures, the culturalist approach, too, has many adherents. The global politics and society approach tends to be both optimistic and all-inclusive, an excellent combination for the production of world-views, but less satisfactory for social science research programmes. Finally, the global capitalism model, by prioritising the capitalist global system and paying less attention to other global forces, runs the risk of appearing one-sided.

There is a growing consensus that global capitalism, driven by the TNCs and fuelled by the culture-ideology of consumerism, is the most potent force for change in the world today, and its importance is hardly controversial. There is, however, a great deal of controversy over its long-term consequences. While some commentators adopt a stance of happy fatalism, assuming that things will get better all the time as a result of economic growth, and the more optimistic see things improving for those who are currently disadvantaged, others suggest that there are problems with capitalism that are a consequence of con-tradictions within the mode of production itself, and that globalisation has intensified these. They identify a crisis of class polarisation – the idea that the rich are getting richer and that gaps between rich and poor classes and societies are widening – and a crisis of ecological unsustainability – the idea that continued capitalist globalisation will eventually make the planet uninhabitable. This has led many to resign themselves to a staunchly 'anti-globalisation' position or to a depressed fatalism, holding that things will probably get worse and may never get much better, but that there is probably nothing anyone can do about it. These controversies suggest an urgent need to consider alternatives to capitalist globalisation, and this may well dominate theory and research on globalisation in the foreseeable future.

Further reading

Lechner, Frank and Boli, John (eds) (2004) *The Globalization Reader*, 2nd edn. Oxford: Basil Blackwell.

Sklair, Leslie (2002) *Globalization: Capitalism and its Alternatives*, 3rd edn. Oxford: Oxford University Press.

Waters, Malcolm (2000) *Globalization*, 2nd edn. London: Routledge.

Leslie Sklair

HABITUS

The concept of habitus is overwhelmingly associated with the writing of the eminent French sociologist Pierre Bourdieu. It is a philosophical term that was used by Aristotle and then intermittently by later authors including Hegel, Husserl, Weber and Durkheim. Bourdieu's development of the concept can most usefully be seen as a synthesising combination of Edmund Husserl's phenomenological rendering of the term, Norbert Elias's use of it to emphasise the socially embedded psychology of actors and Marcel Mauss's focus on bodily habits. Bourdieu set out this idea as a way of resolving his struggles with structuralist anthropology and existentialism, with ideas of **social structure** and **action**.

Bourdieu's habitus is a concept so essential to the analysis of social life that it has found its way into major empirical studies in almost every sphere of sociology, from studies of **poverty** and the underclass, through media and politics, to the consumption of the arts. By habitus, Bourdieu denotes certain properties that are embedded within the minds and bodies of human beings. These properties he defined as the 'transposable and durable dispositions through which people perceive, think, appreciate, act and judge in the world'. By dispositions Bourdieu means the variety of enduring orientations, skills and forms of 'know-how' that people simply pick-up by being socialised into particular **cultures** and **subcultures**. These can range from forms of bodily deportment, speech, gesture, dress and social manners, through ranges of motor and practical skills, to specific kinds of mutual knowledge and collective memory.

Bourdieu emphasised the close match or 'homology' between the social organisation and dynamics of the external world and the embodied, internal, dispositions of individuals. He sees this as coming about through what he calls an 'internalization of externality'. Over the years, human agents gradually take in, or internalise, the kinds of things they need to know about their external social and material milieu in order to engage successfully in a given range of its social practices. This 'know-how' – these dispositions – become so ingrained that they become, for the most part, 'second-nature'. They provide a pool of latent resources, in the form of what Bourdieu calls 'generative schemes' that can be drawn upon whenever circumstances require.

In *Outline of a Theory of Practice*, Bourdieu drew on his earlier fieldwork in Kabylia, the mountainous southern region of Algeria, to elaborate the idea of homologies between the external world and the internal dispositions of habitus. Following Durkheim and Mauss, he focused on the classifications embedded in the Kabylian worldview, and following the structuralism of Claude Lévi-Strauss, he unearthed the binary oppositions that help to arrange these classifications into relations of hierarchy and difference. He avoided the objectivism of this tradition, however, by insisting on the intimate connection between the level of representations and symbols, on the one hand, and the social *practices* mediated by the embodied phenomenology of habitus, on the other. Classifications, representations and binary oppositions are seen as helping to constitute the various 'generative schemes' that are linked to the different domains of practice through which the Kabylians pursue their day-to-day lives. Bourdieu described in great detail the complex classificatory systems and binary oppositions relating to practices in the domains of the agrarian calendar (e.g. wet season/dry season, cold/hot, full/empty), cooking (wet (boiled)/dry(roast), bland/spiced), the rhythms and structures of the day (dark/light, inside/outside), women's work, the cycle of life, the space inside the house and the parts of the body. In their most overt form, contrasts and oppositions are linked to collective ritual practices such as the passage from the wet season to the dry season, which translate directly into changes in routine everyday practices so that, for example, the flocks now go out and return at different times of the day. Certain classifications of the calendar are also, for example, linked to temporal taboos on practices, from pruning, weaving, or ploughing, to celebrating weddings or whitewashing houses.

Most such schemas are taken-for-granted, tacit, ways of being and thinking which guide and orient practices in different but related domains. Habitus acts as a phenomenological mediator between the external social and natural world and the world the agent inhabits experientially. By bringing the outside structures into the agent's mental and bodily structures it also avoids reliance on the subjective will of the agent that is associated with a reliance on existentialism, symbolic interactionism, or ethnomethodology. These latter arguments too often ignore the weight and the limits imposed, by 'past positions in the social structure that biological individuals carry with them, in all times and in all places, in the form of dispositions which are so many marks of social position'.

The world of the Kabyle in the late 1950s and early 1960s was under threat from both **capitalism** and colonial war, but it still remained sufficiently traditional and cyclical for Bourdieu's account to characterise it in terms of what he called 'doxa', a situation in which the external natural and social world appears as self-evident, taken-for-granted, unquestioned, at the level of dispositions. Male values, for example, completely dominate the mythico–ritual system that legitimates the gender division of labour – something Bourdieu returned to in his later book *Masculine Domination* – but this is barely articulated at the phenomenological level of the individual agent. The latent dispositions of habitus are 'transposable' here in that they can be drawn upon in a number of different circumstances. They retain their taken-for-grantedness but just have to be tailored and trimmed to the immediate set of circumstances.

Things change in the more differentiated social formations of modernity and late modernity. Here the plurality of different ways of seeing the world, linked to 'culture–contact', class and other conflicts, to periodic political and economic crises, and to massive changes in the organisation of the division of labour, all combine to undermine a condition of doxa. Many things that were once taken for granted now become aspects of a contested terrain at the explicit level of discourse. The dominant classes try to restore a state of orthodoxy but this is challenged by the heretics, the many groups who can envisage alternative possibilities ('heterodoxy') and who seek to expose the arbitrary character of taken-for-granted ideas. It is important to recognise, however, that whilst habitus often works at the level of doxa, the taken for granted, actors in contemporary societies are increasingly likely to experience aspects of their habitus as dispositions that are contingent and can be reflected upon and contested in **discourse**.

Societies marked by a greater plurality of social roles also complicate what is required from actors as they draw on the transposable dispositions of habitus. Intermediate sets of generative schemes emerge from the plurality of roles that form specific 'fields' of social practices: as artists, writers, journalists, civil servants, CEOs of large conglomerates, military commanders, top politicians, technicians of various kinds, teachers and so on, people become socialised into their respective sub-worlds. Thus, notwithstanding the generalised transposability of some aspects of habitus, an individual in contemporary society will also possess other dispositions that are specific to a specialised field. They will also need to develop the skills to move between different aspects of habitus as they move between fields. So, whilst the disciplinary skills required by the military commander or the teacher in their place of work will be more or less transposable between situations within those social fields, they would be out of place in the home, at a dinner party, or in social interactions with actors from disparate fields.

This lies behind Bourdieu's insistence that the 'capital', or effective power, available to an agent does not only depend on their habitus. Rather, the aspects of habitus drawn upon must be appropriate to the relevant field of practices in order to be effective. This is what he means by the formula: habitus + field = capital. There can be different forms of capital, including **social capital**, **cultural capital**, and economic capital, depending on the type of effective power it denotes. Thus, in *Distinction*, Bourdieu investigated cultural capital by showing how groups inherit dispositional attachments to particular styles and tastes – including the types of art, music, furniture, holidays and films they prefer – that have a close relationship to their position within the social hierarchy, and that this then determines their levels of cultural capital with respect to other groups (i.e. relationally). A favourable disposition towards the waltzes of Johann Strauss or towards a particular news-paper, for example, would confer different levels of cultural capital on actors depending upon the social field or milieu in which they find themselves.

Further reading

Bourdieu, Pierre (1972) *Outline of a Theory of Practice*. Cambridge: Cambridge University Press, 1977.

Bourdieu, Pierre (1979) *Distinction: A Social Critique of the Judgment of Taste*. London: Routledge, 1984.

Bourdieu, Pierre and Wacquant, Löic (1992) *An Invitation to Reflexive Sociology*. Cambridge: Polity Press.

Reed-Danahay, Deborah (2005) *Locating Bourdieu*. Bloomington and Indianapolis: Indiana University Press.

Wacquant, Löic (2006) 'Pierre Bourdieu', in Rob Stones (ed.) *Key Sociological Thinkers*. London: Palgrave Macmillan.

Rob Stones

HYBRIDITY

Cultural hybridity became a central trope of critical studies in the 1990s, celebrated as powerfully transgressive and interruptive of class, national cultural homogeneity and essentialist definitions of race, culture and imperial domination, and as a way of understanding the consequences of **migration and diaspora**. Hybridity has been used to refer to mixed terms and categories or a clash of consciousness, and encompasses terms such as religious syncretism, creolisation, crossover and cyborg politics, which have invaded whole areas of sociological discourse. In studies of **modernisation**, it points to the mixing of 'local' and 'global' cultures in globalisation. As new diasporas continue to emerge and global cultures penetrate further regions, new hybridities are repeatedly discovered, but arguably with little novel theoretical insight.

The notion of hybridity is often criticised for postulating the coming together of two previously closed, bounded and unchanging cultures. This criticism is, however, based on a misunderstanding, as the concept is rooted in a more complex process of cultural meetings. Mikhail Bakhtin distinguished between two forms of hybridisation, both terms referring to the encounter between two registers of language and consciousness. He called these unconscious, 'organic' hybridity and conscious, 'intentional' hybridity. Organic hybridity describes the historical evolution of language through unreflective borrowings, while intentional hybridity is deliberately disruptive, creating an ironic double consciousness, a 'collision between differing points of views on the world'. Bakhtin's distinction thus theorises the simultaneous co-existence of cultural change and resistance to change. What is felt to be most threatening is the deliberate, provocative, aesthetic challenge to a felt social order and identity.

This idea has been especially influential in post-colonial and diaspora studies. The emergence of new South Asian and Black diasporic artists, novelists, film makers and musicians in Britain, hailing from former British colonies, seemed to challenge the Englishness of the English. Homi Bhabha argues that diasporic voices from the margins interrupt national cultural homogeneity, creating an ambivalent, 'liminal', 'third space' that disrupts national grand narratives. According to Paul Gilroy, drawing on the earlier ideas of William Du Bois, hybridity creates a 'double consciousness', a split subject. In similar vein, Stuart Hall sees diasporas as hybrid, reflecting both origins and place of settlement. The global is represented in the prism of the local, the place of settlement. For this reason, Hall sees hybridity as involving a reflexive self-critical distancing from singular identities establishing the grounds for a common political front and 'alliance politics'.

For cultural theorists, aesthetic representations are *constitutive* of the political. Gilroy criticises essentialist 'Afrocentric' invocations of pre-slavery authenticity as well as pluralist deconstructions of black identities as 'multiple'. The continuity of the black subject, he claims, can be found in its simultaneous belonging to and engagement with the darker side of modernity. Similarly, the *Négritude* movement among Francophone African diasporics was fractured into different hybrid identity discourses in the post-colonial era.

The publication of Salman Rushdie's novel *The Satanic Verses* led many anthropologists and sociologists to criticise hybridity theory. From different points of view, they stressed the non-representativeness and alienation of elite intellectuals, who celebrated hybridity, from the wider migrant community. Against hybridity, Ahmad proposed that political agency 'is constituted not in flux and displacement but in given historical locations'. Arguably, however, such critiques do not undermine the central claims of post-colonial theorists – namely, that hybrid cultures enlarge the sphere and inclusiveness of national and global culture, both high and popular.

A materialist critique of hybridity theory's allegedly romantic and utopian vision is that hybrid culture 'sells' within a capitalist mass global cultural industry, infinitely seeking novelty, whether popular or *avant garde*. In globalisation theory, Jan Pieterse criticises linear modernisation models and claims that globalisation always involves hybridisation: local appropriations of global culture create alternative modernities beyond the West. James Clifford invokes an anthropology that attends to colonised people's creativity through their cultural hybridity.

Further reading

Bakhtin, Mikhail (1981) *The Dialogic Imagination*, trans. Caryl Emerson and Michael Holsquist. Austin: University of Texas Press.

Bhabha, Homi K. (1994) *The Location of Culture*. London: Routledge.

Clifford, James (1988) *The Predicament of Culture: Twentieth-Century Ethnography, Literature, and Art*. Cambridge: Harvard University Press.

Gilroy, Paul (1993) *The Black Atlantic: Modernity and Double Consciousness*. London: Verso.

Hall, Stuart (1990) 'Cultural identity and diaspora', in Jonathan Rutherford (ed.) *Identity: Community, Culture, Difference*. London: Lawrence and Wishart.

Werbner, Pnina (2002) *Imagined Diasporas among Manchester Muslims*. Oxford: James Currey.

Werbner, Pnina and Modood, Tariq (eds) (1997) *Debating Cultural Hybridity: Multi-Cultural Identities and the Politics of Anti-Racism*. London: Zed Books.
Pnina Werbner

IDEOLOGY AND HEGEMONY

Destutt de Tracy coined the term 'ideology' around the end of the eighteenth century to indicate a new sensualist 'science of ideas' that would be critical of religion and metaphysics. Soon, ideology itself acquired negative connotations. First, Napoleon labelled his critics as 'ideologues', that is to say, people who deal with speculations and abstractions and know little about practical politics. Later, Marx, by seeking to unmask the new forms of domination and exploitation within **capitalism**, constructed a more substantial critical version whereby ideology became a kind of distorted consciousness that masked the contradictions of society and so contributed to the reproduction of the system. It was through Marx that the term came into sociological debate.

Central to Marx's concept of ideology were the ideas of 'inversion' and 'concealment'. **Religion** was said to be an 'inverted consciousness of the world' because 'man makes religion, religion does not make man'. The inversion produced by German philosophers occurred because they started from consciousness, not from material reality: instead of looking at German reality they merely criticised religious ideas. Marx applied this idea in his study of **capitalism**, where he distinguished the sphere of appearances (the market) from the sphere of inner relations (production), and argued that there is a basic inversion at the level of production. This is apparent in the fact that past labour dominates living labour (the subject becomes an object and vice versa), and that this inversion 'necessarily produces certain correspondingly inverted conceptions, a transposed consciousness which is further developed by the metamorphoses and modifications of the actual circulation process'. The main effect of these inversions was to conceal the real contradictions produced by the capitalist system, thus helping reproduce that contradictory world in the interests of the ruling class. For instance, the values of freedom and equality present at the level of the market are ideological in that they conceal unfreedom and inequality at the level of production and thus force workers to go back time and again to the labour market.

After Marx, the concept of ideology developed in four principal directions, exemplified by the works of Gramsci, Mannheim, Durkheim and the critical theorists. All of these views have influenced contemporary arguments.

Within Marxism, Marx's critical concept of ideology was soon abandoned. Vladimir Lenin and György Lukács introduced the idea of **class** ideologies that are not merely distorted forms of thought but the worldviews of classes. Antonio Gramsci subscribed to this view but gave it a new dimension. For Gramsci ideology was more than a conception of the world or a system of ideas; it also had to do, like religion, with a capacity to inspire concrete attitudes and give certain orientations for **action**. It is in ideology that social classes become aware of their position and historical role, and it is in and by ideology, therefore, that a class can exercise 'hegemony' over other classes. By this, Gramsci refers to the ability of a class to secure the adhesion and consent of the masses. Ideology for Gramsci has an integrating effect, based on its ability to win the free consent of the people. In Gramsci, therefore, this hegemonic quality of a worldview, its capacity to become the common sense of the masses, is the key element in all political life.

This Gramscian view has been at the centre of many new Marxist developments. Although Althusser re-introduced an opposition between science and ideology, he saw the main function of ideology as the 'interpellation' of individuals to constitute them as 'subjects' who either accept their subordinate role within the system or fight against it. The objective of all ideology is to achieve hegemony, to convert individuals into supporters by providing them with articulated concepts and images that help them make sense of their social existence. Both Stuart Hall and the early work of Ernesto Laclau emphasise this aspect and abandon the opposition of ideology to science.

The second approach to ideology is Karl Mannheim's 'relationism'. Mannheim shared some of the ideas of Lukács on ideology as a worldview, and he holds that all points of view have their claims to truth restricted on account of their social determination. At the same time, it is their social determination that gives them a distinctive truth or authenticity. This leads to the theory of ideology being replaced by a sociology of knowledge.

More positivistic social theory retained the idea of a critical 'unmasking' of ideology, but saw this as unmasking non-scientific ideas. This line of thought harks back to Francis Bacon's idea of the false notions that obstruct human understanding and was also central to the Enlightenment view that religious and metaphysical prejudices keep people in ignorance of scientific causes. It was Durkheim who gave this idea currency within the modern social sciences in his efforts to lay the foundations of sociology as a science of social facts. Ideology, for Durkheim, is those preconceptions or illusions that substitute themselves for the real things, thus distorting them and producing an 'imaginary world'. In order for sociology to become a science those pre-notions and preconceptions must be eradicated.

A fourth approach drew on Friedrich Nietzsche to unmask reason itself for its role in concealing the irrational forces that mobilise human beings. Nietzsche carried out a systematic critique of knowledge and reason which become tools in the enhancement of life. They are forms of ideological distortion in three senses: they conceal the reality of a world that is false and cruel, they conceal the fact that the preservation of life requires falsification and deception, and they pretend to be servants of truth. These ideological distortions seduce us to life, but also become weapons to deceive others. Vilfredo Pareto was a transitional figure in developing a sociological approach on this basis. His theory of 'derivations' sought to criticise ideological efforts to explain away the predominance of 'non-logical' actions in society. Unlike Nietzsche, his critique upholds the role of science, but equally minimises its role in society: politics is unavoidably the domain of distorted ideologies. It was the critical theory of Theodor Adorno and Max Horkheimer, however, that was the most influential formulation of this view. They saw capitalism as marked by a growing importance of instrumental rationality and transformed ideology into a purely manipulative force that converges with reality, thus becoming unassailable. Herbert Marcuse took this logic to the extreme in his view that reason and domination have ceased to be contradictory forces: domination no longer requires repression as it can be achieved through the manipulation of needs. This critique of reason influenced post-modernism, but for this position ideology is no longer an important idea.

In contemporary theories of ideology, language and communication have become increasingly important. The early work of Jürgen Habermas drew on critical theory and introduced the idea of communicative rationality as the process of reaching understanding through speech acts in **conversation**. Every speech act posits the goal of un-coerced consensus. When, due to censorship, violence or repression a genuine consensus cannot be achieved, a situation of 'systematically distorted communication' arises. For Habermas, this is the contemporary meaning of ideology. Its content is similar to Freud's problematic of rationalisation and hence his model for a critique of ideology is psychoanalysis. Later, Habermas proposed that in advanced industrial societies ideology has disappeared and has been replaced by 'fragmented consciousness'.

Anthony Giddens abandons the polarity between ideology and science to concentrate on the relationship between ideology and interests and so to use the concept in a critique of domination. Ideology ceases to be a particular system of beliefs and becomes a feature of any symbol-system: 'To analyze the ideological aspects of symbolic orders . . . is to examine how structures of signification are mobilised to legitimate the sectional interests of hegemonic groups', both at the level of discourses and in the daily context of lived experience. John Thompson follows the same idea when he argues that 'to study ideology is to study the ways in which meaning serves to establish and sustain relations of domination'. In order for that to happen it is not necessary that symbolic forms should be false or erroneous.

The 'linguistic turn' in social theory is accentuated in both Michael Freeden's morphological analyses of ideologies and Laclau and Mouffe's post-Marxist account, where discursive practices shape both the subject and reality itself. Freeden holds that ideologies are those systems of political thinking through which individuals and groups construct an understanding of the political world they inhabit, and then act on that understanding. Ideologies 'decontest' or naturalise the meanings of political terms by converting a variety of optional meanings into monolithic certainty. Whereas Freeden limits himself to an analysis of political concepts, Laclau and Mouffe argue that ideologies attempt to naturalise society itself by seeking to re-establish closure wherever a social order has been dislocated. They also seek to create and naturalise subject positions for the construction of political identities. But ideologies never succeed in decontestation or closure. The illusion of closure is the ideological illusion. The concept of ideology has survived both as an illusion that needs to be criticised and as the vehicle for the construction of political hegemony.

Further reading

Eagleton, Terry (1991) *Ideology*. London: Verso.

Freeden, Michael (1996) *Ideologies and Political Theory: A Conceptual Approach*. Oxford: Oxford University Press.

Larrain, Jorge (1983) *Marxism and Ideology*. London: Macmillan.

Norval, Aletta J. (2000) 'The things we do with words – contemporary approaches to the analysis of ideology', *British Journal of Political Science*, 30, 2: 313–46.

Jorge Larrain

INDUSTRIALISM

Industrialism is associated with the emergence of the modern industrial society that was the core concern of the classical sociologists of the nineteenth century. Such a society is based on the unprecedented development of new technologies, a complex division of labour, **urbanism** and the eventual emergence of 'mass politics'. Although it was often regarded as a progressive development in the history of human society, Durkheim, Weber and especially Marx were quite ambivalent about industrial society. Durkheim feared the possibility of social dislocation and even breakdown, while Weber decried the emergence of a one-dimensional formal rationality, which focused on quantity at the expense of quality. The major critic of industrial society, however, was Marx, who argued that the progressive expansion of new technology was actually the product of the competitive accumulation of capital, which concealed the social relations that underpinned this development. Above all, competition between capitals arose as a result of the emergence of generalised commodity production, or 'market society', and this in turn was the result of the separation of producers from direct access to the means of production, which led to the creation of a **class** of landless proletarians. This development occurred first in the English countryside, and laid the basis for competition between rival producers, which in turn led to the development of new technologies, culminating in the industrial revolution. Capitals competed with each other to enhance profits, a compulsion forced on all individual capitals by the emergence of generalised production for the market. The source of profits lay in the exploitation of the proletariat, who were paid a wage lower than the value of the goods they produced. Thus, **capitalism**, a capitalist industrial society, was ultimately one rooted in social conflict, above all between capital – the owners of the means of production – and labour. Marx was however hopeful that such exploitation could be eliminated through a socialist revolution led by the exploited workers, which would lay the basis for an industrial society based on collective ownership, in which conflict could be eliminated, or at least substantially reduced. Indeed, the material basis for such a society was the development of a social surplus product so great that potentially everyone could live comfortably from it, rather than just a minority ruling class. This surplus was the product of the development of the new technologies of capitalist, industrial society. Whatever the political fate of socialism and communism, Marx's assumptions concerning the progressiveness of industrialism were in some respects too conservative, as he too rigidly separated industrial technology from the social relations in which these developed. Many environmentalists, not least those sympathetic to Marxism, have rightly pointed out that much of the technology developed under capitalism is actually socially wasteful or even destructive, and that any alternative society would have to collectively limit the growth of industrialism.

These issues continue to have enormous implications, not least for those (capitalist) development strategies that have seen industrialisation as the best means of promoting development. Too often such 'development' has not benefited substantial sections of the population in developing countries. Whether or not this is the fault of industrialisation *per se*, or the uneven and unequal context in which it has taken place is a matter of great debate.

Finally, it could be argued further that in some respects this debate may be out of date as (post-)modernity is based on the development of the (global) networks of a post-industrial society. This is a contentious point that possibly exaggerates the 'death of industrialism', and in any case, older debates around issues of access to and knowledge of technology, or indeed the context of (capitalist) social relations and instrumental rationality in which such technology exists, be it industrial or post-industrial, have not gone away.

Further reading

Castells, Manuel (1996) *The Rise of the Network Society*. Oxford: Blackwell.

Kiely, Ray (1998) *Industrialization and Development: A Comparative Analysis*. London: UCL Press.

Sutcliffe, Bob (1992) 'Industry and underdevelopment re-examined', in Colin Wilber and Kenneth Jameson (eds) *The Political Economy of Development and Underdevelopment*. New York: McGraw-Hill.

Ray Kiely

INSTITUTION

Institutions are systems of interrelated norms that are rooted in shared values and are generalised across a particular society or social group as its common ways of acting, thinking, and feeling. They are deeply embedded in social life and generate the recurrent social practices through which most social activity is undertaken. As such, institutions are central to the idea of **social structure** and to the structural organisation of human activities.

The idea first appeared among sociologists describing the customs or folkways of a society, which were seen as the central elements in any

culture and cultural tradition. William Sumner, for example, saw them as group habits that develop in unintended and unplanned ways as particular ways of acting, thinking and feeling are adopted and repeated over time to become routinised and taken-for-granted ways of behaving. Herbert Spencer defined societies as comprising, domestic, ceremonial, political, ecclesiastical (or religious), professional (or occupational) and industrial institutions.

This idea was expressed most successfully by Durkheim, who generalised it into the idea of the legal, moral, or customary rules that exist as constraining social facts within a particular society. He argued, for example, that the calculative **rational actions** of people in their economic relations could occur only because these actions presuppose a 'non-contractual element' of normative considerations that gives meaning to them. This element is the institution of contract through which each individual contract is made binding. All social actions are shaped in the same way.

Institutions are built from norms or social expectations that are widely regarded as obligatory and are sustained by strong sanctions that ensure people's conformity to them. They are clusters of associated norms that define social **roles** and the relationships among them. The role of the doctor is defined through the institution of 'professional responsibility', with its constituent norms of trust, honesty, liability and so on. No clear and unambiguous distinction can be made between norm and institution – between norm and clusters of norms – but the basic idea of institutions as central and generalised recurrent normative expectations is clear. Examples of institutions include private property, contract, democracy, free speech, citizenship, motherhood, patriarchy, marriage, professionalism, and such micro-level institutions as turn-taking in **conversation** and gift giving. These organise particular roles or clusters of roles and they combine together into larger institutional structures. It is when people take on and enact the roles associated with these particular institutional structures that they generate particular sets of relations and social organisations. **States**, for example, can be seen as systems of social actions in which the relations among the participants are organised through such institutions as democracy, sovereignty, monarchy and **citizenship**.

The importance of social institutions to social order was especially stressed in normative functionalism, where they were seen as expressing a social consensus and as defining the ways in which social 'functions' could be met in socially approved ways. According to Talcott Parsons, the most important institutions are those that have a 'functional significance' in integrating or adapting people's activities to the world in which they live. It was on this basis that Parsons classified institutions as economic, political, domestic, religious and so on, seeing each type as having a primary concern for a specific social function and as forming the basis of the complex structural parts into which social systems are organised. Such structural parts, he argued, include economies, political systems, kinship systems and so on.

Critics of this approach have pointed to the fact that institutions cannot be separated from the **power** that they embody. Institutions express the power relations of a society and are always, to a greater or lesser extent, imposed by one group on the rest of the society. The situation where there is complete consensus over values, norms and institutions is merely one extreme case and the part played by power and conflict has also to be recognised. This view was taken up by conflict theorists in their view that the institutional regulation of social behaviour can be seen as a form of ideological control or hegemony. Most recently, Michel Foucault has shown how the shared discursive knowledge through which people understand and define their social world has also to be seen as embodying power relations. Social order is a result of the combined application of knowledge/power and cannot be seen as an outcome of either alone.

Although Parsons had been very clear about the fact that institutions had no substantial existence of their own and must be seen as the relatively stable patterns of meaning carried in the minds of individuals, some of his followers tended to reify them and to accord them an existence and reality separate from that of individuals and their actions. The more accurate view of institutions was re-emphasised by the symbolic interactionist critics of structural functionalism who stressed that institutions are elements in the loose organising framework of meanings through which people organise their collective activities. Institutions provide people with the definitions of situations that allow them to identify the roles that they may adopt in the particular situations that they encounter.

In some writers the word institution has also been applied to actual organised social groups such as hospitals, political parties, universities, business enterprises and so on. Because these formal organisations are seen as involving recurrent social practices, they have been described as institutions. Erving Goffman extended this argument to the study of what he called 'total institutions', a phrase by which he referred to organisations in which people are physically isolated from normal everyday activities by being required to sleep, work and spend their leisure within its confines. As a result, they are subjected to an extreme regimentation and discipline over all aspects of their lives — they are subject to 'total' control. As examples of total institutions he cited prisons and mental hospitals, concentration camps, boarding schools, army barracks and monasteries. Although this idea is very powerful, it is confusing to stretch the idea of institution so far, and it is better to distinguish institutions from the organised groupings with which they may be associated.

Further reading

Goffman, Erving (1961) *Asylums*. New York: Doubleday.
Parsons, Talcott (1951) *The Social System*. London: Routledge and Kegan Paul.

John Scott

KINSHIP, FAMILY AND MARRIAGE

The most common mistake found among those commencing their study of kinship is to suppose that the term refers to the biological relations which necessarily exist between all human beings. Kinship relations are not *biological* but that set of *social* relationships that are mapped on to biological relations.

Until there are further developments in reproductive technology, every person who exists is directly related biologically to two other persons. The male is termed the *genitor* and the female the *genetrix*. Together they constitute the *genetic parents* of the child. Since everybody has two such parents, each person may be seen to be at the bottom of an upside-down triangle made up, in *ascending* order, of that person's two parents, four grandparents, eight great-grandparents and so on. Those in the triangle may be termed that person's *parentage*. But if we choose as our point of reference one person from any of the many generations from whom we are descended, then those who share a common *descent* from that person form a triangle (the right way up) with the chosen common ancestor at the top and them at the bottom. Those in the triangle may be termed that reference person's *descendants*. All societies are processes which, simultaneously, create similarities and differences between their members. By establishing *parentage* we *individuate* ourselves from all others except our siblings (brothers and sisters) and complete this individuation by producing children. By establishing *descent* we establish a connection which makes us *the same as others* descended from our common ancestor. Each human individual is born into a web of biological relations which can be used to establish both parentage and descent.

These biological relations are not, in themselves, *social* relations; their existence has no direct effect on human behaviour and they are not therefore appropriate subjects of sociological study. What makes them of prime sociological importance is that not only are they universal – necessarily found in all societies – but all societies understand them to some degree. The major determinants of social behaviour in this area are a people's understandings of the biology and, given that, the cultural meanings with which biological relationships are invested. Central among these is the system of classification by which means the members of a society can establish similarities and differences between each other.

In most societies specific rights and duties attach to genitors and genetrices and the name of the *social* positions thus created can be distinguished from those defined by biology by the use of the terms 'pater' and 'mater'. When we say 'John is Paul's father' we mean both of two things: the existence of a biological relation (genitor) and the occupancy of a social position (pater). The two things do not necessarily go together. In most societies where two sexual partners are married, the male is the 'pater' of all children born to his married partner, even if they have been sired during his marriage by another genitor.

Biological relations are only kinship relations when they are socially recognised, when there are special terms to refer to the different types of relationship to which 'normative expectations' are attached; that is, expectations about how people in one category *ought* to behave to people in another category. When this is the case, then kinship may be said to be institutionalised with the population concerned. Kinship is a social **institution** – a known and accepted way of acting together.

It will be helpful at this point to introduce the term *household*. A household is usually defined as a set of persons who live in the same dwelling and share a common housekeeping. To be a household its members do not have to be related by blood. The criterion for household membership is residence not kinship and its shared activity domestic. There is however a special type of household whose members *are* kin, namely the *family* household. Families are groups of kin which are distinguished from other types of social group by their characteristic activities. Families are bounded social groups created by the procreation of children, i.e. by the same process that generates biological relatedness. Boundedness (in the sense of its not being part of a wider kin *group*) is a characteristic of family groups associated with European and North American cultures and societies and their historical antecedents. Families have typically comprised a pair of married parents and their offspring and are characterised by the parental care of the offspring. This requires that family members live together and share a common housekeeping and that the children are still dependent on their parents. This form of family has been called 'nuclear' because (being two generational) it has been held impossible to form a smaller kinship group. It has also been termed the 'elementary family' because it contains the basic elements of which every kinship system is made up. The two-generational 'nuclear family' is contrasted with the three-plus generational 'extended family' which comprises at least two sets of lineally related parents (e.g. a married couple and their married child and spouse and the younger couple's children) all of whom reside in the same household.

Now if kinship is confined to blood relationships, then the family is not a kin group since it includes two people who are not blood relatives: the parents of the children. Parents in elementary families have typically been related by marriage. The technical term for 'relatives by marriage' is *affines*. In everyday speech, 'affines' have sometimes been seen as the opposite of 'kin' in the restricted sense of 'blood relatives'. However it is preferable to use 'kin' to refer to both, distinguishing among kin between 'consanguineal kin' and 'affinal kin'.

Marriage is an institutionalised form of sexual partnership. As an institution it is an arrangement made publicly between two partners and their families which establishes a relationship between the partners' elementary families of origin and any future grandchildren the couple may have. It also defines the rights and duties of the spouses to each other. A partnership is only a marriage where that partnership is recognised by third parties. In modern societies, third-party recognition is provided by state registration and therefore state definition of 'marriage'.

'Kinship' and 'family' are often used as opposed terms: an endlessly ramifying kinship network versus a bounded interactive group. To understand either, the two phenomena must be related. The knots that tie together the strands of the kinship network are the result of the extension of relationships founded within the nuclear family into the social world beyond the domestic group. Marriage partners do not cease to be the children of their parents just because they have got married though they may no longer reside with them. The most important of these extra-domestic ties are therefore those between members of networks who, had they been co-resident, would have formed 'extended families'. The members of this kin category have come to be referred to as 'extended (family) kin'.

Further reading

Harris, C. C. (1990) *Kinship*. Milton Keynes: Open University Press.

Chris Harris

McDONALDISATION

McDonaldisation is a concept designed to bring the idea of rationalisation into the twenty-first century and to extend it from its roots in production (the capitalist system) and work (the **bureaucracy**) to the realms of **consumption** (the fast food restaurant) and **culture** (valuing efficiency, rationality and so on) more generally. It is based on Max Weber's theory of **rationalisation**, but goes beyond it not only to apply it to the realm of consumption, but also to argue that this is the realm in which the great advances in this process are now taking place. While Weber saw the bureaucracy as the paradigm of the process of rationalisation, the fast food restaurant is the contemporary paradigm of McDonaldisation.

McDonaldisation describes the spread of a set of principles pioneered by the fast food restaurant, but derived from a variety of sources such as the bureaucracy, the assembly line and scientific management: *efficiency* (finding the best route to whatever goal is sought); *predictability* (that things be the same or very similar from one time or place to another); *calculability* (an emphasis on that which can be quantified, often to the detriment of quality); and *control* over employees and customers usually through the *substitution of non-human for human technology*). Systems based on these principles have been enormously successful and they have spread from their base in the American fast food industry to many other sectors of society (e.g. religion, agriculture, politics and so on) and to most of the developed world. Indeed, they have been so successful that other nations have developed their own McDonaldised systems (e.g. Ikea, Body Shop) and exported them throughout the world, including back to the United States.

In spite of the many advantages associated with highly McDonaldised systems, there is a wide range of disadvantages associated with them. These disadvantages can be discussed under the broad heading of the *irrationality of rationality* that seems to be an inevitable accompaniment of increasing McDonaldisation. First, McDonaldised systems often do not operate in accord with their basic principles so that, for example, there is often great *inefficiency* (e.g. long lines at the drive-through or walk-up windows) associated with fast food restaurants. McDonaldised systems also tend to be associated with *dehumanisation*, either for those who work there or who are served by them. At one level, McDonaldised settings are inhuman, perhaps alienating, places in which to work and to be a consumer. At another, they can be even more directly destructive of human life as, for example, in the health threats posed by fast food high in cholesterol, fat, salt and sugar. Similarly, they pose a danger to humans in the various ecological problems that arise from the way their foods are grown and from the high level of consumption they encourage. Most generally, McDonaldised systems tend to produce a *disenchanted* world in which life itself is robbed of much of its mystery.

It is important not to think of McDonaldisation in either/or terms, but rather in terms of matters of degree. Thus, while the fast food restaurant is highly McDonaldised, other settings may be McDonaldised to a moderate or even small degree.

The concept of McDonaldisation has increasingly wide applicability to many parts of the world and to many sectors of society. Thus, there is growing literature on such topics as McUniversities, McDoctors, McPrisons and so on. While the spread of McDonaldisation may not end in the 'iron cage' that Weber so feared, it is already creating, following Michel Foucault, a carceral archipelago of highly McDonaldised islands (amidst a sea, perhaps shrinking, of non-McDonaldised settings). These islands can be thought of as housing the 'living dead' because of their propensity toward dehumanisation and the exercise of great control over human life.

Further reading

Ritzer, George (ed.) (2002) *McDonaldization: The Reader.* Thousand Oaks, CA: Pine Forge Press.
Ritzer, George (2003) 'McDonaldization: Chicago, America, the world', *American Behavioral Scientist*, 47, 3.
Ritzer, George (2004) *The McDonaldization of Society*, revised New Century Edition. Thousand Oaks, CA: Pine Forge Press, (original edition 1993).
Smart, Barry (ed.) (1991) *Resisting McDonaldization*. London: Sage.

George Ritzer

MASCULINITY

Under the impact of second-wave feminism, sociologists developed the concept of masculinity for two main reasons. It was claimed that the founding fathers and most pre-feminist sociology had simply equated the study of men with the study of people as such, and so the concept of masculinity enabled men to be analysed henceforth as 'gendered' persons. Thus, for example, studies of miners hitherto seen as analyses of **class**, could now also be read as studies of masculinity. Second, as 'masculine', the position of men could be seen as a function of socially constructed **gender** relations rather than of sexual difference or biology. Connell's influential study *Gender and Power* argued that men's superior power, resources and status were a function of the historical development of a form of gender identity, *hegemonic masculinity*, that socially reproduced their dominance. The recognition that not all men, such as men of colour or gays, benefited equally from this 'patriarchal dividend' led to analyses of multiple 'masculinities'. This generated a profusion of studies of heterogeneous masculinities, since even 'powerful' men might exercise hegemony in different ways. The reality or threat of physical and sexual violence might be one of the few resources open to otherwise powerless men. Connell's emphasis on 'embodied masculinity' spawned studies of sport and the sociology of the body, while other work examined the connections between organised militarism and violence. Men's domination of the public world of work led to studies on masculinity and management, politics, economics and the environment; as well as studies of discourse, the various forms of the men's movement and fatherhood, where sociology rediscovered the 'absent father' (often unaware that this was a theme with a long pedigree).

The quantity of work on masculinity has unfortunately not always been matched by quality of analytical rigour. Few theorists have attempted even to define the object of study, clarified how 'the masculine' can be studied empirically or distinguished from the behaviour of 'men', or wondered how the profusion of masculinity studies in romance languages which lack distinct terms for 'male' and 'masculine' has even been possible. Masculinity has been treated variously as what men empirically do, an ideal type model of their social action, the discursive representation of the latter, or discourses that legitimate either **patriarchy** in general or particular groups of men. Few convincing attempts have been made to link the concept of masculinity to patriarchy, nor has there been much reflection on the lack of symmetry in the use of the terms *femininity* and *masculinity*. There has been a dearth of empirical studies of the material and discursive impact on men of changing gender relations, or their agency in that process, despite the rapid pace of gender change in such spheres as education, the division of paid and unpaid labour, leisure and consumption, the law and politics.

Finally the break with the patriarchal sociology of the past has perhaps been overstated. Parsons' concepts of instrumental and expressive sex roles is remarkably close, in practice, to Connell's definitions of hegemonic masculinity and emphasised femininity, while pre-feminist sociology was hardly the uniformly sex-blind exercise it has sometimes been portrayed as being.

Further reading

Connell, Robert W. (1995) *Masculinities*. Cambridge: Polity Press.
Duneier, Mitchell (1994) *Slim's Table*. Chicago: University of Chicago Press.
Kimmel, Michael S., Hearn, Jeff and Connell, Robert W. (eds) (2004) *Handbook of Men and Masculinities*. Urbana: University of Illinois Press.
MacInnes, John (1998) *The End of Masculinity*. Buckingham: Open University Press.
Mann, Michael (1986) 'Persons, households, families, lineages, genders, classes and nations,' in Rosemary Crompton and Michael Mann (eds), *Gender and Stratification*, Cambridge: Polity Press.
Parsons, Talcott and Bales, Robert (1956) *Family Socialisation and Interaction Processes*. London: Routledge and Kegan Paul.

John MacInnes

MEDICALISATION

Medicalisation refers to the processes by which medicine as a social institution takes over a range of activities that formerly fell outside its boundaries. According to the Oxford English Dictionary, the first English-language use of the concept came in a letter concerning sexually active teenage girls published in the *New England Journal of Medicine* in 1970. This referred to the deterrents to their use of contraceptive services, and described the medical examinations and tests to which they were subject as a 'medicalization of sex that is probably self-defeating'. It is interesting to note the oft-echoed implication that this medicalisation was not desirable. The concept was first defined and examined in detail in a paper by the American sociologist, Irving Zola, entitled 'Medicine as an institution of social control', published in 1972, but first presented at the British Sociological Association Medical Sociology Conference in September 1971. The paper referred both to the 'medicalization of society' and the 'medicalizing of daily life' and drew on, and was shaped by, Eliot Freidson's two studies, *The Profession of Medicine* and *Professional Dominance*, both published in 1970. Talcott Parsons, in his extensive writings on medicine in the 1950s and 1960s, had contended that illness constitutes a form of social **deviance** that needs to be controlled by society, and had pointed to medicine's power to determine whether a person who was behaving as sick, was actually sick or not, and to legitimate their illness. Freidson, however, went beyond this, arguing that medicine could determine what illness is. It could decide whether a particular set of phenomena should be viewed as an illness or not, and Parsons's formulation of illness in terms both of deviance and role performance lent itself to just such an interpretation. Zola adopted Freidson's explicitly social constructionist stance, quoting his comment that 'The medical profession has first claim to the jurisdiction over the label of illness and *anything* to which it may be attached, irrespective of its capacity to deal with it effectively.' He then proceeded to gloss Freidson's claims about medicine's tendencies 'to label as illness what was not previously labelled at all', by using the term medicalisation, which he defined as the process that makes 'medicine and the labels "healthy" and "ill" *relevant* to an ever increasing part of human existence' (Zola's italics). Medicine, Zola suggested, was becoming a 'major institution of social control' and 'the new repository of truth'.

Zola identified four components of the medicalisation of society. First, the expansion of what is deemed relevant to the good practice of medicine, arguing that the shift to multi-causal models of illness was leading to more and more aspects of a person's life becoming relevant to their illness – with medicine exploring these wider aspects in order to diagnose and treat illness, and also to prevent it. Second, medicine's absolute control over certain procedures, particularly treatments such as surgery and drugs, permitted the extension of medicine well beyond the diagnosis and treatment of organic disease, as with cosmetic surgery or the prescription of many psychotropic medicines. Third, medicine's absolute access to certain 'taboo' areas – the inner workings of our bodies and minds – meant that anything that could be shown to affect either body or mind could be declared an illness: hence, for instance, the increased use of doctors to deal with personal problems, alcoholism and drug addiction. Fourth, medicine was increasingly deemed to be relevant to the 'good practice of life' and so had greater authority to tell people how to live their lives. Zola contended that by means of such processes medicine was replacing religion and law in many areas. One consequence was that issues were being depoliticised and other avenues of intervention closed off, because medicine is seen as a scientific and technical enterprise even though in practice it involves moral values as much as religion and the law. However, critical though Zola was of medicalisation, he argued that the process did not result from professional imperialism. Rather medicine's potential to help people, the increased reliance on the expert in an increasingly complex and technological world, and the belief as to 'how much can be done to make one feel, look or function better' were crucial, along with the high value attached to health. In his view the explanation of medicalisation lay outside the motives and actions of doctors.

The concept of medicalisation came to the attention of a wider audience through the polemical writings of the Austrian refugee and former Catholic priest, Ivan Illich. In his *Medical Nemesis* of 1975, modified and republished as *Limits to Medicine* in 1977, Illich offered a forceful critique of modern medicine, claiming that 'the medical establishment has become a major threat to health' and providing a dossier of medicine's adverse effects – the wrongs and harms it has done – through processes of clinical, social and cultural 'iatrogenesis' or doctor-induced conditions. Consequently, the careful separation Zola attempted between medicine as a profession and practice, and medicalisation as a process, was lost and medicine and the actions of doctors were as much the object of attack as medicalisation itself. Such a view was given a more sociological interpretation by writers such as Howard Waitzkin who, drawing on the tradition of political economy, argued that medicine and health care were being increasingly transformed into large-scale business enterprises with doctors and health care companies keen to expand their empires.

As one might expect given these early theoretical contrasts, the concept of medicalisation – and less frequently its corollary 'demedicalisation' – has been used in a variety of ways within medical sociology and with varying degrees of hostility to the changes it describes. Fostered by the second-wave feminism of the second half of the 1960s and 1970s, some feminist scholars in the 1970s and early 1980s took up the concept with enthusiasm using it to describe the increased medical involvement, usually male, in the functioning of women's bodies, especially childbirth. This medicalisation was most obviously evidenced by the rapid rise in many countries in the number of births taking place in hospital rather than at home during the second half of the twentieth century, but also by the far more extensive use of medical technologies such as induction, episiotomies, foetal monitoring and caesareans. Feminists were generally highly critical of these changes, arguing for greater control over the process of childbirth by women themselves and a reduction of medical power. The classic feminist handbook *Our Bodies: Ourselves* (1973) was followed by a range of sociological studies, including Ann Oakley's *Women Confined* and *The Captured Womb* and Michelle Stanworth's *Reproductive Technologies* 1987.

In the 1980s the term medicalisation was also extensively used in discussions of crime and wrongdoing, which were held to be being increasingly medicalised. Peter Conrad and Joseph Schneider in their well-known text *Deviance and Medicalization: From Badness to Sickness* attempted, following Zola, to identify the conditions under which behaviours are medicalised, pointing to a range of social forces such as the decline of religion, and the entrepreneurial endeavours of pharmaceutical companies. But they also argued that 'Medicalization is not possible without the complicity or willingness of at least some part of the medical profession' adding that 'Often there are medical professionals who act as entrepreneurs for medicalization.'

Notions of medicalisation have also been shaped by the work of Michel Foucault, although he rarely if ever used the term, and his work may have helped to reduce its use. In a series of books such as *Madness and Civilisation*, *The Birth of the Clinic* and *The History of Sexuality*, Foucault emphasised the increasing penetration of medical ideas and practices in Western ways of thinking, particularly from the period of the Enlightenment onwards. However his conception of **power** differed from that of writers such as Zola or Illich. In Foucault's view, power and knowledge are inextricably linked and power operates through the development and construction of discourses. These constitute ways of seeing and understanding the world and are not just constraining but also productive. Medical discourses are guidelines as to how patients should understand and regulate their bodies, and they create new ways of thinking, new possibilities and new opportunities. For Foucault power does not exist in doctors considered as 'figures of domination'. Instead it exists in relationships between people.

The concept of medicalisation has proved a useful descriptive tool for sociologists and other intellectuals and is still used quite frequently, almost invariably with critical force. Some, following Illich, have also been critical of the power medicalisation gives the profession and of the ideas and practices of medicine, and some have suggested it is to blame for the power it exercises. These negative views of medicine and of its possible role in medicalisation, are regarded by others as misplaced or simplistic and this, along with the spread of theoretical ideas such as those of Foucault, may help to account for the fact that the term is now less widely used than formerly. Yet it continues to have value as a descriptive term to highlight an important set of social changes.

Further reading

Conrad, Peter and Schneider, Joseph (1992) *Deviance and Medicalization: From Badness to Sickness*, 2nd edn. Philadelphia: Temple University Press.

Friedson, Eliot (1970) *The Profession of Medicine*. New York: Dodd, Mead.

Illich, Ivan (1977) *Limits to Medicine*. Harmondsworth: Penguin.

Zola, Irving K. (1972) 'Medicine as an institution of social control', *Sociological Review*, 20, 4: 487–504.

Joan Busfield

MIGRATION AND DIASPORAS

Though humans had a common origin in Africa, their subsequent fate was characterised by dispersion and migration. People moved in defensive bands in search of food and in response to climatic changes. The very ubiquity of migration generated the social construction of communities. Eventually these socialities developed largely incommensurate languages, **religions**, histories and political **institutions**. In particular, nation-states sought to develop secure borders and create fixity, consensus and homogeneity. However, the enhanced mobility of people in a global age has led to uncertainty and **hybridity**, with certain immigrants being stigmatised as being incapable of integration into the preferred norms and languages of the dominant populations.

Why do contemporary migrants generate such profound anxieties? The numbers alone do not provide convincing evidence of potential impact. Worldwide the number of migrants is 175 million, set against a world population in excess of six billion. Take the example of the USA. While the proportion of foreign-born population reached a ninety-year high in 2000 at 10 per cent, it was nowhere near the 14.7 per cent record achieved in 1910. Measuring migration alone, however, is misleading insofar as international mobility of all kinds (measured by number of arrivals) reached 700 million worldwide in 2004. Migrants are also often different from the settlers of old, who were looking to put down new roots. With increased global inequalities, violent political conflict and threats to livelihoods, illegal and refugee migration has risen relative to the number of migrants regulated by entry permits and work programmes. The unpredictability of migrant flows, the sense that governments are losing control of their borders and the relative lack of integration of the newcomers have fuelled nativist fears.

However, we must not forget that migrants are social actors with wills of their own. Retaining an old identity in a new setting is often a matter of choice. Migrants are more than ever prone to articulate complex affiliations, meaningful attachments and multiple allegiances to issues, people, places and traditions that lie beyond the boundaries of the resident nation-state. This holds especially members of diasporas and other transnational communities, including faith communities. For diasporas, as traditionally defined, this is not unexpected. Groups like the Jews, Armenians and Africans were dispersed by force. They ended up where they were more by accident than intent. The traumatic events were so encompassing that such populations remained psychologically unsettled. They characteristically manifest a dual loyalty to their places of settlement and also to a place, often invented, of origin.

What has changed is that considerably more migrants are now attracted to a diasporic consciousness. People move to trade, to study, to travel, for family visits, to practise a skill or profession, to earn hard currency, or to experience an alternative culture and way of life. Many either are prevented, or have no intention, of settling, adopting an exclusive citizenship, abandoning their own language, or cutting off the possibility of return to a familiar place. These 'fluid' transnational migrants and the increasing numbers of refugees, legal foreign workers and undocumented entrants, have altered many societies, making them much more socially diverse and culturally complex.

Further reading

Brubaker, Rogers (2005) 'The "diaspora" diaspora', *Ethnic and Racial Studies*, 28, 1: 1–19.
Cohen, Robin (1997) *Global Diasporas: An Introduction*. London: Routledge.
Cohen, Robin (2005) *Migration and Its Enemies*. Aldershot: Ashgate.

Robin Cohen

MOBILITY

The metaphor of individuals moving between positions is a common tool for understanding some features of social life. An obvious move to make for any sociology that uses the notion of a structure of positions – **roles**, **status** groups, **kinship** groups, occupations, **classes** – is to ask questions not just about the origins and characteristics of the structure itself but also about the causes and consequences of movement between the positions that constitute it. These questions may be posed at both the micro and the macro level. For example we might be interested in the causes that explain why some individuals are able to move from a **childhood** spent in a working-class home to an adulthood of middle-class affluence whilst others from similar origins retain their working-class position. This is obviously a micro-level question. Also pitched at the micro level is a concern with the individual consequences of mobility. Are the socially mobile more psychologically insecure than the socially immobile? Do they vote differently? Do they have less (or more) children? Do they have a subjective awareness of mobility? Do they have less contact with their socially immobile kin?

Macro-level questions are usually about the implications of aggregate rates of mobility for the functioning of the society as a whole. Consider two societies A and B. Both contain just two groups, the sky blues (SB) and the leek greens (LG). In both societies the SB are five times as wealthy as the LG and the LG are five times as numerous as the SB. However in society A the child of LG parents has a one in two chance of becoming an SB whilst in society B the child of LG parents has only a one in 100 chance of becoming an SB. Despite having a very similar structure of positions, upward mobility is common in society A and uncommon in society B: they are in fact very different types of society. By making some assumptions about rates of downward mobility we can imagine polar types of society, one in which the SB are mostly first-generation recruits and another in which they are mostly hereditary aristocrats. In cross-section the societies look similar, but the demographic dynamics give them a very different character. If we add detail about the prevailing mechanisms of mobility and the ideologies that legitimate mobility or immobility, we start to get (a little) closer to descriptive models of actually functioning societies.

The measurement of trends in the degree of openness (in the sense of lack of constraint on mobility) of societies and the degree of demographic identity (in terms of exposure to mobility or immobility experiences) of the groups that occupy the positions within them have been the subject of sustained empirical investigation by Richard Breen, Robert Erikson and John Goldthorpe. The empirical investigation of the macro-level consequences of openness for, say, economic performance or of group demographic identity for micro-level action or the macro-level political economy of distributional struggles is much less developed. Significant progress may well have to await the collection of more and better quality data.

There is considerable scope for muddleheaded thinking occasioned by the failure to distinguish between very different ideas about the positions between which mobile individuals are supposed to move. The terms 'social mobility', 'class mobility', 'social class mobility' and 'occupational mobility' are treated by some writers as synonyms while others draw quite careful distinctions between them. The water can be further muddied in investigations where social mobility is equated with movement either over a generation or within a single life-course between different nominal income or earnings percentiles. Especially pernicious is the assumption that more mobility is necessarily a good thing both for the individuals concerned and for the society as a whole. Few political parties advocate increasing the rate of downward mobility.

Most empirical sociological work has been focused on class mobility with class membership defined in terms of positions within a system of employment relations and operationalised in terms of aggregations of occupations that, on the average, share similar characteristics. Whether these classes are genuine social classes in the sense that they form discrete boundary-maintaining groups with distinct cultures and self-conscious identities is usually not an issue of concern and attempts to empirically identify such groups from mobility data itself are commonly held to have failed.

Social mobility is a much more capacious concept and when used with precision can be taken to imply a much broader conception of the types of social positions between which individuals can move than those defined simply by class or social class alone. Positions in status hierarchies implying relations of derogation and deference between social superiors and inferiors are the most common examples here. The boundaries around status groups and therefore the size of the barrier the aspirant has to traverse to gain acceptance must, by definition, be readily observable in order for a status hierarchy to exist. Political struggles for the collective (upward) mobility of a status group, for example, *jati* in the intricately differentiated caste system in rural India, are common and imply self-consciousness about social position in the (local) pecking order but also, especially in the middle of the order, a certain amount of status ambiguity. Those who are socially mobile in status terms can scarcely fail to notice it or be noticed by others and though after the dust has settled they may be accepted at the dinner table or the wedding altar it may take several generations before their origins are forgotten (or covered up).

Whether in modern industrialised nations any generally accepted status order of positions exists for people to move between is rather doubtful. Generalised derogation is now more likely to be met by defiance than deference. Attempts to discern status groups by examining either who marries whom or friendship choices, are ambiguous in what they reveal. Clearly the marriage market and the friendship market are structured, but usually it is not possible to tell whether this structure is the consequence of attempts to impose social closure or simply a function of the opportunity made available by the social geography of the housing and labour market. What is clear is that industrialisation leads to a substantial correlation between positions in the economic hierarchy and positions in a social status hierarchy. As Weber observed:

> in the so-called pure democracy, that is, one devoid of any expressly ordered status privileges for individuals, it may be that only the families coming under approximately the same tax class dance with one another.

Class mobility can bring with it the trappings of status mobility. The minuet of assimilation that brought the scions of industrial and financial magnates into the matrimonial circle of the landed aristocracy of late nineteenth-century Britain shows this.

Further reading

Breen, Richard (ed.) (2005) *Social Mobility in Europe*. Oxford: Oxford University Press.

Erikson, Robert and Goldthorpe, John H. (1992) *The Constant Flux: A Study of Class Mobility in Industrialised Societies*. Oxford: Clarendon Press.

Goldthorpe, John H. (1987) *Social Mobility and Class Structure in Modern Britain*. Oxford: Clarendon Press.

Jonsson, Jan O. and Mills, Colin (eds) (2001) *Cradle to Grave*. Durham: Sociologypress.

Weber, Max (1968) *Economy and Society*. Berkeley: University of California Press.

Colin Mills

MODERNISATION AND DEVELOPMENT

The status of the concepts of modernisation and development in the light of contemporary, 'post-colonial' theory is particularly controversial. Classical social theories of the nineteenth century all contrasted modern and pre-modern society. Durkheim focused on the distinction between organic and mechanical **solidarity**, Weber theorised the development of **rationalisation** and Marx examined the transition from feudalism to **capitalism**. Each has been accused of adopting a linear model of development, in which the supposedly advanced European societies show to the less developed societies the image of their own future. In this way, modernisation is simply a process of catching up, as the 'backward' progresses by catching up with the 'advanced'. This involves a transition from rural to urban, from feudal to capitalist, from agrarian to industrial, from irrational to rational, and from traditional to modern.

This linear model was formalised in the post-1945 era in the context of the end of empire and – in the case of the capitalist world – the desire of ideological social theory to avoid the spread of communism, although the communist world too had its own version of linear Marxism. It was explicitly linked to the idea of development, which was theorised as a process in which the 'backward' societies of the 'third world' would catch up with the 'advanced' West through a process of modernisation. The idea of nation-states passing through similar stages of development on the path to (Western) modernity – a crude caricature of the concerns of Durkheim and Weber – came to be associated with the modernisation theories of Walt Rostow, Shmuel Eisenstadt, Bert Hoselitz and David McClelland.

These theories briefly dominated Western sociological thinking in the 1950s and early 1960s. But they were subject to a number of devastating critiques by radical political economists such as André Gunder Frank and Immanuel Wallerstein. Following some of Marx's rudimentary attempts to theorise capitalism, not in one country, but as a world system, they argued that lack of development was not a pre-existing condition but was one that was strongly influenced by the actions of the 'developed' states. In other words, the alleged 'backwardness' of 'underdeveloped' countries, regions and peoples, was itself a product of the development of the core, developed areas. Development and underdevelopment could not be considered in isolation, and nor could it be assumed that contact with 'the West' was a benign process; indeed, the development of 'the West' rested on the underdevelopment of 'the Rest'. **World systems** and underdevelopment theories were themselves problematic in that the original division between core and periphery was never properly explained, and neither were the mechanisms that sustained this process. If 'the West' developed by underdeveloping 'the Rest', then presumably this was through trade and investment, but in fact such trade and investment has historically tended to concentrate among the 'developed' countries – a process that continues to this day. Indeed, insofar as we can talk about divisions between cores and peripheries, a more convincing political-economy-based explanation focuses less on the *exploitation* of the periphery, and more on this concentration of trade and investment, which has the effect of (relatively) *marginalising* the periphery. While these points undermine some of the central claims of underdevelopment and world systems theory, they share with these theories the idea that nation states do not develop in isolation. Moreover, they also show that while that contact with the West does not necessarily lead to a zero-sum game of development and underdevelopment, it equally does not lead to inevitable modernisation. This focus on the international political economy of uneven development thus has devastating implications for the nation-state centrism, linearity and Eurocentrism of the crudest theories of modernisation and development.

However, the problems run deeper than this. In putting forward 'the West' as a model for the rest of the world, this theory was unconvincing not only about the capacity of the rest to follow 'the West', but also about the reasons why 'the West' developed in the first place. This was in part because it neglected the contribution of 'the Rest' to the development of 'the West' which, even if it did not adequately theorise, underdevelopment theory at least pointed to some of the malign connections. Equally, however, modernisation theory generally saw development within 'the West' as a conflict-free process (and indeed homogenised Western development into the bargain). This was as unconvincing an explanation of the segregated United States of the 1950s as of the bloody process of urbanisation and industrialisation in nineteenth-century Europe. Indeed, classical social theory has theorised these processes in a far more critical way than mid-twentieth-century modernisation theory implied – Weber's account of rationalisation was as pessimistic about modernity as Rostow was optimistic.

Increasingly, it is this contemporary sense of pessimism about Western societies that has served to further undermine the idea that modernisation and development automatically represent progress. Some of this can be traced back to the concerns of classical social theory: to Durkheim's **anomie**, Weber's **rationalisation**, Marx's **alienation** and exploitation. For similar reasons, although the study of development has long since moved on from the crude theories of the 1950s and early 1960s, it continues to be accused of adopting a linear and Eurocentric account of social change. In the context of a broad acceptance by mainstream development studies that there is no alternative to capitalism, where 'Western capitalism' (and possibly even neo-liberalism) has been said by Francis Fukuyama to represent the most advanced form of capitalism, this accusation is not without merit.

Insofar as it still exists, critical development studies now focuses less on the political economy critique of (capitalist) modernisation, and more on cultural critiques of the homogenising discourse of development. This is perhaps not surprising in a 'post-communist' world but, in searching for alternatives through solely imagining new worlds, theories of 'post-development' stand accused of wishful thinking and ignoring the ways in which global capitalism continues to structure core inequalities in the international order. Moreover, in rejecting development wholesale, they also tend to hold on to the binary divides of crude modernisation theory, although in this case they favour the 'pre-modern' as opposed to the 'modern'. This ignores the power relations that existed in 'pre-modern' societies, and the (uneven) impact of capitalist modernity throughout the globe. For these reasons, and despite the enormous problems associated with them, modernisation and development continue to be key concepts in sociological analysis.

Further reading

Escobar, Arturo (1995) *Encountering Development*. Princeton: Princeton University Press.

Frank, André G. (1969) *Capitalism and Underdevelopment in Latin America*. New York: Monthly Review Press.

Hoselitz, Bert (ed.) (1960) *The Sociological Aspects of Economic Growth*. New York: Free Press.

McClelland, David (1961) *The Achieving Society*. New York: Free Press.

Rostow, Walt W. (1960) *The Stages of Economic Growth: A Non-communist Manifesto*. Cambridge: Cambridge University Press.

Ray Kiely

MODERNITY

In its original and most general sense, the word modern means something that is contemporary, up-to-date, or of today. The word contrasts the music, clothing, architecture, attitudes, and social patterns of present and recent times with those of the more remote past. In sociology, it is used in this way when referring to modern social theory, contrasting it with older, 'classical' theory. It is also used to contrast modern Britain – present-day British society – with earlier periods in British history.

Early writers on modernity – the modern social condition – contrasted the emerging commercial and national societies of seventeenth-century Europe with the waning structures of feudalism and all other forms of traditional society. The word modern was used to describe the specific social conditions of post-medieval Europe.

The modern society, born by the seventeenth century, was seen as a new historical epoch that would develop and endure for some time. Modernity, then, came to be associated with the specific social institutions of this post-medieval society. These institutions are marked by a strong and increasing emphasis on purely rational considerations and a corresponding decline in **tradition and traditionalism**. The modern social condition comprises a rationally organised way of life in which social actions take the form of techniques or strategies that use the most appropriate and exact means for pursuing goals. The core forms of **rational action** found in the institutions of the nation-state and capitalist **industrialism**, and their political and economic practices come to dominate and shape all other areas of social life. Social theorists, especially those of the formative period of sociology, tended to see the growth of rational forms of action as an inevitable long-term tendency in modern societies. They have depicted a relentless **rationalisation** of the world and it was generally assumed that all societies would follow a similar developmental path of **modernisation** that would lead them to adopt the same modern institutions that had emerged in Western Europe. Theses are the social institutions that solidified in the West in the late nineteenth century: centralised and interventionist nation-states, monopolised markets, large-scale productive and financial enterprises, mass production systems, mass consumption, mass movement and settlement through transport and urban forms, mass communications and mass culture.

Rationalisation is unlikely ever to be complete. Modernity can, therefore, be said to exist if the key **institutions** of a society are rationalised in all key respects and its general logic of development tends to increase its level of rationalisation. In such a society, challenges and resistance to rationalisation are both weak and marginal. A society is modern only ever to a greater or lesser extent, and there will always be residual, non-modern elements.

Recent social theorists have questioned the inevitability of modernity and have suggested that even modern social institutions might change. If the scale of such change is great, they hold, then it may no longer make any sense to describe them as modern. It has been suggested that the second half of the twentieth century may, in fact, have seen such a change and that the Western world has entered a new 'postmodern' condition. These theorists held that fundamental cultural changes had undermined the rationality of the Enlightenment and had stalled the process of rationalisation and so had initiated major social transformations.

These cultural changes had begun in the nineteenth century. The initial cultural forms of modernity had been highly rational and were those of representational realism in the visual arts, classicism in architecture and music, and linear narrative and naturalism in literature, which shared a concern to present a 'realistic' and technically accurate image of the world and reinforced the realism and objectivity of natural science, industry and politics. In the late nineteenth century, cultural commentators began to diagnose a break with this outlook across all the arts. The new aesthetic outlook that they identified they described – paradoxically and unhelpfully – as 'modernism'. This aesthetic modernism rejected any search for eternal truths and principles and sought to bring out the transience and fluidity of all cultural forms. 'Modern art' aimed to be sceptical: reflexively aware of the arbitrariness of its own forms. It abandoned fixity, certainty, absolutes and order, stressing instead flux, contingency, relativity and fragmentation. From the mid-1960s this cultural outlook was renewed in ever more reflexive forms as aesthetic modernism itself came under attack. Hippies and other radicals mounted a politicised challenge to the technology and bureaucratic rationality of the 1950s and 1960s in the name of impulse and pleasure, psychedelic expressivity and cultural freedom. What came to be known as 'post-modernism' built on this and relentlessly pursued the cultural radicalism that had been unleashed by aesthetic modernism. Post-modernists held that no foundations could be established for intellectual certainty. There could be no 'totality', no 'grand narrative' or 'big picture' that could make sense of the world, which had to be accepted as chaotic and ephemeral.

These arguments influenced the theories of writers such as Jacques Derrida, Michel Foucault and Jean Baudrillard, who emphasised the relativity of values and ideas and pointed to the eroding effects of this cultural change on social structures. If social life is culturally formed, then cultural post-modernism must involve the transformation of social institutions in a post-modern direction. The growth of post-modernity has been identified in such things as the weakening of nation-states, the disorganisation and fragmentation of national economies, the growth of transnational transactions and population movements, the growing significance of flows in information and knowledge, the growth of risk, uncertainty, and anxiety, the massive expansion of consumerism and popular culture in everyday life, and the global extension and inter-connection of human activities. These arguments point to crucial social changes in the structures of contemporary societies, but many of these changes can be seen as deepened and intensified shapings of modern social institutions. Modern social institutions have continually been transformed since their first appearance. The claim that we have reached the end of modernity remains highly contentious.

Further reading

Bauman, Zygmunt (1992) *Intimations of Postmodernity*. London: Routledge.

Castells, Manuel (1996) *The Rise of the Network Society*, Volume 1 of the Information Age: Economy, Society and Culture. Oxford: Blackwell Publishers.

Harvey, David (1989) *The Postmodern Condition*. Oxford: Basil Blackwell.

Kumar, Krishan (1978) *Prophecy and Progress*. Harmondsworth: Penguin.

John Scott

NARRATIVES AND ACCOUNTS

The concepts of 'narrative' and 'accounts' are quite closely related, but have different histories in the social sciences and are used for somewhat different analytical purposes. Both concepts refer to linguistic or textual devices for reconstructing past events and thereby conferring meaning on those events. Those reconstructions are regarded by scholars in the human sciences as intrinsic to and necessary for human conduct of any scale, ranging from interpersonal relationships, such as friendships, to inter-group relations, such as labour negotiations, and to international relations, such as trade agreements or waging war.

While scholarly work on accounts is conventionally traced to C. Wright Mills's article 'Situated Actions and Vocabulary of Motives', Marvin Scott and Stanford Lyman actually introduced the concept into the sociological literature. According to those authors, accounts are verbal statements actors use to explain behaviour that is unexpected or regarded as deviant. Accordingly, accounts are seen as ways for people to manage problematic situations. Scott and Lyman classified such verbal statements into two general analytical categories. The first category is justifications, in which actors accept responsibility for an act but deny that the act was deviant (i.e. it was the right thing to do), and the second is excuses, in which actors accept that an act was a breach of acceptable norms but deny responsibility (i.e. it was an accident or done without intention). Both types of accounts involve actors dealing with normative codes and standards of conduct and offering interpretations of conduct as a means of creating a measure of congruity between the conduct itself and cultural expectations. Scholars such as Terri Orbuch relate accounts to what Gresham Sykes and David Matza called 'techniques of neutralization', which include denial of responsibility, denial of injury, denial of the victim, or condemning the condemners. In this sense, accounts are seen as processes central to a society's moral order and are generic to what Randall Stokes and John Hewitt have called 'aligning actions', actions that involve the ways that actors configure ongoing cultural and personal meanings and constraints in relationships.

Work on accounts has developed into a lively focus of scholarship. Some have focused on questions of the degree to which accounts will be accepted or honoured, sanctions assessed, and actor credibility appraised in situations calling for or giving rise to accountability. Other work has focused on the abilities of various groups that can both require accounts, as in cases of employee evaluations, and are situated in asymmetric relationships and hierarchies of credibility. Still other work has focused on life course disruptions, as in instances of illness or unexpected crisis events. Some accounts involve specific audiences (parents, employers, police) pertaining to acts within a bounded jurisdiction, while other accounts may involve less specific audiences (neighbourhoods, peers) and pertain to more ambiguous forms of conduct, such as lifestyles or expressions of values.

While a portion of the research on accounts has dealt with types of accounts and the situations that mobilise them, other work has focused on their functions. Psychologists have studied confiding accounts; James Pennebaker documents the negative psychological and physical effects of not confiding about traumatic events, whereas, conversely, other research shows that confiding accounts can ease stressful life transitions and occurrences. Accounts also function as explanations and attributions of causation. When done consensually and within a common framework of values, they provide acceptable reasons for action, whether pertaining to national policies adopted by legitimate authorities, administrative decisions that might affect broad categories of employees, revisions of official theology promulgated by clergy, or parental decisions about family matters. Scholars who more centrally use attribution theory often view accounts as ways for people to maintain consistency of self and identity as well as self-esteem. As these approaches developed, scholars began regarding accounts, in Orbuch's words, as 'packages of attributions including attributions of causation, responsibility, and blame and trait ascriptions both to other and to self' rather than as disparate attributions.

While scholarly work on accounts has been primarily social psychological in approach, the work on narrative has been decisively and broadly interdisciplinary. Traditionally regarded as belonging solely to the humanities, narrative analysis now finds itself in all of the social science disciplines. Sociologists have come to study narratives in the recognition that story-telling activities are fundamental to personal and collective life. That centrality includes most of what sociologists have conventionally studied – from **self and identity** to family, political arrangements, social **class**, **race**, **gender**, social **change**, aging and the life course, organizations, health and illness,

urbanism and so on down the list of topics common to sociological scholarship.

There are a number of terms referring to narrative phenomena, such as rumour, chronicles, tall tales, propaganda, autobiography, history and gossip, but generically narrative pertains to some kind of reportage. There are three minimal components of a story: an event or occurrence, a time frame or sequence that organises the event and meaning attached to the event or what is commonly called the point of the story. Other elements can be added, such as story-telling competence, audience and situation, but these three components identify stories as a category of communicative behaviour. By using and combining these elements in different ways, people can configure personal and collective meanings in a variety of relationships to help explain and share their experiences and bring individual and collective pasts into the present.

Stories, as acts of telling and reporting, can be distinguished from the concept of narrative structures. This concept refers to cultural paradigms, cultural framings and ideologies that can prefigure stories insofar as group beliefs and values contain already articulated plots. These narrative structures frequently have a taken-for-granted quality of commonsense reality that resonates with local populations and constituencies, and they function to confer degrees of believability to stories that are told. Norman Denzin, for instance, shows how stories of drinking and abstinence told at Alcoholics Anonymous meetings are interpreted by members inside the dominant frame of AA stating that one cannot control alcohol and never fully recovers from alcoholism. Likewise, Patricia Turner describes how specific stories of racial oppression told by African-Americans are given legitimacy in terms of conspiracy narratives that circulate among Black communities. Such cultural frames, as shown by David Maines, serve as plausibility structures that prefigure and precede actual story-telling occasions, and help us understand better how a given story can be fiction to one group and reality to another.

Scholarly work on narrative also include a growing literature on what Donald Polkinghorne has called 'narrative knowing'. There are two dominant aspects to this area of concern. First, there are conventional methodological issues of data collection and analysis. James Holstein and Jay Gubrium treat the interview as a social occasion that constructs the data gathered. In those encounters, respondents are seen as narrators who tell their stories, usually in an interactive and negotiated process with the interviewer. Elliot Mischler addresses the diversity of narrative analysis by offering a typology of analytical modes: those that focus on the correspondence between temporal sequences and actual events and their textual representations, those focusing on how types of stories acquire structure and coherence, and those focusing on the content and function of stories. And Diane Holmberg, Terri Orbuch and Joseph Veroff in their book, *Thrice Told Tales*, show how narrative data can be incorporated into conventional longitudinal designs and converted to the methods of quantitative analysis. A second issue pertains to writing as a way of knowing and thus draws attention to scholars as narrators themselves. Laurel Richardson, in her book, *Fields of Play*, discusses a number of interesting issues relating to writing as a form of inquiry, and provides detailed autobiographical information about how context influences writing. Her account includes her family, academic departments, networks of colleagues and students, and how these relationships and experiences were intrinsic to what she wrote as a scholar. Her work illustrates how the 'knower ' and the 'known ' collapse into one another and thus how acts of writing are tied to the construction of knowledge.

The related concepts of 'accounts' and 'narrative' share some important similarities. Both are forms of communication that reconstruct the past; both are central to meaning-making activities; both allow scholars to focus on human agency, and both link personal and collective phases of human group life. Orbuch brings focus to these similarities in her analysis of how accounts are 'story-like' constructions and in what respects accounts–as–stories are 'central to the enterprise and endeavours of contemporary sociology'. Although there are no hard and fast distinctions between the two concepts, they have been used in rather different ways. Accounts by and large have been treated as objects of inquiry, and scholars have investigated their nature, how they are formed and their function in human lives. Narratives, however, have been treated as objects of inquiry, just as have accounts, but also have been regarded as methods of inquiry as well as the outcomes of inquiry. These differences reflect the narrower disciplinary origins of work on accounts as well as the literary and post-structuralist influences on narrative analysis and inquiry. Furthermore, the analysis of accounts has tended to be more focused on strategic interaction, reflecting the influence of Erving Goffman's work, whereas narrative analysis has tended to have a broader focus to include cultural forms and collective structures.

Further reading

Denzin, Norman (1987) *The Recovering Alcoholic*. Newbury Park, CA: Sage.

Maines, David (2001) *The Faultline of Consciousness: A View of Interactionism in Sociology.* Hawthorne, NY: Aldine de Gruyter.

Mills, C. Wright (1940) 'Situated actions and vocabulary of motives', *American Sociological Review*, 5: 904–13.

Mishler, Elliot (1995) 'Models of narrative analysis: a typology', *Journal of Narrative and Life History*, 5: 87–124.

Orbuch, Terri L. (1997) 'People's accounts count: the sociology of accounts', *Annual Review of Sociology*, 23: 455-78.

Scott, Marvin and Lyman, Stanford (1968) 'Accounts', *American Sociological Review*, 33: 46–62.

David Maines

NATION

What is a nation? This question was addressed in one of the most celebrated accounts by the French writer, Ernest Renan in 1882, and remains one of the puzzles of the twenty-first century. According to Renan, 'a nation is . . . a large-scale solidarity, constituted by the feeling of sacrifices that one has made in the past and of those one is prepared to make in the future'. In that short sentence, Renan captured much of the essence of the nation: it is a macro-social phenomenon, binding people together; emotions are key, encouraging sacrifice on its behalf; it spans past into an indeterminate future.

Why, then, does defining the nation seem to cause much difficulty? Let us begin by saying what 'nation' is not. Despite its use in everyday speech and political rhetoric, it is not a synonym for the state. Politicians make appeal to 'this nation of ours', but they are probably referring to the territorial-political entity of the state. Talking about the 'nation-state' is of little help, because that implies either that they are the same thing, or that they reinforce each other. Put simply, whereas the state refers to the political-constitutional realm which binds people to it as 'citizens', the nation is in essence a cultural concept, a solidarity – which implies that its members have more in common than they have dividing them. Neither is a nation a **society**, which is defined by its institutional reach, such as its system of governance – education, administration, law and so on. In short, while state is a political concept, and society a social one, nation is a cultural expression of commonality, in Benedict Anderson's famous phrase an 'imagined community'. It is important to stress that it is imagined, not imaginary, for nation is not, as language has it, a figment of the imagination, but a **community** imagined by people as they go about their daily business. In essence, this means that nation is an ideological construction, seeking to fuse a culture with a people, and hence, it is close to, but not coterminous with nationalism, which is a political ideology which claims that a people, usually territorially defined, have the right of self-determination. Are nations about **ethnicity**? Not if by that we mean, as in everyday language, simply issues of 'race' and minority groups; yes, if we mean groups who consider themselves, and are so considered by others, as culturally distinct. In short, ethnicity is the politicisation of culture.

In truth, nations may exist without nationalism, though more usually, as Ernest Gellner had it, nationalism makes nations rather than the other way around. By this he meant that the political project created the idea of the nation, rather than preformed nations demanding territorial sovereignty and self-government. Part of the difficulty, then, of defining nation lies in its close association with nationalism. As Rogers Brubaker observed, '"nation" is a category of "practice", not (in the first instance) a category of analysis. To understand nationalism, we have to understand the practical uses of the category "nation", the ways it can come to structure perception, to inform thought and experience, to organise discourse and political action.' Does 'nation' have to be territorial? True, one can speak of the 'black nation' and the 'Islamic nation', for example, but it is much harder to translate that sense of solidarity and shared experience into self-government if people are spread across different states. In essence, however, as Josep Llobera observed, a nation is a 'cultural community endowed with political relevance'.

Can one identify the key characteristics of 'nationness'? Cultural characteristics such as shared language, **religion**, ethnicity, even material circumstances (nations as classes) have been put forward as likely candidates. It is however too easy to find instances of 'imagined community' where one or more, even all, are absent. We search in vain for the key, common cultural identifier which unlocks in an 'objective' sense the idea of the nation. Some, such as Jürgen Habermas, have even argued that a contentless national identity is possible, even desirable, what he called 'constitutional patriotism', that citizens can generate a shared sense of community simply by virtue of being citizens, and being governed in a particular territory. Others have argued that one cannot make national bricks without a modicum of cultural straw, that there has to be some perceived shared characteristic even if it is not difficult to show that it has been manufactured. In like manner, territorial communities may have much that separates them from their neighbours, but seeking political self-determination is not an automatic outcome simply of the existence of these differences. For example, the very different territories of Bavaria in Germany, and Shetland in Scotland, have more than enough cultural raw materials to build political movements to break away from the bigger states, but they do not, at least at present, have the social, political and cultural grievances for that to happen in the foreseeable future.

In short, imagined communities – nations – can be embryonic, even fully developed, but there is nothing inevitable about the political-constitutional outcomes. Much depends on how cultural differences are interpreted and, if necessary, mobilised. Nations are neither simply ancient nor modern; ethnic nor civic; political nor cultural; collective nor personal. Indeed, they can be all of these things. While there is much debate about the historic origins of nations, whether they are in essence modern state constructions, or have their roots in history, there can be little doubt about their capacity to move people to die, to kill, to love and to hate. Being 'national' is a deeply personal thing, as well as a property of a larger collective, in Renan's words a soul, a spiritual principle, a kind of moral conscience. It can be both/and as well as either/or ethnic and civic, deriving from some perceived cultural characteristic as well as from the commonality of shared territory. In a world in which cultural and territorial groupings are subject to rapid social change, to globalisation, there is little doubt that the 'nation' will not wither away, but adapt in new forms to people's needs for community and solidarity. In Renan's words: 'the essence of a nation is that all individuals have many things in common, and also that they have forgotten many things'.

Further reading

Brubaker, Rogers (1996) *Nationalism Reframed: Nationhood and the National Question in the New Europe.* Cambridge: Cambridge University Press.
Eriksen, Thomas H. (1993) *Ethnicity and Nationalism.* London: Pluto Press.
Gellner, Ernest (1983) *Nations and Nationalism.* Oxford: Blackwell.
McCrone, David (1998) *The Sociology of Nationalism.* London: Routledge.

David McCrone

ORGANISATION

Until recently the term organisation was used almost exclusively to designate 'formal organisation'. By this is meant social groups specially set up for particular purposes. In the words of Peter Blau, 'The defining criterion of formal organisation – or an organisation, for short – is the existence of procedures for mobilising and coordinating the efforts of various, usually specialised, subgroups in the pursuit of joint objectives.'

The model for organisation was the business firm or government agency, and the most developed form of the general type was the **bureaucracy**. Defined thus, organisation is difficult to imagine without other features of modernity, such as **rational action**, literacy and a system of law. Indeed, in the classical literature, organisations are specifically held to be modern, and the idea of organisation is used in ways that draw on and support a distinction between **modernity** and **traditionalism**.

Giving priority to organisation as an object developed with functional sociology, where social relations were thought to contribute something necessary to the entities of which they are parts. In the functional analysis of organisations that emerged in Britain and the USA, elements of organisations were considered as contributing to the integrity of the organisation as a whole. From the beginning, however, the most sophisticated analysts were aware that formal organisations embody the exercise of power, being primarily constituted by authority. As such, they were seen routinely to provoke resistance from groups within them and so, often, did not function as expected. For this reason, many system theorists have suggested that organisations often function sub-optimally. Conflict theorists, utilising Marxian and neo-Weberian concepts, drew more extreme conclusions.

Partly in response to such critiques, and partly as a process of development, the mainstream of organisational studies began to perceive that differences between contemporary organisations and other types of institution could be exaggerated, and that irrationality and sub-optimal performance were normal features of organisations. Although thinking about organisations in terms of performance is still common, there is now more awareness of the implications of this sort of approach and a willingness to entertain other perspectives. Organisation is now conceived as an activity as well as an object.

Eventually, mainstream organisational analysis came specifically to define itself in institutional terms that are little different, in principle, from those found in traditional societies. There is a valuable recognition that formal organisation is not the limit of organisation. Under diverse sources of intellectual inspiration, such as ethnomethodology and phenomenology, new perspectives on organisation have made generic processes of organising the centre of attention. The value of this is clear in the era of the 'virtual organisation', in which an organisation may never actually be constituted in the sense of all the participants in the organisation interacting in one place at one time. As Robert Cooper rightly suggests: 'In its most fundamental sense, organisation is the appropriation of order out of disorder.'

Further reading

Blau, Peter and Scott, William R. (1963) *Formal Organizations: A Comparative Approach*. London: Routledge.
Clegg, Stewart (1990) *Modern Organisations*. London: Sage Publications.
Cooper, Robert (1986) 'Organisation/disorganisation', *Social Science Information*, 25, 2: 299–335.
Powell, Woody W. and DiMaggio, Paul J. (1991) *The New Institutionalism in Organisational Analysis*. Chicago: University of Chicago Press.
Westwood, Robert and Clegg, Stewart (2003) *Debating Organisation*. Oxford: Blackwell.

Stephen Ackroyd

PATRIARCHY

Patriarchy is a **social system** of **gender** relations in which there is gender inequality. Gender relations are the social relations between men and women and are embedded in a range of social **institutions** and **social structures**. The concept of patriarchy incorporates the concept of gender relations, and goes beyond it in two respects. First, it includes the inequality that routinely exists in gender relations. Second, it draws attention to the inter-connectedness of different aspects of gender relations, which together form a social system.

In many aspects of social life there is gender inequality, in that women are typically disadvantaged as compared with men. The following are some examples of this. In employment, there is a gender pay gap, in that women are on average paid less than men. Women do disproportionate amounts of **domestic labour**, such as housework and childcare. Women are more likely than men to experience **poverty**, especially in old age. Men disproportionately take up the positions of political **power**, such as being Members of Parliament. Women experience violence from men, such as domestic violence and sexual assault. Men are more likely than women to have the influence to shape **cultural** and moral standards, for instance, as newspaper editors and religious leaders. Of course, there are individual exceptions to these statements, since they are about average gender inequality, not about every individual man and woman. These patterns of gender inequality are replicated over time within social structures.

There have been some differences in the definition of patriarchy. Some of the early definitions tended to focus on the role of the eldest male as head of the family household (see **kinship, family and marriage**), that is, including a focus on generation and one specific social institution. More recent definitions have not been so restrictive, noting that many social institutions contribute to patriarchy, of which the family is but one.

The concept of patriarchy captures the inter-relatedness of different aspects of gender inequality. There are causal connections between gender inequality in one domain and that in another. For example, gender inequality in political representation is linked to inequalities in the workplace. When gender inequality in political power declines, if women increase their representation in parliaments and Cabinets, there tends to be an increase in the laws supporting women in employment, which in turn tends to narrow the gender pay gap. The different aspects, dimensions or domains of patriarchy are connected. This connectedness means that there is a system of gender inequality, not merely a set of separate and unrelated occurrences.

The implied notion of **social system** within the concept of patriarchy is important for a sociological analysis of gender inequality as it enables a deeper and more powerful explanation of different aspects of gender relations. It enables the linking of different levels of analysis, of social structures with phenomena at a more individual level. For example, women make choices but not in circumstances of their making: as when 'choosing' a low paid part-time job because that is the only employment that fits in with a child's school hours in the absence of affordable quality childcare. The explanation of her 'choice' is more powerful if these wider social institutions and social structure are brought into the analysis.

There are variations in the forms that patriarchy takes in different times and places. One dimension of variation is a continuum from domestic patriarchy to public patriarchy. This dimension varies according to the extent to which women are contained within the domestic sphere and the extent to which they are present in public institutions, such as employment, universities and parliament. A second dimension is that of the degree of gender inequality, for example, the size of the gender pay gap. **Modernity** has seen a tendency for a transformation of the form of patriarchy from domestic to public forms. This transformation is only partly associated with changes in the degree of inequality, hence the need to keep these dimensions analytically distinct. The trajectory of the **modernisation** of patriarchy is not uniform or universal, but path dependent, in that the earlier changes and other sets of social relations affect the path of change.

Patriarchy exists in interaction with other systems of social relations, such as capitalism and systems of ethnic relations. These interactions change the nature of gender relations within the system of patriarchy.

In particular, they differentiate the experiences and practices of women in different **class** and ethnic locations.

The concept of patriarchy has sometimes attracted controversy. This has often been because of misunderstandings. In particular, it has sometimes been assumed that analysis using the concept of patriarchy must be universalist and essentialist, reducing social differences between men and women to biological differences, and ignoring differences in the patterns of gender relations in different times and places. While some early versions of the analysis of patriarchy did have a tendency to simplification, this tendency to essentialism is not found in more recent analysis. A further source of controversy is to be found in the use of the concept of system.

As a consequence of this controversy, there has been a development of terms in addition to patriarchy to capture the concept of a social system of unequal gender relations. This includes, for example, the term 'gender regime'. The use of gender rather than patriarchy removes any lingering ambiguity about the nature of the social rather than biological basis of this social system. Further, the term 'regime' has softer connotations than that of system, signifying the importance of the interactions of other sets of social relations, such as class and **ethnicity**, in shaping gender relations. In practice, the two terms are effectively interchangeable, meaning the same thing, that is, a social system of unequal gender relations.

The addition of the concept of patriarchy to the sociological vocabulary facilitates the analysis of gender relations at the level of social structure and social system, going beyond conceptions of gender as determined by biology or psychology.

Further reading

Walby, Sylvia (1990) *Theorizing Patriarchy*. Oxford: Blackwell.
Walby, Sylvia (2006 forthcoming) *Complex Social Systems: Theorizations and Comparisons in a Global Era*. London: Sage.

Sylvia Walby

POVERTY AND INEQUALITY

Poverty can be defined in a range of different ways: as lack of resources (income) available to purchase necessities or to achieve an acceptable standard of living; through actual levels of expenditure; as deprivation indicated by the lack of essentials; as lack of the capability to achieve a particular standard of living, whether or not that standard of living is achieved; or as inability to participate in the activities of everyday life. At the same time, sociological attention to inequality has focused on a range of different inequalities: inequality of income; health inequalities; educational inequalities, or inequality of educational opportunity. Where poverty and inequality overlap is in the area of income poverty and income inequality, which will provide the main focus of this discussion. However, many of the other inequalities are typically associated with poverty or differentials in command over resources: poorer people are more likely to be ill, to have more limited educational opportunities, to have poorer quality housing and so on. Moreover, research into poverty and inequality has paid attention to differences between groups in their poverty and in their inequalities, rather than simply to the number of poor people or overall gaps between rich and poor. Thus, not only is the amount of poverty of interest but also which groups – for example, women versus men, different ethnic groups – are over-represented in poverty. In relation to inequality, levels of income inequality as they differ between groups are of interest, and also the concentration of different groups at different parts of the income distribution has been explored. Indeed, inequalities more generally can be defined as the differences between groups rather than simply the range of different outcomes: for example, health inequalities are the different chances of sickness or death for different sections of the population, most often those from different social classes but also those from different ethnic groups, or those living in different regions, and according to sex.

While there has always been poverty, the modern conceptualisation and measurement of income poverty is widely regarded to have been initiated as recently as 1901 by Seebohm Rowntree's study of poverty in York. Since then, definitions of poverty have multiplied, as indicated in the first sentence of this entry, with the work of Peter Townsend being important in stressing the relational aspects of poverty and its impact on participation. Even in the area of income poverty there have developed a range of ways of establishing the point at which the poor are separated from the not-poor: the poverty line. Attention has also been paid to a range of other issues in the conceptualisation and measurement of income poverty. Many of these have been concerned to differentiate the experience of poverty, rather than conceiving of 'the poor' as a homogeneous group. For example, differences in the depth of poverty – 'the poverty gap' – have been considered and measured; and how this gap varies between groups and over time has been explored. The length of time people are in poverty has also been seen to be crucial to understandings of poverty – being poor for five years is clearly very different from falling below the poverty line for three months; and studies have also examined the factors associated with both falling into poverty and escaping from it.

The starting point, however, is to fix some form of poverty line which separates those considered poor from those considered not poor at any point in time. Simple 'head count' measures of the poor as well as measures of poverty gaps and poverty durations all require such a line – or a series of such lines. There have been two main approaches to calculating such lines, which are conventionally termed absolute and relative approaches (though for a critique of this distinction see Platt, 2006). Another way of describing these two types of line is as a fixed line or one which moves with changes in the overall distribution of income. The fixed line specifies a minimum amount of resources that allows people to avoid poverty. If an individual has this minimum or more, then they are not poor; if they have less, they are poor. The implication of a fixed line is that poverty is linked to the satisfaction of minimum needs and is largely unaffected by the experiences of others in the same society – poor or not poor. This fixed line is not affected by increases (or reductions) in inequality, and does not necessarily take account of changes in society or in social norms. An example is the US poverty line introduced in 1969 and based on work on poverty thresholds using food budgets by Mollie Orshansky

The moving line relates to the overall income distribution and specifically to the mid-point of that distribution – the 'average'. The implication is that people's living standards are related to each other: it is not just what you have – or rather don't have – that makes you poor, but also what other people around you have and the social norms and the patterns of expenditure implied by that. The moving poverty threshold will therefore be affected by changes in income distribution and also by changes in inequality. It will go up with increasing average prosperity – you will need more money to avoid poverty as those around you become better off, on average; and it will also tend to go up with increasing inequality, though this will depend in part whether inequality is increasing because of more people falling to the bottom of the income distribution or because of the better off having big gains. The increase in the moving poverty line with increasing prosperity does not necessarily mean that there will be more poor people – those near the poverty line may also increase their incomes. But the number of people in poverty will tend to go up with increasing inequality. An example of a moving poverty line is that utilised by the annual *Households Below Average Income* statistics produced in the UK.

Investigation of income inequality, rather than being concerned with fixing a line and exploring the number and characteristics of those below it, examines the overall distance between rich and poor and the shares of total income that are held by those better or worse off. It is typically summarised by the Gini coefficient, a single number between zero and one which has the value zero if everyone has the same income (complete equality) and a value of one if a single person has all the available income and no-one else has any (complete inequality). Clearly these two extremes are hypothetical, but the extent to which the Gini tends in one direction or the other can indicate the levels of inequality in any country or group of people and enables comparison over time and across space. In developed countries the Gini is typically between 0.25 and 0.35. In high inequality countries, such as Brazil or South Africa, it can exceed 0.5 or even rise as high as 0.6. Inequality has increased in Britain since the 1970s from around 0.25 to around 0.35.

Those who are concerned with poverty and inequality are often concerned from the point of view of social justice: reductions in poverty or inequality are argued to create a fairer society and to be beneficial not just for the poor but for society as a whole since social cohesion is increased and the chances of the social exclusion of the poorest are reduced. However, the two are conceptually distinct and thus the arguments for tackling poverty or inequality are somewhat different. As Tony Atkinson has pointed out, it is perfectly possible to be concerned about one without being concerned about the other. Concern with the situation of the most disadvantaged is not incompatible with a belief in a system of differential rewards and thus in the necessity of inequality. On the other hand, Richard Wilkinson has argued that once countries have attained a certain level of economic development, it is not levels of prosperity but the extent of inequality in a society that results in worse outcomes for those at the bottom of the income distribution and in negative impacts on society more generally. Moreover, while poverty is necessarily a concept that focuses on those with the least resources, it is the incomes of the wealthiest that invite attention from those concerned with income inequality as they will tend to be driving changes in income inequality.

As mentioned above, the issue of whether differences between groups are of fundamental interest is also an important one. Then, regardless of whether poverty itself is conceived of as problematic the different risks of different groups of being in poverty may be seen as unfair, or as a challenge to a meritocratic society. Conversely, the link between inequalities in resources and other inequalities may direct attention to those who are disadvantaged (in health, education, or housing) rather than simply to the size of the gap between the best and the worst off.

Further reading

Atkinson, Anthony B. (1998) *Poverty in Europe*. Oxford: Blackwell.

Lister, Ruth (2004) *Poverty*. Bristol: The Policy Press.

Orshansky, Mollie (1965) 'Counting the poor: another look at the poverty profile', *Social Security Bulletin* 28.1: 3–29.

Platt, Lucinda (2006) 'Poverty', in G. Payne (ed.) *Social Divisions*. Basingstoke: Palgrave.

Rowntree, B. Seebohm (1901) *Poverty: A Study of Town Life*. London: Macmillan.

Townsend, Peter (1979) *Poverty in the United Kingdom: A Survey of Household Resources and Standards of Living*. Harmondsworth: Penguin.

Wilkinson, Richard G. (1996) *Unhealthy Societies: The Afflictions of Inequality*. London: Routledge.

Lucinda Platt

POWER

Power, in its most general sense, is simply the production of causal effects, and social power is an agent's intentional use of causal powers to affect the conduct of other agents. Social power is a relation between two agents, one of whom is the 'principal' or paramount agent, and the other is the 'subaltern' or subordinate agent. The principal has or exercises power, while the subaltern is affected by the power of a principal.

This general view of power is common to all who write on the subject, though many different interpretations have been given to the core idea. A mainstream approach has focused on the actual exercise of power: seeing a principal actually making a subaltern do something. A second approach, however, focuses on a principal's capacity or potential to do something or to facilitate things.

The mainstream approach, influenced by the ideas of Weber, looks particularly at the exercise of decision-making powers in sovereign organisations – such as **states**, business enterprises, universities and churches – through the use of elections and administrative mechanisms. Such power relations are asymmetrical and are organised around the conflicting interests and goals of the participants. Power is fixed in quantity and because one agent can gain only at the expense of another, there will always be winners and losers in any power relationship. There are two faces to sovereign power: formal decision-making and the 'nondecision-making' that occurs when some have the power to keep matters off the decision-making agenda. Steven Lukes extended this approach to power from the actual intervention of a principal in the life of a subaltern to the enduring structural constraints that shape the exercise of power.

The second approach to power has started out from such structural concerns, though it has stressed the cultural construction of institutional structures rather than the relational structures emphasised by Lukes. This approach developed in the diverse arguments of Antonio Gramsci, Talcott Parsons and Michel Foucault. It concerns itself with the strategies and techniques of power, seeing it as diffused throughout a society rather than concentrated in sovereign organisations. Power is a collective property of **social systems** of cooperating actors that facilitates both collective empowerment and collective discipline. What Foucault referred to as the 'discursive formation' of power operates through mechanisms of **socialisation** and **community** building that produce individuals as subjects with particular kinds of mental orientation and routines of action. While the principals in power relations are formed as those who are 'authorised' to discipline others, the most effective and pervasive forms of power occur where people have learnt to exercise a self-discipline over their behaviour. They have been discursively formed into subalterns who conform without the need for any direct action on the part of a principal.

Only a combination of these two approaches to power can provide a basis for developing a nuanced understanding of the various social forms that power can take. Each approach has highlighted different, but complementary, sets of mechanisms, and it is possible to combine them into a more general account of the mechanisms of power, working from the most elementary forms to the more complex patterns of domination found in states, economic structures and other associations.

The two elementary forms of social power can be called corrective influence and persuasive influence. Corrective influence, analysed mainly within the mainstream approach, involves a rational, calculative orientation to others and operates through the use of punishments and rewards. The two main forms taken by this are force and manipulation. Force involves the use of negative physical sanctions to prevent the actions of subalterns, while manipulation involves the use of both positive and negative sanctions (for example, money, credit and access to employment) as ways of influencing subaltern decisions. Persuasive influence, on the other hand, depends on the rhetorical use of arguments, appeals and reasons that will lead subalterns, by virtue of their socialisation, to believe that it is appropriate to act in one way rather than another. The two main forms of persuasive influence are signification and legitimation, operating respectively, through shared cognitive meanings and shared value commitments. These make a particular course of action seem necessary or emotionally appropriate to other actors.

These elementary forms of power are found in numerous day-to-day acts of interpersonal power. Power depends on personal attributes and characteristics as much as it does on office holding or formal resources. A married woman with no alternative sources of support may depend entirely on her husband for material support, and her dependence will be the basis for the man's power over her. Household and family structures and the private sphere of intimacy and sexuality are crucial contexts in which interpersonal power is honed and exercised, giving many other power relations a patriarchal form.

Elementary forms of power	corrective influence		persuasive influence	
	force	manipulation	signification	legitimation
Developed forms of power	domination			
	through constraint		through discursive formation	
	coercion	inducement	expertise	command
	counteraction			
	protest		pressure	
	interpersonal power			

Source: Scott (2002: Figure 1.1).

The elementary forms of power are the building blocks from which more fully developed power relations can be built as structures of domination. Domination is power that is structured into stable and enduring social structures, as shown in the diagram. It is the means through which **elites** are formed as dominant groups. Coercion and inducement are structures of domination that operate through constraint and correspond to the elementary forms of force and manipulation. Constraint is what Weber called 'domination by virtue of a constellation of interests' and Giddens called 'allocative domination'. Principals are able to influence subalterns by determining the action alternatives open to them and the considerations that they take into account in choosing between them. The resources controlled by the principal, within the overall structural distribution of resources, shape the constellation of interests within which both principal and subaltern must act. Expertise and command are structures of domination that operate through discursively based structures of authority. They correspond to the elementary forms of signification and legitimation and can be regarded as organised forms of persuasive influence that work through institutionalised commitment, loyalty and trust. Weber defined this as 'domination by virtue of authority', while Anthony Giddens called it simply 'authoritative domination'.

The gendered nature of much interpersonal power has been the basis on which **patriarchy** has come to permeate the public sphere of domination. Gendered regimes of recruitment to positions of command and gendered relations between professional experts and their clients, for example, embody patriarchal patterns of power, rooted in the private sphere of the household and the family, that shape the ways in which formal powers of domination will be exercised and that articulate with them in complex ways.

There has been much debate about the relationship between the constraining mode and the discursive mode of domination, and this has been focused particularly around the idea of legitimacy as the basis of state authority. Domination through command, as it has been defined here, works through the structuring of rights and obligations: the *right* of the principals to give orders and a corresponding *obligation* for the subalterns to obey. Subalterns show a willing compliance because of their commitment to a belief in the legitimacy of the command and of those who issue these commands. Legitimacy exists whenever there is a belief that a pattern of domination is right, correct, justified, or valid in some way. Agents who have internalised the prevailing cultural values will identify with those who occupy positions of domination that are defined in terms of these values. It is this internalisation and identification that creates principals and subalterns and that defines the rights and obligations that underpin the power of command that are available to the principals. The work of Foucault has stimulated a great concern for domination by experts, understood as power that is rooted in the signifying practices through which their expertise is discursively constructed. Subalterns recognise and so accept the knowledge on which a professional expert relies as the basis for an express or implied agreement with their recommendations for action.

Power researchers have emphasised that any exercise of power will tend to generate resistance, and that this resistance is also a form of power. In the case of structures of domination, subaltern resistance takes the form of counteraction to the structure of domination. This may be manifest in inchoate resentment, hostility, or withdrawal, or in isolated acts of disruption and sabotage. The most important forms of counteraction, however, are those that involve coordinated or collective action. Counteraction is power from below, rather than power from above, and it derives its significance from the number of subalterns that unite together and the kind of solidarity that they are able to achieve

When oppositional action is institutionalised and counteracting groups are given a degree of recognition and legitimacy within the established structure of power, they can be said to exercise 'pressure' as formal participants in the institutionalised structure. Pressure groups, for example, have a legitimate role within the state. 'Protest', on the other hand, is subaltern counteraction that occurs outside the formal institutions of power and that poses a challenge to these very structures. It is subaltern resistance that is exercised as a counter-mobilisation to the existing structure of domination. These analytical distinctions are often difficult to disentangle in concrete situations. Protest groups may achieve some of their goals and accommodate themselves to the established framework of power, transforming themselves into pressure groups; and pressure groups may be frustrated in their actions and mount progressively more confrontational protests. Pressure groups may be subverted from within, becoming progressively more challenging to the existing system; and protest groups may be subtly transformed into more quiescent resistance where their oppositional ideology obscures a *de facto* accommodation with the system.

Further reading

Lukes, Steven (2005) *Power: A Radical View*, 2nd edn. London: Palgrave.
Scott, John (ed.) (1994) *Power*, three volumes. London: Routledge.
Scott, John (2001) *Power*. Cambridge: Polity Press.

John Scott

RACE AND RACIALISATION

According to Michael Banton, the first person to systematically lay out a theory of the relations between races was Robert Knox, a medical doctor from Scotland. Knox published *The Races of Men* in 1850, arguing that the world was naturally divided into a limited number of distinct races, each with its own mental and physical attributes, and that racial membership determined ability and the relations between the races. Knox believed that each race was suited to its own climate – Africans to hot climates, Europeans to cold climates – and that they could not successfully live outside their own climate. This began a long line of racial theorising.

The classification of races used in this theorising, and still the most widely used system of classification today, originated in the earlier work of Johann Freidrich Blumenbach, in his 1775 publication *On the Natural Variety of Mankind*. Blumenbach had classified humanity into five races: Caucasian (white), Mongolian (yellow), Ethiopian (black), American (copper-coloured) and Malay (tawny coloured). These theories were elaborated in a context in which Europeans had conquered what was to become the Americas, and Africans were being enslaved by the millions on plantations producing cotton, sugar and coffee. Popular stereotypes held by plantation owners – for example, that African men could work longer hours in the sun, African women could more easily endure the perils of childbirth and return to work in the fields, while both were mentally inferior to whites – influenced theories of racial ability.

Charles Darwin, who published *The Origin of the Species* in the 1850s, demonstrated that the basis of such thinking was wrong. Humanity cannot be classified into distinct races, but rather we all share the same genetic origins, and have become differentiated over time, due to migration and geography and to genetic variations developed to adapt to different environments. Most biologists at the end of the twentieth century believed that race was not the best way to think about human variation. A better concept was that of populations that shared common genetic pools.

So, race began as an idea, a concept, or a theory to describe and classify human variation. We see too, that it is a relatively recent concept – only around 250 years old – and that academic writing was very strongly influenced by social factors such as slavery and colonisation.

Since the end of the nineteenth century, most academic work on race has sought to identify the social factors that led people to believe in races, and the benefits that arise from this for different groups. Emphasis is laid on a range of economic, political and religious factors. Eric Williams argued that racism was developed to meet the economic demands of Europeans for a controllable labour population to colonise the Americas. Racism, and the alleged inferiority of races was simply a justification. Others point to political power and control, with beliefs about race being used, for example, in the 1882 Chinese Exclusion Act, to deny American citizenship to Chinese immigrants. Still others believe that religion is more important, as with the Boers of South Africa whose beliefs led to the system of apartheid.

The concept of racialisation is usually used in two senses. One describes a historical process during which social significance has become attached to certain human features (skin colour, hair texture, shape of nose) and on the basis of which people are classified into distinctive groups. Thus, the racialisation of the West refers to the ways in which race was applied within and across Europe to classify the English, Irish, French and Spanish into different races; and the racialisation of the world refers to the ways in which Africans, Native Americans and Asians became distinctive races. It is used in a second sense as a theoretical framework, as a model for evaluating competing explanations of race. In this sense it might best be thought of as answering a question: if race is not biology, then what is it? Sociologists usually point to a variety of social factors – culture, economics, politics, 'common sense' – as the basis of racialisation. Many analysts argue that we have seen an increasing racialisation of the world along with **globalisation**, as more and more diverse populations have come into contact with one another.

Another useful concept for understanding race and racialisation is 'racial projects', introduced by Michael Omi and Howard Winant. A racial project is an interpretation, representation, or explanation of racial dynamics and an effort to reorganise and redistribute resources along particular racial lines. This concept highlights the motivations of groups who find the idea of race to be a useful organising tool. The promoting of segregation by the Ku Klux Klan is one type of racial project; so, too, were efforts by President Reagan to abolish affirmative action. In Britain a good example of a racial project is the effort made by Margaret Thatcher to win votes over from the racist political party the National Front. A key dimension to racial projects is the use of 'code words'. These are words that do not mention race but that have a racial meaning that is understood by everyone: law and order (black criminals), welfare cheats (black women), reverse discrimination (affirmative action). Margaret Thatcher, in the run up to the 1979 election, said that British people were afraid of being 'swamped' by people of a different culture. The white British public clearly understood that she meant Indians and Caribbeans, and not immigrants from the Republic of Ireland, or from Australia. Thus groups or individuals motivated by race no longer have to even use the word

Since the 1990s there has been a set of developments, which reinforces beliefs in race, and a set of developments that breaks down such beliefs. In the fields of biomedicine and genetics the quest to explain biological variations in terms of race have met with renewed vigour. Since the completion of the sequencing of the human genome, much biomedical literature now purports to document difference in disease and social behaviour (e.g. crime) that can be attributed to race. At the same time, the massive increase in a population in the USA and Britain increasingly likely to call itself mixed race, has led to a challenge to race thinking. Mixed-race individuals, who number in the millions in the USA, and hundreds of thousands in Britain, refuse binary explanations and have a wide range of hyphenated categories for classifying themselves: for example, as Irish/Vietnamese/Native American. As these groups grow larger – and the patterns of inter-racial marriage and dating continue to grow at a phenomenal rate – then ideas about race will become far more varied and far more complex, more characterised by **hybridity**. Once again, this demonstrates that in the process of racialisation it is social factors that provide the best explanations for shifting attitudes towards race.

Further reading

Banton, Michael (1977) *The Idea of Race*. London: Tavistock Publications.
Omi, Michael and Winant, Howard (1994) *Racial Formation in the United States. From the 1960s to the 1990s*, 2nd edn. London: Routledge.

Stephen Small

RATIONAL ACTION

Rational action is **action** that is based on a calculation of the most efficient means of accomplishing an end. A discussion of rational action, and social **action** more generally, can be found in the work of Weber, a key figure in the development of sociology. Weber argued that sociology should be concerned with understanding (*Verstehen*) social action. It was only by understanding social action that we could make sense of social structures since they are simply the product of lots of individual actions. This perspective is referred to as methodological individualism.

Weber outlined four types of action. First, there is instrumental rational action when people use the most efficient means to obtain their objective. There is a clear purpose for the action and the means are chosen as the most effective way of achieving that goal. Second, there is value rational action where people are committed to a value or set of values that guide their actions. Such values are less tangible than goals and the way of obtaining these values is not necessarily efficient or effective. That said, Weber thought this type of action was rational in employing means to obtain an end.

Third, Weber identified traditional action that people undertake in a habitual and unreflective fashion. It is a type of action that involves little conscious thinking of ends and means. Much mundane everyday action is not especially rational in this respect. Fourth, he considered affective action that results from the expression of emotions such as lashing out at someone in a flash of anger. Again, Weber did not see this action as rational because it is not necessarily directed towards goals or values. Of the four types of action, Weber identified two as rational and two as irrational or non-rational.

Weber saw these four types of actions as ideal types: namely, conceptual constructions highlighting the key aspects of the different types of action. He did not believe they existed in real life in such discrete forms. Rather, Weber thought that most actions could be seen to have elements of the four types he identified. The role of the sociologist, he argued, is to understand these actions and especially the meaning people attach to their actions, their motives for action, their assessment of the situation in which they find themselves, the choices they have and the decisions they make to act one way or another.

Weber claimed that in seeking to understand social action, sociologists could rise above the chaos of life to see patterns and regularities in how people behave in certain situations. If people act rationally in any given situation, it is likely that they will act in the same way that produces similarities and continuities. It is possible to predict behaviour and thereby offer a causal explanation of individual action and its consequences. Indeed, Weber argued that such uniformities arising out of rational action were the basis of social order and social structure rather than any shared norms or values.

Weber believed that rationality as a way of thinking was becoming increasingly dominant in the modern era. He described this process as **rationalisation**. Medieval and feudal societies, he argued were dominated by value-rational action or traditional action. Weber cited the dominance of religion as an example of value-rational action in earlier epochs. In modern societies, however, he claimed that most actions would be instrumental rational action and the deliberate calculation of ends and means would pervade not just economic activities but other aspects of social life too.

Other German sociologists, including Georg Simmel, subscribed to Weber's view of the importance of understanding social action and interaction. This starting point was influential on American sociology such as the Chicago School and, later, symbolic interactionism and other perspectives within the interpretative tradition. This tradition was critical of Talcott Parsons's structural functionalism – dominant in 1950s American sociology – and his focus on shared norms and values as the basis of social order. That said, these perspectives did not take up Weber's particular interest in rational action.

It was another critic of Parsons, George Homans, who developed rational choice theory drawing on economics and psychology. Focusing on processes of interaction, he termed this exchange theory. Rational choice theories, which look at the many permutations of rational calculations and decision-making that occur in a given situation, have been very popular among American sociologists, including Marxists such as Jon Elster and non-Marxists such as James Coleman. It has become increasingly characterised by formal game theory and mathematical modelling which is increasingly popular in discussions of public choice in political science in both the US and the UK.

In British sociology, John Goldthorpe's development of a rational action theory has taken up Weber's focus on rational action. Having built up a substantial body of empirical work describing the stability of class inequalities and patterns of social **mobility**, he then turned his attention to explaining such continuities with rational action theory. **Class** structures, he argues, have self-maintaining properties because those in positions or privilege and power act rationally to secure the transmission of their advantage from one generation to the next. Macro-level regularities are to be explained with reference to micro-level actions.

Goldthorpe argues that middle-class parents' mobility strategies ensure their children enjoy educational and occupational success and thereby secure their advantaged positions. They employ their resources: economic assets, cultural capital and social networks to circumvent any constraints and exploit any opportunities. Working-class parents may want their children to be upwardly mobile but they do not have the necessary resources to do so. They do not have the means to achieve them and do not pursue an end they cannot have. Working-class mobility strategies are directed elsewhere.

Differential rates of educational progression and attainment can be explained, therefore, with reference to the mobility strategies of middle-class and working-class parents. Detailed empirical studies show that parents do not rationally pursue educational success for their children as a single-minded goal however. It is often one of many aspirations for children and balanced alongside others. If action is not characterised by the pursuit of a singular end, nor are means chosen for their efficiency. Parents are not constantly engaged in a cost/benefit analysis in the pursuit of their children's educational success.

Rational action theory, therefore, does not capture the complexity of rational action. More often than not, human action departs from rational action theory rather than confirms it. It is assumed, for example, that information is collected as evidence on which people make informed decisions when people often misinterpret evidence in support of their beliefs and values. Decisions about choice of school, for example, can be influenced by political values. People's beliefs about themselves – their **self**-identity – also shape their actions and interactions.

Micro studies of families highlight the continuing importance of other forms of social action of a non-rational kind. Rational choice theory has long been criticised for neglecting the influence of norms on action and rational action theory suffers the same problem. It ignores the ways in which shared views about appropriate or desirable behaviour shape people's actions. It does not consider where norms come from, how they are internalised and how they influence the way in which parents help their children into jobs. Local traditions of employment, for example, might be influential in this respect.

Finally, micro-level research on social action highlights the importance of a huge range of **emotions** – happiness, anger, regret, disappointment – on people's actions. Parents feelings for their children are very influential in how they help them in life. Emotions are not unpredictable natural impulses. They are socially constructed and culturally variable. Rational action theory is a cognitive theory of action that assumes a high level of awareness of a situation before actions are taken. Increasingly, social scientists are turning their attention to the interplay of cognition and emotion.

For all of these reasons, Goldthorpe's rational action theory, with its singular emphasis on instrumental rationality, cannot explain the stability of class relations. Social action is shaped by instrumental rationality and rational action is a very important type of social action. Rational action theory has a strong sense of agency. Nevertheless, other types of action are very important too and a sophisticated theory of social action has to incorporate the full range. The unintended consequences of social action certainly cannot be forgotten either.

Further reading

Devine, Fiona (2004) *Class Practices*. Cambridge: Cambridge University Press.

Goldthorpe, John H. (2000) *On Sociology*. Oxford: Oxford University Press.

Fiona Devine

RATIONALISATION

There are many theories of rationality and the rationalisation process in sociology and the social sciences more generally, but the most famous, by a wide margin, is Max Weber's theory of the rationalisation of the Occident and the barriers to that process in other parts of the world.

Weber distinguished among four types of rationality. *Practical rationality* exists everywhere and at all times in history. In involves the everyday search for the best means to whatever goal or objective we might have. *Theoretical rationality*, involving the effort to achieve cognitive mastery over the world, also exists everywhere and throughout history. The same is true of *substantive rationality* involving the search for optimum means to an end, but this time guided by a larger set of social values. What most interests Weber is the type of rationality – *formal rationality* – that is both distinctive to the modern world and to the Occident. Such rationality involves, once again, the search for the best means to an end, but this time guided by rules and regulations. It is the progressive spread of formal rationality, at first throughout the Occident, and then throughout the rest of the world, that is Weber's primary concern in his theory of rationalisation. While the progressive spread of formal rationality brings innumerable advantages (e.g. greater efficiency), Weber was also concerned with problems associated with it, especially the development of an *iron cage* of rationality from which people would have a harder and harder time escaping.

Weber's interest in formal rationality, including its rule-guided behaviour, led him in the direction of a concern for **bureaucracy**. The bureaucracy is the organisational form most suited to a society characterised by formal rationality. Choices of means to ends within the bureaucracy are dominated by its rules and regulations. And the bureaucracy comes to be dominant within many sectors of society – the state, the economy, education, the Church and many more. Indeed, it is possible to think of the process of *bureaucratisation* as closely aligned with rationalisation.

This is all closely related to Weber's thinking on three ideal-typical authority structures. The first is *traditional authority* dominated by decisions based on time immemorial customs. There are various organisational forms associated with traditional authority, but they tend to be staffed by the traditional leader's personal retainers who are usually organised in a loose and haphazard fashion. Charismatic authority is derived from a belief on the part of the followers of the exceptional qualities of a leader. The organisation of disciples associated with charismatic authority tends to be weak and unstable, although over time, through the process of the *routinisation of charisma*, more stable organisational forms develop. However, these organisations then tend to evolve in the direction of traditional authority, or Weber's third type – *rational-legal authority*. The leader's ability to lead in such a system is derived from the rules and regulations of the larger system (for example, the President of the United States derives his authority from having been elected with a majority of votes in the electoral college). The organisational form most associated with this type of authority is the bureaucracy and it tends to be superior in terms of its functioning than the organisational forms associated with the other types of authority. Thus, Weber sees a long-term trend away from traditional and charismatic authority and in the direction of rational-legal authority. This is a key aspect of his more general theory of progressive rationalisation.

Thus, there is a close association among increasing formal rationality, bureaucratisation and rational-legal authority and they all can be subsumed under the broad heading of rationalisation. Rationalisation has influenced a wide range of social theorists, perhaps most notably critical theorists such as Theodor Adorno, Herbert Marcuse and Jürgen Habermas, and became the basis, at least in part, for their analysis of technocratic domination and one-dimensional thought. Important to Weber in his day, rationalisation is, if anything, more significant today, although it may now be somewhat different as reflected in the tendency to use the term **McDonaldisation** to describe at least some of its most important contemporary manifestations.

Further reading

Kalberg, Stephen (1980) 'Max Weber's types of rationality: cornerstones for the analysis of rationalization processes in history', *American Journal of Sociology*, 85, 1980: 1145–79.

Weber, Max (1921) *Economy and Society* (three volumes). Totowa, NJ: Bedminster Press, 1968.

George Ritzer

RELIGION

No sociologist has matched the intellectual effort Durkheim devoted to defining religion. After several false starts, his considered definition, given in *The Elementary Forms of the Religious Life*, was: 'a unified system of beliefs and practices relative to sacred things, that is to say, things set apart and forbidden – beliefs and practices which unite into one single moral community called a Church, all those who adhere to them'. This formulation illustrates many of the crucial dilemmas that continue to confront the sociological analysis of religion.

Durkheim was anxious to define religion as a phenomenon that could be analysed sociologically. He deliberately excluded any reference to God, the gods, or the supernatural, thinking that some religions, such as classical Buddhism and Jainism, operate without such beliefs. If he was right (which is questionable), to define religion in those terms would be narrowly ethnocentric. His approach was essentialist: he looked for the common factor in all religions. He started with what he took to be its most 'primitive' form, the totemic religion of the aboriginal peoples of Australia, from which he generalised to all others. The essence of religion, the sacred, is not as the faithful imagine. Its source is not God but society; it is not divinely ordained but socially constructed.

For Durkheim, religion and the sacred were essentially social: individual beliefs and practices were secondary. Hence he drew a sharp distinction between religion and magic. Priests minister to a community, whereas magicians have individual clients looking for specific solutions to their personal problems and desires. Unlike magic, religion for Durkheim necessarily involves obligation, which is why he insisted that it requires a moral community. Religion stands over against us as a constraining force – as the **power** of society. From this Durkheim derives his thesis that religion is 'society worshipping itself' (an idealised version of itself, it should be noted).

Sacred and profane, society and the individual: to Durkheim, these are sharp dichotomies. Yet, they can be transcended through ritual. Rituals are rule-governed actions that are strongly charged with symbolism. Through rituals, we are brought into communion with the power of the sacred. Robert Bellah pursued this idea in his work on what he called 'civil religion' in America. This is a set of beliefs, practices and values that pervade American society without being dependent on the state or on religious organisations. The political rituals of civil religion, such as the inauguration of a President, the commemoration of martyrs and the celebration of victories, involve invocations of sacred symbols and myths and the shared values they embody. Unlike Durkheim, Bellah and other contemporary sociologists stress that rituals can be vehicles of social protest as well as social cohesion. Rituals, myths and sacred symbols are not just given: they can be deliberately created and manipulated in pursuit of politicised agendas such as glorifying dictators or campaigning for civil rights. They have been just as important to the political culture of the former Soviet Union and other officially atheist regimes.

In contrast to Durkheim, Weber refused to define religion at the outset of his study. He argued that a definition could only be given at the conclusion – though he did not attempt it himself. He also contended that sociologists should be concerned with the social structuring and social impact of religion, not with its essence. Weber's work focused not on religion but on religions, and on the effects that different religions have had on the course of history. The intimate link Weber emphasised between the Protestant ethic and the spirit of capitalism has its counterpart in his attempts to show that other religions, such as Hinduism, Buddhism, Confucianism and Islam, lacked the impulses necessary to give an impetus to rational forms of capitalism.

Echoing Weber's anti-essentialist position, Talal Asad rejects definitions of religion that treat it as fundamentally the same thing in all **cultures** and historical periods. Drawing on Michel Foucault, he sees religion as a key component in discursive formations of power: it is a social construct that serves to legitimise distinctions between true and false claims. For example, distinctions between 'real' religion and bogus 'cults', genuine miracles and fakes, and 'true' and 'nominal' Christians. Nation-states have an interest in such distinctions, in order to determine the scope of the rights they grant selectively to the various faith communities within their jurisdiction. The UK prison chaplaincy service, for example, classifies Scientology, the Nation of Islam and Rastafarianism as 'non-permitted religions'. Thus, people detained in British penal establishments have no right to practise these faiths. In Germany, recognised religions enjoy legal privileges; neither Jehovah's Witnesses nor Scientology qualify. The German approach is partly explained by the Nazi past, as the constitution has a range of provisions designed to prevent authoritarian movements from subverting democratic institutions.

Religion is a troublesome category to legislators and sociologists. The obvious reason for this is that other-worldly concepts are incompatible with this-worldly disciplines. A related reason is that religion radically breaches the culture/nature dichotomy. Sociologists treat religion as a cultural phenomenon, but that is not how the faithful typically see it. To Christians, Jews, Muslims and many others, religion is a gift from God, the creator of the world and all things in it. The term 'religion', with its cultural overtones, is problematic for many believers, who often prefer to speak of their 'faith'. This may explain why the issue of same-sex relations has been so divisive within Christian churches: they are held to contradict not only God's commandments but also the natural order He created. A comparable issue in the Muslim world is apostasy – the renunciation of Islam – which is a serious sin. When someone becomes a Muslim they are said not to have converted to Islam, but *reverted* to it; this is because, in an Islamic perspective, human beings are Muslims by nature.

Contemporary sociology of religion has been preoccupied with debating the relative merits of inclusive and exclusive definitions of religion. Inclusive definitions, such as Durkheim's, avoid reference to the gods, the supernatural or the transcendent. Instead, they define religion in terms of the ultimate meanings of life. Inclusive definitions tend to emphasise the 'functions' that religion performs for individuals (generating motivation and morale) and for society (strengthening social integration). Inclusive definitions are carefully crafted by sociologists and anthropologists, with the explicit aim of avoiding ethnocentric assumptions that apply only to a few religions in a particular cultural context.

Advocates of exclusive definitions often claim that they are simply reflecting common usage, and that the definition of religion is straightforward. Bryan Wilson worked with a minimal definition of religion as humanity's orientation to the supernatural, while Steve Bruce refers to beliefs, actions and institutions that assume the existence of gods or moral powers governing human affairs. Crucially for Wilson and Bruce, exclusive definitions enable us to investigate empirically whether or not religion is losing social significance. Inclusive definitions, they say, make empirical research redundant: the persistence of religion becomes not a finding but true merely by definition.

The debate about exclusive versus inclusive definitions of religion is closely linked to the secularisation thesis, which holds that religious beliefs, practices and institutions are losing social significance in modern societies. Peter Berger identified three dimensions of secularisation in the West. These are: 'social-structural', marked by a transfer of functions from churches to publicly funded welfare services; 'cultural', shown in the rise of secular sciences and decline of religious content in art, music, literature and philosophy; and 'individual', as fewer and fewer people think in religious terms.

Sociologists have identified various root causes of secularisation. For

Weber, the replacement of traditional and charismatic forms of authority by rational-legal systems enshrined in soulless bureaucracies has led to a disenchantment with the social world. For Wilson, the erosion of local communities has destroyed the necessary social foundation on which religious belief and practice are based. For Berger, the move to a pluralist, consumer-oriented society has undermined the authority of religious institutions.

Secularisation was never plausible as an account of the condition of religion in the United States, where participation rates are high and religion plays a key role in the public sphere. Many critics of the secularisation thesis argue therefore that the process is neither universal nor irreversible, but applies only to European societies in the heyday of industrial **modernity**. In that socio-historical context, the Weberian themes of **rationalisation** and disenchantment were a plausible diagnosis – though even in Europe, explicit atheism has only ever been a minority option, while secularist social movements have generally lost credibility. As we move into late- or post-modernity, possibilities have opened up for the resurgence of religion and re-enchantment of the world. Traditional authority structures have lost some of their powers, but a differentiation of functions does not necessarily mean a decline. The quest for spirituality flourishes: 'believing without belonging' is Grace Davie's phrase to capture the cultural shifts under way. **Globalisation** has intensified social inequalities and destabilised national and local communities; religion is a resource for mobilising the Third World's dispossessed, and a source of meaning and cultural identity for the ethnic minorities and anxiety-prone consumers of the affluent West.

Further reading

Aldridge, Alan (2000) *Religion in the Contemporary World: A Sociological Introduction*. Cambridge: Polity.

Asad, Talal (1993) *Genealogies of Religion: Discipline and Reasons of Power in Christianity and Islam*. Baltimore: Johns Hopkins University Press.

Beckford, James (2003) *Social Theory and Religion*. Cambridge: Cambridge University Press.

Bruce, Steve (2002) *God is Dead: Secularization in the West*. Oxford: Blackwell.

Casanova, José (1994) *Public Religions in the Modern World*. Chicago: University of Chicago Press.

Davie, Grace (1994) *Religion in Britain since 1945: Believing without Belonging*. Oxford, Blackwell.

Alan Aldridge

ROLE

Roles exist where social groups have established norms that are valid only for certain categories of individual. They imply or create a social differentiation of individuals according to the particular part that they are expected to play in the life of the group. Social theorists have long recognised this effect of social expectations, using such terms as character, mask and persona to explore the incorporation of cultural patterns into individual personality and the ways that individuals came to act in socially approved ways in specific tasks. It was not until the 1930s, however, that the term 'role' became firmly fixed as the basis for exploring this.

It was thanks to cultural anthropologist Ralph Linton that this occurred, and his terminological innovation became the basis on which Talcott Parsons constructed the model of the normative regulation of social behaviour that formed the basis of mainstream sociology. Critics such as Ralf Dahrendorf, who rejected Parsons's reliance on normative consensus, nevertheless saw the value of the concept of role to refer to the structured social expectations to which individuals orientate themselves. A more radical view, associated in particular with symbolic interactionism, saw this idea of role as being over-deterministic and stressed that roles should be seen simply as the shared and inherited ideas that guide and inform behaviour but do not determine it. Individual actors should be seen as improvisers rather than mere automatons. In creatively enacting the roles that they inherit, individuals are also transforming them and making these transformed roles available to others. This reconstruction of social roles is an aspect of the constant negotiation of social definitions in which individuals are engaged and through which they establish a sense of order and stability.

Linton distinguished two aspects of social roles. These are the static 'positional' aspect (which he misleadingly called 'status') and the dynamic aspect of the role behaviour itself. Cultural systems define the positions in terms of which people identify themselves and others as members of a society or social group. These positions are cultural ideals or exemplars characterised by their specific rights and obligations and marked out by particular identifying labels: worker, mother, politician, criminal, citizen, student and more diffuse categories such as celebrity or elder. Role behaviour comprises the enactment or performance of the rights and obligations associated with the position. Position and role behaviour, then, have typically been treated by role theorists as integrally linked aspects of the generic idea of role. In Parsons's social theory, roles are defined as the organised expectations relating to particular contexts of interaction that shape the motivational orientations of individuals towards each other. They are the cultural patterns, blueprints, or templates for behaviour through which people learn *who* they are in the eyes of others and *how* they should act towards them.

Robert Merton proposed that the role behaviour associated with the particular position could be seen as comprising a whole set of complementary behaviours towards specific others, to which he gave the name 'role set'. The ways in which a person is expected to behave towards the occupants of each other role encountered will tend to be quite distinct. A medical student, for example, faces specific and distinct expectations concerning how it is appropriate to behave towards fellow students, teachers, doctors, nurses, patients and so on. There is no guarantee that these differing expectations will be complementary with each other, and individuals may face various degrees of 'role conflict' in their relationships with others. Such role conflicts are experienced whenever the shared expectations that define a role set are mutually contradictory or incompatible. A teacher, for example, may be expected to behave towards pupils in one way by the head teacher, in another way by parents and in quite different ways by the pupils themselves. Although there may be a core of common expectations, the specific expectations may differ quite considerably. Individuals rarely occupy just one role, and further dilemmas of role behaviour may result from contradictions between the expectations imposed by their different roles. Thus, a woman may face conflicting demands placed on her in her roles as wife, mother and employee.

The symbolic interactionist criticism of mainstream sociology emphasised that roles and role expectations must not be treated as fixed and given determinants of individual action. Ralph Turner stressed that they are acquired as loose guidelines within which people must improvise if they are to enact them at all. The scripts provided in the cultural templates are mere outlines that define only the broad shape of a role and cannot give detailed guidance on how to act in particular situations. In any interaction, therefore, individuals must negotiate the situational meanings and applicability of specific role expectations. Individuals tentatively interpret and reinterpret each other's actions in particular situations and so recreate their roles from the blueprints provided by their socialisation.

The implications of this were taken further by Erving Goffman in his account of the relationship between roles and the **self**. The private self – the 'I' – is the focus of autonomous agency and is distinct from the self displayed in any publicly enacted role. This autonomous agency is the basis of the choices and decisions made and is the means through which impressions are managed or calculatively manipulated in role performances. This allowed Goffman to develop such concepts as 'role distance' to describe those situations where a person seeks to distance himself or herself from a role that must be enacted but with which they do not wish to be identified by others. They may, for example, seek to maintain a degree of personal autonomy by engaging in the minimum of overtly expected behaviour or acting in ways that exhibit their lack of commitment to the role.

Further reading

Banton, Michael (1965) *Roles: An Introduction to the Study of Social Relations.* London: Tavistock.

Biddle, Bruce J. (1979) *Role theory: Expectations, Identities, and Behaviours.* New York: Academic Press.

Gross, Neil, Mason, Ward S. and McEachern, Alexander W. (1958) *Explorations in Role Analysis: Studies of the School Superintendency Role.* New York: John Wiley and Sons.

Jackson, John A. (ed.) (1972) *Role.* Cambridge: Cambridge University Press.

John Scott

SELF AND IDENTITY

Sociological accounts of the self have been enormously influential in the development of classic and contemporary social theory. While it may seem counter-intuitive to theorise something as private and internal as the self in terms of social forces and processes, this approach reveals a great deal about the relationship between individuals and the societies in which they live. In contrast to psychological theories of the self as an essential core of the personality, sociological theories emphasise the way in which selves are socially shaped and managed through the processes of **socialisation**, interaction and biographical identity work.

Perhaps the most influential theory of the self in the twentieth century was that of George Mead, who described his approach as one of social behaviourism. Mead argued that humans, unlike other animals, do not simply respond passively to stimuli in their environment but rather are actively engaged in creating the social world. Everyday life comprises 'social acts' performed by individuals as they perceive and attribute symbolic meaning to the 'social objects' around them. These social objects include other people and, as such, Mead suggested that interaction unfolds as a 'conversation of gestures'; but more importantly, they also include the self. That is, by taking the role of the other towards oneself, we can reflect upon ourselves as we think that we appear to other people, and adjust our behaviour accordingly. Mead therefore conceived of the social self as an internal conversation of gestures between two parts, or phases: the 'I' and the 'Me'. Drawing on Kant and William James, he described the 'I' as the creative, impulsive and unknowable agent of the self who was responsible for thinking, feeling and responding to situations, while the 'Me' was a reflexive awareness of oneself as a social object, as seen from the perspective of others. The 'Me' comprised all those attitudes towards oneself that the individual had learnt from interaction, and this image would be constantly revised as they encountered new experiences. The importance of social audiences in shaping one's self-concept was also central to Charles Cooley's account of the 'looking glass self'.

Other sociologists have focused on the way in which we acquire and learn to perform social **roles** in everyday life. Traditionally, role theory has followed a Parsonian, structuralist approach, focusing on the way in which social behaviour could be organised in terms of the normative aspects of roles and statuses, stressing the expectations concerning the conduct of role incumbents. This rather rigid idea of role-*taking* has been criticised by those who emphasise the agency of individuals in the interpretive act of role-*making*. George McCall and Jerry Simmons, for instance, proposed that a sense of social selfhood is developed by performing 'role-identities', or characters devised from the imaginative view of oneself as the occupant of a particular social position. The same social role (for example, 'teacher' or 'mother') might then be interpreted and performed in an infinite number of ways, depending on the individual's personal experiences and situation.

Symbolic interactionist theorists elaborated on this view of the self as a social actor, arguing that roles are 'negotiated' or collectively defined. Actors tailor their role performances to the perceived demands of each situation and the others present, meaning that a person can have as many different selves as there are distinct groups of persons with whom he or she interacts and whose opinion matters. Perhaps the most influential proponent of this approach was Erving Goffman, whose dramaturgical perspective identified the various strategies of 'self-presentation' that actors devise to create particular impressions upon others. Goffman saw the self as constantly moving between two distinct regions: the 'frontstage' arena, where publicly visible social characters are performed, and the 'backstage' area in which actors keep their props or 'identity equipment' and can relax out of role. Implicit in this is the notion of a true or authentic self that is rarely allowed expression in the company of others As Norbert Elias argued, the civilising process of socialisation leads people to present only those parts of themselves that are deemed appropriate to the norms of each situated encounter. Nevertheless, through repeated patterns of interaction, the individual may come to think of themselves in terms of one particularly dominant role or 'master status'. The labelling theory of **deviance** advocated by Howard Becker illuminated this process of *becoming* a certain type of person, such as a marijuana user, insofar as social reactions to norm-breaking behaviour serve to define it as deviant and limit the courses of action left open to the individual.

In more recent years, sociologists have considered the fate of the self in a culture that is undergoing rapid social, economic and political changes. Ulrich Beck, for example, identifies a growing climate of risk awareness that appears to permeate the consciousness of social actors, while Anthony Giddens points to the 'tribulations of the self' in late modernity. As globalisation and systems of mass communication have undermined the sense of social identity, he says, people have begun to turn inwards and focus on the self and personal relationships. Giddens sees the self as a 'reflexive project' that the individual is constantly striving to perfect, and this has been said to extend into practices of the body, health and beauty and to **narrative** strategies for telling what Ken Plummer has called 'stories of the self'.

In contemporary Western societies, the self is increasingly seen as fragmented, multifaceted and unstable. In contrast to the essentialist views of the self found in Enlightenment thought, post-modern and post-structuralist writers have argued for a more fluid notion of subjectivity, defined at the more abstract, superficial level of language and representation. Some of these theories have drawn upon Jacques Lacan's psychoanalytic theory, which sees the self emerging out of the 'mirror stage' of development when infants begin to inhabit the symbolic realm of language. Others, meanwhile, have abandoned the idea of selfhood altogether, in favour of the more pluralistic notion of 'identities'. The work of Michel Foucault has been highly significant in this regard, for he suggested that identities were formed by discourses, or ways of representing knowledge about people and their behaviour. Thus historically, identities such as the 'hysterical woman' or the 'lunatic' could be seen not as essential types of self, but rather as subject positions constructed by the dominant forms of **discourse** in a particular social and historical context. Consequently, more overtly critical theories have developed about the way in which powerful groups can use forms of knowledge to subjugate those with less power, by positioning them as 'others' or outsiders. For example, within feminism, this argument has been used not only to criticise the male bias implicit in traditional social theory, but also to challenge the feminist project itself, by questioning the assumption that 'women' comprise a homogeneous social group whose interests can be adequately represented by just one form of knowledge. Sociologists of 'race' and ethnicity have argued extensively about the political struggles involved in establishing cultural identities, particularly in post-colonial societies, and how this affects the knowledge produced about minority ethnic groups. Meanwhile, proponents of the social model of disability have voiced their dissatisfaction with the way in which disabled people are defined as 'others' by a society that creates barriers to their participation and discriminates in favour of the able-bodied. Such examples of 'identity politics' show how sociological theories of the self have been revisited and transformed to reach a new understanding of the relationship between the individual and society.

Further reading

Becker, Howard S. (1963) *Outsiders: Studies in the Sociology of Deviance*. New York: Free Press.

Cooley, Charles H. (1909) *Social Organization*. New Brunswick, NJ: Transaction, 1983.

Foucault, Michel (1976) *The History of Sexuality: Volume 1: An Introduction*. New York: Vintage, 1980.

Giddens, Anthony (1991) *Modernity and Self Identity*. Cambridge: Polity Press.

Goffman, Erving (1959) *The Presentation of Self in Everyday Life*. Harmondsworth: Penguin.

McCall, George J. and Simmons, Jerry L. (1966) *Identities and Interactions*. New York: Free Press.

Plummer, Ken (1998) *Telling Sexual Stories*. London: Routledge.

Susie Scott

SEX AND SEXUALITY

The term 'sexuality' encompasses all erotically significant aspects of life – including desires, practices, relationships and identities. Sexuality is thus a rather slippery concept. What is sexual or erotic depends on what is defined as such, and this varies historically and from one culture and context to another. The words 'sex' and 'sexual' are, moreover, ambiguous. They can be used to refer to the erotic (e.g. 'having sex', 'sexual fantasies') or to denote differences between men and women (as in 'the two sexes' or 'the sexual division of labour'). This semantic confusion reflects some of the taken-for-granted assumptions underpinning everyday understandings of sexuality: that to be born with a particular set of genitals (sex organs) defines one as a member of a particular 'sex' (male or female) and as destined to be erotically attracted to the other 'sex'. In subjecting sexuality to critical scrutiny sociologists seek to question the assumed naturalness of this linkage between sex, **gender** and heterosexuality and to demonstrate that our sexual lives are as social as any other aspect of our existence.

Differing approaches to the study of sexuality have affected the way in which it is conceptualised. Within the psychoanalysis of Sigmund Freud, the term 'sexuality' often subsumes gender (or 'sex' in psychoanalytic terminology), since each is seen as inextricably bound up with the other. Becoming masculine or feminine requires fixing our erotic choice in the appropriate direction: to be one sex is to desire the other. Sexuality is understood as a libidinal drive, initially without direction or boundaries, repressed and channelled from infancy through the emotionally charged relationship between child, mother and father. Psychoanalysis, in the many variants that have developed since Freud, remains influential in contemporary social thought.

The first fully sociological account of sexuality, produced by John Gagnon and William Simon, constituted a direct challenge to this Freudian view. Where psychoanalysts conflate sexuality and gender, Gagnon and Simon distinguish between them and argue that the acquisition of gender shapes sexuality rather than vice-versa. Human sexuality does not result from the repression of an innate drive, but from a process of social construction occurring in and through everyday social life. For them, no act or experience is sexual in itself: what is sexual is a matter of social definition. Further, to be able to mobilise these social definitions, to recognise feelings, desires and situations as sexual and to enact sexual conduct depends on learning and deploying the 'scripts' that govern contemporary sexual life.

Since the 1980s, the work of French theorist Michel Foucault has become increasingly influential. Like Gagnon and Simon, Foucault criticises the concept of repression, but from a different angle. Seeing power as productive rather than repressive, he argues that the Victorian era was not one of repression but of a discursive explosion around sexuality. This effectively brought sexuality into being as an object of **discourse** and as a means of ordering 'bodies and pleasures'. Whereas in previous eras it was particular sexual conduct that was policed, with particular acts condemned or outlawed, in the late nineteenth century categories of sexual persons were created – it became possible to *be* a homosexual, for example. Foucault enables us to explore how our pleasures are ordered by a particular construction of sexuality and how and why we have come to see sexuality as an intrinsic 'truth' of our being.

Sociological investigations of sexuality have been immensely influenced by feminist, gay and queer scholars. The rise of gay liberation and second-wave feminism in the late 1960s and early 1970s created a political motivation for contesting the naturalness of existing sexual arrangements, giving social constructionism a vital critical edge. Heterosexuality was redefined as an oppressive social institution rather than a normal and natural relationship – hence such concepts as 'compulsory heterosexuality' introduced by Adrienne Rich. Feminists documented sources of women's discontent within heterosexual relationships and barriers to their sexual autonomy; they questioned the myth of the vaginal orgasm and thus the definition of 'the sex act' as penetrative vaginal intercourse. They also paid considerable attention to sexual coercion and violence – although some argued that this focus on sexual dangers denied women's sexual pleasures. Feminist work on sexuality has, since the 1980s, followed a number of different paths, informed by different theoretical perspectives, but taken as a whole it has radically undermined the idea of a natural heterosexual order.

Gay politics and scholarship has also undergone changes. In the 1990s, Foucault's arguments contributed to a new form of theorising called queer theory. While a contested term, 'queer' generally denotes approaches that seek in some way to trouble heterosexuality, interrogate and destabilise the binaries of gay/straight and man/woman, and reveal the ways in which heterosexuality depends upon its excluded 'other' to secure its own 'normality'. Queer theory represented a break with earlier gay theories, which had embraced gay identity, seeing sexual identities as fluid, shifting and contingent rather than as fixed aspects of the self. There is some overlap and ongoing dialogue between queer theory and feminism; the former tends to be more concerned with destabilising what it calls 'heteronormativity' and the latter with the relationship between sexuality and gender divisions.

Critical perspectives on sexuality have facilitated a great deal of empirical work revealing a diversity of sexual lifestyles, practices and identities within contemporary society. It is now common to talk of sexualities in the plural to capture these variations. On the other hand, certain persistent patterns have been documented, such as sexual violence and continuing gender asymmetries in heterosexual relations. In recognising sexuality as fully social, its interconnections with other spheres of life, such as work, are also subject to investigation. Importantly, sexuality has now been thoroughly denaturalised – no longer treated as a pre-social given but as open to continued critical questioning.

Further reading

Gagnon, John and Simon, William (1973) *Sexual Conduct*, 2nd edn. 2004. Chicago: Aldine.

Foucault, Michel (1976) *The History of Sexuality Volume 1*. New York: Random House, 1978.

Jackson, Stevi and Scott, Sue (eds) (1996) *Feminism and Sexuality: A Reader*. Edinburgh: Edinburgh University Press.

Seidman, Steven (1996) *Queer Theory/Sociology*. Oxford: Blackwell.

Seidman, Steven (2003) *The Social Construction of Sexuality*. New York: W. W. Norton.

Stevi Jackson

SOCIAL CAPITAL

Social capital has been the focus of intense debate since the early 1990s. At its heart is the idea that people can treat their connections with others as an important resource, which they are able to draw on for a variety of purposes. Individuals call on friends and family when they face problems or make changes in their lives; groups of people band together to pursue common interests; at a broader level, all forms of social organisation rest on complex webs of interpersonal connections to hold them together. In Robert Putnam's words, 'the core idea of social capital theory is that social networks have value . . . social contacts affect the productivity of individuals and groups'.

While others have recognised that relationships are an asset, what was new in the 1990s was the argument that social capital served a wider public good, and that when levels of social capital fell into decline, the **community** as a whole would suffer. Putnam's name is widely associated with this argument, thanks to a series of polemical articles during the mid-1990s, followed in 2000 by a empirically detailed and analytically ambitious book. His vivid image of Americans playing on their own at the bowling alley, where once teams competed in organised leagues, neatly encapsulated his view. Buttressing his argument with hefty blocks of data on the declining membership of civic associations, Putnam argued that community in the United States is collapsing, thanks partly to the disappearance of a 'long civic generation' who grew up in war and depression, partly to the spread of home-based electronic entertainments.

This line of thinking appeals directly to long established American preoccupations with the way in which voluntary associations help to integrate individuals into the wider whole. Putnam has brought a new vigour to a tradition in political sociology that dates back to Alexis de Tocqueville's early nineteenth-century observations on the way in which American democracy was held together by constant interaction through interest groups and civic associations (by contrast, de Tocqueville believed that a time-honoured social order headed by the monarchy and aristocracy ensured internal stability in Europe). Putnam appeared on countless television and radio shows to put his case, and advised two presidents as well as a number of European prime ministers. Putnam's influence, then, has spread beyond the social sciences.

Putnam was not the first social scientist to use the concept in this way. This distinction goes to Jane Jacobs, who thought levels of crime varied between different cities because of dissimilarities in social relationships. The concept was then taken in a rather different direction by Pierre Bourdieu, who was interested in its role in explaining the reproduction of socio-economic inequality. Social capital, Bourdieu and Löic Waquant wrote, is 'the sum of resources, actual or virtual, that accrue to an individual or a group by virtue of possessing a durable network of more or less institutionalised relationships of mutual acquaintance and recognition'. Social capital explained why some groups were able to hand on their privileged socio-economic position: they mobilise by proxy the capital of an entire group, such as powerful family members, old pupils of elite schools, members of a select club, or the nobility. As a form of capital, network resources required an investment of labour, of constant sociability, so as to maintain its value.

Bourdieu's work was set within what was essentially a neo-Marxist framework of analysis, focusing on network assets as a property of elite groups. James Coleman, by contrast, emphasised the value of interpersonal connections to less advantaged groups, such as young African-American high school students. In a series of empirical studies, Coleman showed that family and community characteristics could outweigh other factors, such as low income or features of the school. He subsequently published a very influential paper on the relationships between social and human capital, which argued that strong shared social ties were often complementary with high levels of educational attainment. For Coleman, social capital comprised 'the set of resources that inhere in family relations and in community social organisation and that are useful for the cognitive or social development of a child or young person'. Coleman was a sociologist with strongly developed interests in economics, working within the framework of rational choice theory. Theories of **rational action** assume that actors' behaviour is driven by the goal of rational individual self-interest; it therefore has a problem in explaining cooperative behaviour, particularly where it is altruistic. For Coleman, then, social capital does not simply explain why pupils in some disadvantaged communities do much better educationally than their peers, it also resolves this basic problem in rational choice theory.

Bourdieu and Coleman were both prominent sociological thinkers whose work is still very influential today, and with Putnam they have heavily influenced the debate over social capital. The debate itself is a far-reaching one, which encompasses vigorous theoretical challenges to the concept, as well as a mounting volume of empirical studies and a number of policy-oriented discussions. Theoretically, it has been suggested by sociologists that the concept concedes too much to economics, and by economists that it is too sociological; it has also been criticised for its breadth and lack of precise boundaries. It is not entirely clear how far the term 'capital' is to be seen as a kind of metaphor, or whether on the contrary social capital can be measured and subjected to the kind of rate of return analysis that is applied to financial and physical capital. Moreover, the concept of social capital has a strong normative dimension; in Bourdieu's hands it was rather negative, since it reinforced privilege and wealth; in Putnam's hands, it is positive, the glue which holds us all together. Yet some of the empirical studies have shown that people can use their network assets for anti-social purposes (such as organised crime), and some networks reinforce values and behaviour that prevent people from tackling problems effectively.

Increasingly, researchers have adopted a differentiated view of social bonds. At the most basic, Putnam accepts a distinction between bonding social capital, based on family and other close ties, and bridging social capital, which brings people together with others from different backgrounds; there has also been interest in the idea of linking social capital, to denote ties between people with different types of network that give access to very different types of resource. Again, this has echoes of earlier sociological perspectives. In particular, there seem clear parallels with Durkheim's notion of social **solidarity**: bonding social capital seems similar to Durkheim's mechanical solidarity, resting as it does on direct and 'obvious' ties to known individuals, placed in an established hierarchy, while bridging social capital seems akin to Durkheim's organic solidarity.

Empirical challenges have also been thrown down, especially to Putnam's account. He has been attacked for focusing on old, formal, declining organisations; other studies have examined newer social movements, or virtual and other remotely networked communities. Nevertheless, the empirical studies have tended to confirm that social networks are indeed a significant factor in determining people's well-being; conversely, research into social isolation has shown how a serious lack of connections can adversely affect people's lives. So whether or not the concept itself will stand up to the test of debate over time, it has helped draw attention to an important feature of social life, as well as prompting new investigations around pressing research questions, while bringing social scientists into dialogue with policy makers and others.

Further reading

Bourdieu, Pierre and Wacquant, Löic (1992) *An Invitation to Reflexive Sociology*. Chicago: University of Chicago Press.
Coleman, James (1994) *Foundations of Social Theory*. Cambridge, MA: Belknap Press.
Field, John (2003) *Social Capital*. London: Routledge.
Putnam, Robert D. (2000) *Bowling Alone: The Collapse and Revival of American Community*. New York: Simon and Schuster.

John Field

SOCIAL MOVEMENTS

At its most basic, the concept of social movement focuses on political protest, and examines the link between **civil society** and the political system outside of the institutionalised patterns of political participation. Various aspects of this link have been stressed over the years and by different research traditions.

Work on social movements developed initially in the United States after the Second World War. In its earlier formulations social movements were examined either in psychological terms, through an approach that focused on 'collective behavior', or in terms of a structural functional approach that focused on their role in overall societal stability. Psychologists studying mass society often concep-tualised social movements as individuals' dysfunctional adaptations to personal stress, while structural functionalists saw them as indications of tensions in the social system. Prominent authors of this period include the structural-functionalist Neil Smelser, the mass society theorist William Kornhauser and later the social psychologist Ralph Turner, who drew on symbolic interactionism.

A major paradigmatic innovation took place in the 1970s, with the rise of the new student movement and its spin-offs. A new theory of 'Resource Mobilization' saw social movements as normal social processes in which political and social change were pursued by political entrepreneurs through the rational accumulation and deployment of resources. Rather than social psychology or general social theory, the inspiring paradigm became organisational behaviour. In this perspective, social movements were seen as similar to other organised groupings, such as business **organisations**. Authors who worked in this framework included Mayer Zald. Over the years, several proponents of this approach have paid specific attention to the interaction between social movements and regular politics, developing what has come to be known as the 'Political Processes' perspective of Charles Tilly and others. These approaches were complemented in the 1980s by authors who stressed the relationship between social movements and their opponents in the public sphere and examined, from a cognitive perspective, the framing strategies utilised to win public support.

Left-libertarian movements appeared as prominent actors in Europe and, particularly in the 1980s, displayed distinctive features such as a preference for flat organisational structures and rotating or informal leadership. Research in the field developed with a distinctive European perspective, which, in opposition to the American approach, emphasised issues of **culture**, **identity**, and the novelty of the repertoire of political protest adopted by movements such as the environmental and women's movements. Prominent authors of what has come to be known as the 'New Social Movements' perspective include Alain Touraine, Alberto Melucci and Klaus Eder.

Most recently, a gradual convergence has developed between European and North American researchers. New themes have emerged more prominently, such as a specific attention to the network aspect of social movements, the role of **emotions**, the role of the press (especially in the perspective known as 'protest event analysis'), and studies of the newly emerged anti-globalisation movement. Recently, the examination of the impact of social movements on public policy has also begun to receive attention.

Further reading

Della Porta, Donatella, Kriesi, Hans-Peter and Rucht, Dieter (1999) *Social Movements in a Globalizing World*. Basingstoke: Macmillan.

Diani, Mario and McAdam, Doug (2003) *Social Movements and Networks: Relational Approaches to Collective Action.* Oxford: Oxford University Press.

Melucci, Alberto, Keane, John and Mier, Paul (1989) *Nomads of the Present: Social Movements and Individual Needs in Contemporary Society.* London: Hutchinson Radius.

Ruzza, Carlo (2004) *Europe and Civil Society: Movement Coalitions and European Governance.* Manchester: Manchester University Press.

Tilly, Charles (1978) *From Mobilization to Revolution.* Reading, MA: Addison-Wesley.

Zald, Mayer N. and McCarthy, J. Doug (1987) *Social Movements in an Organizational Society: Collected Essays.* New Brunswick, NJ: Transaction Books.

Carlo Ruzza

SOCIAL STRUCTURE

Social structure is one of the fundamental concepts in sociology and its theorists are often seen as stressing one side of the dichotomy between 'structure' and 'action' around which much contemporary sociology has been organised. The concept was set out by Comte, Spencer and Durkheim to describe the organised pattern of social activity. It became the central organising idea for the structural-functionalist theories that formed the mainstream of sociology for much of the twentieth century, and it was developed in novel directions by structuralist writers. Towards the end of the century, it was radically modified by post-structuralist theorists who disliked its apparent implication that social life is organised through a monolithic organising framework. These writers stressed, instead, the dispersed and fragmentary character of 'structural' processes.

The word 'structure' refers to the act of building something and the end-product of that act of building. It originally referred to an actual physical construction and the inner balance of physical forces that give it its solidity. From this core meaning it has been extended to the combination of connected parts that make up a biological organism and its various organs, the rock formations of the earth, and the arrangement of atoms into molecules. The pioneer sociologists used the term in this sense to refer to societies as organised wholes irreducible simply to individuals and their actions. Spencer, for example, saw societies as being internally organised into clusters of individuals that are specialised around particular tasks or activities.

Social structure, then, has most typically been seen as a way of describing and explaining the recurring and enduring patterns that are found in social behaviour and the various elements that make up any **social system**. It comprises a social arrangement, social organisation, or social framework and can be contrasted with random, chaotic, or disorganised activities. Durkheim saw the **collective representations** of a society organising people's expectations into a pattern of social **institutions**, of social norms that define people's expectations towards each other. These institutions in turn shape the collective relationships into which people enter and the causal interconnections among them and their actions. These social relations cluster into distinct arrangements that are the structural 'parts' of a society, the specialised sets of social relations with particular 'functions' within the whole society. This emphasis on the patterning of social activity through 'institutional structures' and 'relational structures' was the basis of structural-functionalist sociology and other mainstream approaches to the subject. Thus, Parsons defined a social structure as 'a set of relatively stable patterned relationships of units' that results from the normative orientation of action.

Parsons's main emphasis was on the institutional aspects of social structure, which he saw as the framework or skeleton of a society. A social structure comprises the 'normative patterns which define what are felt to be, in the given society, proper, legitimate or expected modes of action or of social relationship'. They regulate and channel people's actions by providing them with predefined patterns of conduct. Merton described this as the 'cultural structure', and the focus on normative patterns led many to describe this position as 'normative functionalism'. This approach has been criticised for assuming that a consensus over social norms is necessary as the basis of social order. Critics have pointed out that the level of consensus in a society is generally quite low. More typically, institutional structures are characterised by malintegration, incompatibility and contradictions in normative patterns. From within structural functionalism, Merton recognised this fact in his account of **anomie**. Parsons also recognised the importance of this point and held that social institutions may simply comprise the '*dominant* structural outline' of a society. Subordinate groups may have their own, quite distinct, norms and values that sustain counter institutions. The constraining force of an institutional structure, then, results from a combination of value commitments and power, rather than on a complete consensus.

Parsons's approach left relational structure as an almost residual category in structural analysis, but this aspect of social structure has been taken more seriously by other writers. Radcliffe-Brown saw social relations existing among individuals whenever their actions involve a mutual adaptation of interests. A social structure comprises a complex network of such relations and interconnections that organise the flow of interactions among specific people at any given moment. Relational structure consists of the general and enduring relations of actors to each other – the 'structural form' that lies behind the particular instances of interaction. In a similar vein, Simmel stressed what he called the 'forms of sociation' that can be analysed independently of the specific normative 'content' that they have. These forms are relations among individuals in which there is a reciprocal effect, interdependence, or interweaving of their actions. Social structures, then, are crystallisations, constellations, configurations, or concatenations of social relations. These relational ideas informed a number of theorists who explored the ways in which social relations could be seen as varying in their frequency, duration and direction, and as forming complex networks with varying degrees of 'connectedness', density and integration.

Social structure as a fully developed idea must be seen as comprising both institutional structure and relational structure. It is their combination that leads to the kind of structuring that interests sociologists. The distinction between norms and social relations is important, but they depend upon each other. Social relations exist only by virtue of the norms or rules that people apply in their actions, but these relations cannot simply be read off from the rules and there is no one-to-one relationship between the two.

Recent work by structuralist writers produced a rather different view of social structure that was taken up by Anthony Giddens and Pierre Bourdieu. Their arguments have provided an account of a further aspect necessary in a comprehensive concept of social structure. Structuralists have been influenced by the arguments of linguists such as Chomsky and have seen social structure as analogous to the grammatical structures of speech and writing in a language. Chomsky had argued that people are able to produce well-formed sentences only because they possess an in-built linguistic competence that allows them to build mental structures of grammatical rules. These rules are the unconscious linguistic skills that are involved in the production of speech. Giddens follows this line of thought and argues that social structure has to be seen as the unconscious 'generative' system of rules that allows people to engage in particular courses of interaction.

Bourdieu has developed this approach most fully. He stresses that rules become 'embodied' as dispositions and tendencies of action. These dispositions are 'infraconscious' and 'infralinguistic', existing below the level of consciousness. They are coded into the brain and other organs in such a way that people can act in routine ways without thinking about what they are doing. The social relations and social institutions of a society become 'incorporated', or taken into the corpse, as dispositions to act in particular ways. They are fixed in the body as a posture or gesture, or as ways of standing, walking, thinking and speaking. These 'embodied social structures' are internalised and generalised reflections of the institutions and relations in which individuals are positioned. Bourdieu refers to this system of bodily dispositions as a **habitus** comprising specific and durable 'generative schemes' that can be applied to the various situations that people encounter.

According to this point of view, institutional and relational structures result from the actions of individuals who are endowed with the capacities or competencies that enable them to produce them by acting in organised ways. At the same time, these institutional and relational structures provide the conditions under which people act and from which they derive their embodied habitus. Social structure in its fullest sense, then, refers to the combination of each of these structural phenomena – the institutional, the relational and the embodied – into the recurring and enduring mechanisms that generate the patterns that Durkheim described as social facts.

Further reading

Crothers, Charles (1996) *Social Structure*. London: Routledge.
López, José and Scott, John (2000) *Social Structure*. Buckingham: Open University Press.

John Scott

SOCIAL SYSTEM

Use of the concept of the social system has been intended to highlight the interdependence of individuals in a social whole and its possession of distinctive properties that can be analysed in their own terms and without detailed reduction to the individual courses of action that produce them. The general idea of the system originates in the natural sciences, where system concepts have been pursued in two main directions. These are the mechanical systems that have been studied in physics and the organic systems studied in biology. Analogies with these two concepts have provided the principal sociological models for social systems, though this work has always sought to recognise the additional and distinctive features of systemic organisation at the socio-cultural level. While some contemporary views do still reflect one or another of these analogies, most approaches combine elements from each.

Mechanical models of the social system drew on the ideas that emerged in physics during the eighteenth and nineteenth centuries, where systems were seen as fields of forces and energies existing in a state of equilibrium. In the second half of the nineteenth century, the advances in physics made by James Clerk Maxwell and others introduced the idea of 'energy' as the fundamental physical force, and this also proved influential among social theorists. The mechanical model appeared in social theory as the advocacy of a 'social physics' through which laws of social equilibrium might be discovered. Economists such as Friedrich List and Henry Carey proposed that individuals and groups actions could be studied in terms of their 'distance' from each other, their 'mass', and their consequent 'attraction' or 'repulsion' of each other. This attraction was seen as a parallel to – even a reflection of – the gravitational attraction that stood at the heart of classical physics, and many sought the ultimate unification of such sociological theories with physical theory. Carey proposed models of population movement and city formation using these ideas, and proposed that urban systems would tend towards a state of equilibrium. Friedrich Engels recast Marx's model of **capitalism** as a mechanical system of forces in an equilibrium that would be disrupted as these forces came into ever sharper contradiction with each other. This view was later elaborated by Nikolai Bukharin, who saw equilibrium in social systems resulting from the interchange of energy among its parts

Lester Ward and Vilfredo Pareto produced influential formulations of this point of view. According to Ward, equilibrium could be described as involving a 'synergy' among social forces, with the changing balance of forces producing a constantly moving equilibrium as a social system adapts to its environment. Pareto reconstructed economic laws and their statistical investigation as equilibrium states of a system of actions and proposed the extension of this idea to political processes such as the formation of elites and the occurrence of revolutions.

Advances in biological knowledge during the nineteenth century – most particularly, the emergence of developmental and evolutionary ideas – led to the idea of systems of circulating flows and the metabolism of environmental resources as the basis for models of the physiology and anatomy of 'organisms'. Auguste Comte and Herbert Spencer pioneered ideas of the 'social organism', depicting socio-cultural systems as complex wholes that could be seen in terms of the 'static' analysis of social structure and the 'dynamic' analysis of social change. Their social statics saw the coexistence and interdependence of social phenomena in systems characterised by varying degrees of solidarity and integration as 'anatomical' structures. As such, social systems can be seen as existing in states of equilibrium or disequilibrium with respect to their environment. The social dynamics of Comte and Spencer saw movement and circulation among these phenomena as leading to their development over time from one structural state to another. Spencer characterised the specific features of social systems as 'super-organic': they had the organic properties of physically connected matter but also had properties that resulted from their communicative connections. Super-organic social systems are built and maintained through the communicative, linguistically mediated actions of their members.

Such organicist views of social systems were pursued by a variety of theorists. Towards the end of the nineteenth century, Pavel Lilienfeld, Albert Schäffle, René Worms and others systematically pursued the parallels with organic systems and made numerous analogies between physiological processes and the mental tissues of communication, flows of ideas and expulsion of waste products. Differentiated aspects of social systems were seen as the 'organs' of societies and social groups. While this language often implied a close reliance on biology – even a bio-logical reductionism – their purpose was to use such terminology to illustrate distinctively social processes. They saw the connections that comprised the 'physiology' of a social system as 'functional' connec-tions, highlighting the contribution that each organ or 'part' of a system makes to its continuing existence.

Durkheim was the most sophisticated social theorist to pursue this idea of the functional connections from which social solidarity and social integration result. In his *Rules of the Sociological Method*, he held that the 'causal' or historical analysis of how social facts come into being must be distinguished from the functional analysis of their consequences once they exist. Functionally integrated societies are to be seen as realities *sui generis* and the task of sociology is to study these systems of relationships using statistical and other methods of analysis that might, ideally produce 'laws' that describe the empirical regularities found in social life. Durkheim's arguments were elaborated by his own colleagues and students, but found their particular expression in the 'functionalism' expounded as the heart of the anthropological studies of Alfred Radcliffe-Brown and Bronislaw Malinowski.

The work of Pareto proved especially influential among those whose work produced the first comprehensive integration of mechanistic and organic ideas in social theory. The physiologist Lawrence Henderson was the leading figure in the development of sociology at Harvard in the 1930s and he led Talcott Parsons to explore the emerging frame-work of systems theory. He drew on the functionalist ideas in anthropology to produce a powerful fusion of Durkheim with Pareto, seeing social systems as shaped by processes of integration and adaptation. These arguments proved compatible with the 'general system theory' that emerged during the 1950s. Research into 'cybernetics' and control systems saw the 'closed systems' studied in mechanics as particular cases of the 'open systems' studied in biology. According to this position all systems are open to environmental influences through a constant flow of energy and information, but certain environmental conditions may allow a system to be studied in an equilibrium state, in isolation from its environment and as if it were closed. Environmental changes, however, ensure that most real systems must constantly struggle to achieve such equilibrium and will typically be in a dynamic 'homeostatic' state that depends upon the 'feedback' of energy and information into the system.

The social system theory that Parsons eventually constructed saw social systems as having to evolve ways of meeting the requirements imposed by their environment if they were to survive. Social systems that failed to do so would break down or would be transformed in some way. He explored this by identifying the four basic functional requirements that he termed adaptation, integration, goal attainment and pattern maintenance. **Institutions** and **social structures** could be seen as more or less specialised responses to these requirements, which therefore formed the cornerstone of any sociological analysis. Institutions can be seen as formed into 'subsystems' of the overall social system, each subsystem (such as an economic, political, or religious subsystem) being primarily concerned with a specific function and so contributing to the overall cohesion of the social system through the 'interchange' of energy and information among them. Equilibrium exists only when there is a balance or reciprocity in the interchanges among the various subsystems.

Critics of Parsons's system model suggested that he overemphasised the integration of social systems. Although he saw that social systems might fail to meet the functional requirements imposed on them, his work stressed those situations in which societies were relatively successful in meeting them. Critics such as Alvin Gouldner and David Lockwood, therefore, proposed that the Parsonian model be modified by a greater recognition of the relative autonomy of subsystems and the existence of contradictions and incompatibilities among system parts. These criticisms encouraged the building of a so-called neo-functionalism and more general system theory. Jeffrey Alexander in the United States and Niklas Luhmann in Germany have been the leading figures in developing these ideas, building a more complex and flexible understanding of the relationships between social systems and their subsystems. Luhmann's work depicts social systems as comprising dispersed and fragmented subsystems with varying degrees of autonomy and distinct *sui generis* mechanisms.

Similar views have been proposed by writers such as Michel Foucault and Pierre Bourdieu, though they eschew the terminology of 'system' and return to the earlier idea of 'fields' existing within a social space. A whole society – as a social system – is a social space within which numerous overlapping fields of action, each with their distinctive developmental dynamics, coexist. This terminology highlights a convergence with new ideas within physics, where the emergence of complex organisation is seen as a result of 'chaotic' movements and 'catastrophic' transformations. Social theorists have begun to explore the implications of this 'complexity theory' for the received idea of the social system.

Further reading

Buckley, Walter (1967) *Sociology and Modern Systems Theory*. Englewood Cliffs, NJ: Prentice-Hall.
Russett, Cynthia (1966) *The Concept of Equilibrium in American Social Thought*. New Haven: Yale University Press.

John Scott

SOCIALISATION

Socialisation is a process of learning to be a member of a society, and through which we become social beings. Becoming social is a lifelong experience, accomplished through interacting with others and participating in the daily routines of everyday cultural life. Socialisation is a concept which recognises that social identities, **roles**, and personal biographies are constructed through a continuous process of cultural transmission.

A distinction is usually made between primary and secondary socialisation. Primary socialisation is associated with the foundational or early years of personhood, and is the process by which children start to accumulate the knowledge and skills needed to become a member of a particular society. This process is accomplished through various activities – play, imitation, games, observation – and in interactions with important agents of socialisation; significant others such as parents, carers and siblings. It is during this phase of socialisation that primary social identities begin to be formed – for example with regard to

gender, **ethnicity** or **religion**. The important thing is that these identities are actively learnt and constructed. They are often understood as core aspects of a person's social identity, and as relatively stable. However, even if these identities are challenged in later life (for example through gender reassignment or religious conversion), it is still against a backdrop of knowledge and understanding of cultural norms and practices acquired during primary socialisation.

Secondary socialisation recognises the complex and lifelong experiences of *becoming* and *being* a member of a society or cultural group. It thus refers to a broader range of skills, knowledges and roles acquired and learnt over the life course. Secondary socialisation is a process of understanding and making sense of the various cultural scripts with which we are presented over the whole of our lives. Education is usually seen as a prime site for secondary socialisation. Schooling is where children and young people are formally exposed to knowledge and skills (through subjects and curricula) required to function as part of a particular society, and where teachers act as important agents of socialisation. However, educational arenas are also sites for more informal, cultural learning. Through a wide range of interactions and experiences in educational settings, roles are learnt, values understood and identities shaped. Peer groups can be significant agents in this process of acculturation.

Socialisation does not, however, stop at the school gates. During our transitions to adulthood, and throughout our adult lives we continue to *become*. Personal biographies and social identities are actively constructed and reconstructed, as we continue to come to terms with new roles and the nuances of the culture within which we are located. Thus we both acquire and lose secondary identities over the course of our lives – occupational identities, leisure identities, identities associated with particular kinds of consumption practices and so forth. Occupational socialisation is a term used to describe the processes of learning and becoming associated with professional or employment identities. Thus there is a process of socialisation that takes place in order to *become* and *be* a medic, builder, hairdresser or accountant. Of course, this includes the acquisition of formal 'taught' knowledge and skills – medicine, surgical procedures, bookkeeping, cutting hair, laying a brick wall and so forth. But it also includes the acquisition of more tacit and indeterminate sets of knowledge – learnt *in situ*, through trial and error, observation, imitation and through interactions with peers and significant others. Hence occupational socialisation also requires 'learning the ropes' – categorising patients, looking 'busy' when there are no clients in the hair salon, getting to know who the significant individuals are in the office, figuring out how to pick up casual work on the building site and so on. Learning the subtleties of the occupational setting is as important as acquiring the technical skills – for establishing and maintaining a credible occupational identity; for being socialised into the occupational culture.

The same rules apply to the construction of other identities – where the teaching and learning of formal knowledge and skills is only at best part of the process of socialisation. Being an accomplished musician is not a sufficient prerequisite, or even necessary, to a successful musical career. Indeed there are 'successful' musicians who cannot read music, play an instrument or sing in tune. Playing a passable game of golf will not guarantee access to and acceptance by the golfing fraternity, where membership of the 'right' golf club may matter more. Indeed some identities are almost entirely 'learnt' through the informal understandings of cultural scripts. There are no courses to attend or books to study on 'how to become' a gothic punk, train spotter, nightclub participant or homeless person. There are roles – such as that of hospital patient, theatre audience or hair salon client – that have rules and patterns of behaviour attached to them, which are rarely, if ever, written down. These cultural scripts, and the social identities that are shaped by them, are learnt through continual processes of engagement and interaction.

There are a number of theories of socialisation. These include theories which suggest that individuals have no agency or choice in the construction of their social identities – social roles are to be learnt rather than negotiated in order for society to function. There are also psychoanalytical theories which focus on the unconscious and emotional processes of selfhood. In sociology, the work of American philosopher and social reformer George Mead and sociologist Erving Goffman has been particularly important in recognising that the **self** is a social construct, and that individuals are *active* agents in the processes of socialisation and identity construction. Mead identified the emergence of the self through social experience, and the importance of social communication and reflexivity. Goffman contributed to our understanding of the ways in which social identities are the outcomes of social processes and interactions located with/in particular times and places. He adopted the theatrical metaphors of 'frontstage' and 'backstage' in order to understand both the visible and the 'behind the scenes' work involved in socialisation – as the construction and management of social identities.

Further reading

Giddens, Anthony (1991) *Modernity and Self-Identity*. Cambridge: Polity Press.

Goffman, Erving (1959) *The Presentation of Self in Everyday Life*. Harmondsworth: Penguin.

Jenkins, Richard (2004) *Social Identities*, 2nd edn. London: Routledge.

Melia, Kath (1987) *Learning and Working: The Occupational Socialisation of Nurses*. London, Tavistock.

Amanda Coffey

SOCIETY

When asked 'what is sociology', it is normal to answer that it is the study of society, or perhaps of societies. This answer sounds clear and straightforward but it is not. There is indeed little agreement on what is a society, especially in the contemporary era.

Indeed former British Prime Minister Margaret Thatcher once declared that 'there is no such thing as society', there are only 'individual men and women and their families'. Many sociologists rejected her claim by declaring that there is obviously such a thing as society. But although pretty well all sociologists do agree that there is something 'more' to social life than only 'individual men and women and their families', exactly what this extra amounts to is not so obvious.

Sometimes society means that there is a realm of the social or of social facts that are in some way separate from, or of a different kind, from facts about individuals. There is a social level, best articulated by Durkheim's arguments as to how there is a realm of social facts and that one set of social facts should be explained by other social facts. Society is here taken to be a reality *sui generis*, of social facts and their interrelationships. Studying this *sui generis* level enables sociology to develop a distinct and unambiguous object of study.

Sociology in the twentieth century took up this Durkheimian challenge and developed the notion of an organised 'society' as its object of study. This was especially so from the 1920s onwards as sociology came to be institutionalised within American universities. In various textbooks and key writings sociologists referred to the network of relationships that comprise society, which was seen as possessing certain powers that subordinated individual people to it. The theorist of the prototypical modern society, Talcott Parsons, defined 'society' as the type of social system characterised by the highest level of self-sufficiency relative to its environment, including other social systems.

What this notion of sociology was based upon (and which main-stream sociology did not fully reveal) was the system of nations and of separate and competing nation-states. To the extent there is something called 'society', then this should be seen as a sovereign social entity with a nation-state at its centre that organises the rights and duties of each citizen. The economy, politics, **culture**, **classes**, **gender** relations and so on, are structured by such a society that regulates the life-chances of each of its members. Such a society is not only material but cultural, so that its members believe they share some common identity which is bound up in part with the territory that the society occupies or lays claim to. Central to most such societies is a banal nationalism that is part of how people think of and experience themselves as human beings. This has many features: the waving of celebratory flags, singing national anthems, flying national flags on public buildings, identifying with one's own sports-teams, being addressed in the media as a member of a given society, celebrating independence day and so on. Members of each society do similar kinds of things as each other, share similar beliefs, eat similar food, think of themselves as characteristically 'French', 'American', or whatever.

Over the past two centuries, this conception of society has been central to North American and Western European notions of what it is to be a human being, as someone possessing the rights and duties of social citizenship. To be human, from this point of view, means that one is a member or citizen of a particular society. Society here is understood as ordered through a nation-state and with clear territorial and citizenship boundaries and a system of governance over its par-ticular citizens. National societies were based upon a concept of the citizen who owed duties to, and received rights from, their society through the core institutions of the nation-state. Governing such societies has been in part effected through new forms of expertise, partly based upon sociology as the science of such societies. Indeed, the mainstream view of the subject matter of sociology reflects the relative autonomy exhibited by American society for much of the twentieth century.

Such societies are, moreover, well-organised to mobilise human capacities and to exploit nature, as well as less developed societies. Sociology took for granted the success of modern societies in their overcoming of nature. Sociology specialised in describing and explain-ing the character of these modern societies based upon industries that enabled and utilised new forms of energy, transportation, com-munication and patterns of social life. These modern societies were presumed to be qualitatively different from the past.

It was also presumed that most economic and social problems and risks were produced by, and soluble at, the level of the individual society. Each society was sovereign. The concerns of each society were to be dealt with through national policies, especially from the 1930s onwards through a Keynesian welfare state that could identify and respond to the risks of organised **capitalism**. These risks were seen as principally located within the geographical borders and temporal frames of each society. Political solutions were devised and implemented within such societal frontiers.

However, what seems to have developed from the 1980s onwards is a powerful array of 'global' processes that are re-drawing the contours of human experience. There are exceptional levels of global inter-dependence – of **globalisation** – with shock waves spilling out 'chaotically' from one part of the globe to the other, obliterating some of the differences between societies. Events in one place (in Chernobyl in what is now the Ukraine in 1995 or in New York on 11 September 2001) have many powerful unforeseen consequences in other places. There are not just 'societies' at large but powerful 'empires' (Microsoft, McDonalds, Ford) roaming the globe. There is mass mobility of peoples, objects, and dangerous wastes and risks (nuclear contamination, terror-ism, SARS) that know few societal boundaries. Human powers increasingly derive from complex interconnections with material objects that are rarely embedded within single societies. There is the miniaturisation of electronic technologies that are connected with humans (laptops, iPods, mobile phones); the transformation of biology into genetically coded information; the increasing scale and range of mobile waste products and viruses; changing technologies of road, rail and air travel that facilitate rapid mobility; and informational and communicational flows which compress differences of time and space.

These transformations weaken the power of societies to draw together their citizens as one, to endow them with national identity and to speak with a single voice. Thus while many authorities still speak of society, the very meaning and salience of this term is under question as other kinds of social groupings seem to capture people's attention (such as environmentalists, supporters of Manchester United, vege-tarians, Chinese people living abroad, gay and lesbian people, fans of Michael Jackson, refugees, consumers of McDonalds and so on). All of these might be seen as new kinds of 'society' but ones that are not coterminous with the boundaries of nation-states. To the extent to which societies remain they are only one of a large number of powerful entities. Nation-**states** are less the regulator of peoples that are unambiguous citizens of such a society, and more the facilitors that regulate and respond to the consequences of the diverse mobilities flowing in and through its often very porous borders.

Sociology's mission should thus be to analyse these intersecting and diverse mobilities flowing in and through national territories, to see what remains of 'societies' as such, and to see what new emergent social forces are arising and to examine their interdependent effects around the world.

Further reading

Frisby, David and Sayer, Derek (1986) *Society*. London: Tavistock.
Urry, John (2000) *Sociology Beyond Societies*. London: Routledge.
Urry, John (2003) *Global Complexity*. Cambridge: Polity Press.

John Urry

SOLIDARITY

The concept of solidarity relates to people's identification with and supportiveness of other members of groups to which they belong. It is associated primarily with Durkheim, whose first book *The Division of Labour in Society* traced the implications of the shift from what he termed mechanical to organic solidarity. Durkheim argued that societies differ in how they achieve order, with simpler societies held together by the sameness of their members while more complex societies are held together by social differences. This paradoxical path of social evolution he explained by pointing to the increased inter-dependence of individuals as they develop more specialised roles in a modern industrial economy. This essentially optimistic perspective challenged more backward-looking thinkers such as Ferdinand Tönnies who associated **industrialism** and **urbanism** with the erosion of traditional **community** solidarities and their replacement by more shallow and fleeting social relationships. Although Durkheim's later work did not build directly on the rather simplistic terminology of mechanical and organic solidarity, the essential idea of a shift in the basis of social order continued to influence his thinking and that of the Durkheimian school of sociology and social anthropology. From this perspective, solidarity is more of a cultural than an economic phenom-enon and is instilled in people through religion or its secular equivalents, such as the cult of the individual. People are solidaristic because they share common values that are reinforced through rituals.

A different tradition of analysis is associated with Marx's analysis of **class** relationships, in which solidarity is rooted in class members' recognition of their shared interests against common opponents. From this point of view solidarity is a rational phenomenon of people coming together in pursuit of their common interests. Working-class solidarity finds its expression in organisations such as trade unions, whose members join forces to secure objectives that promise to benefit them all, such as an increase in wage rates. Solidarity may entail group members foregoing individual interests in the short term for the longer-term common good; rising incomes may be achieved by strikes that involve a period of deprivation before they succeed. Marx's appeal to workers of the world to unite was regarded by Weber as idealistic, given the many cleavages that exist between workers along lines of locality, industry, gender, age, religion, ethnicity and nationality. Weber saw social closure around sectional interests as working against broadly based class solidarity, promoting instead competition for scarce resources between rival social groups. Georg Simmel added the further observation that solidarity is at its most intense in the relationships between members of exclusive secret societies such as the mafia who have a heightened sense of their interdependence and collective fate.

The contemporary relevance of these legacies from classical sociology continues to be much debated. Various authors such as Ulrich Beck and Anthony Giddens have argued that the processes of economic and social change, notably the trends of increased social and geographical **mobility** and of individualisation and **globalisation**, have undermined traditional class and community solidarities. Their analysis suggests that there have been important changes in people's perceptions of the risks to which they are exposed and that new forms of solidarity are emerging as a result, for example the solidarity between members of new social movements. This changed perception has been prompted in part by the failure of welfare states to deliver the degree of economic and social security that was promised to their citizens. It is also possible to argue, as Zygmunt Bauman does, that welfare states have revealed limited popular support for the ethic of solidarity among groups whose members perceive themselves to be net contributors to collective welfare provision on a national scale. Such an attitude of being prepared to support others only where there is an obvious personal benefit in doing so is regarded as the antithesis of solidarity by Mary Douglas, for whom solidarity necessarily involves self-sacrifice rather than self-interest. She recognises that the altruism for the good of the group that is involved in solidarity makes its explanation more challenging than explaining self-interested actions.

Another perspective on solidarity is found in contemporary writings on communitarianism. The foremost proponent of this perspective is Amitai Etzioni, whose central idea is that supportiveness of others is best promoted through community organisations rather than through the market or the state. Solidarity based on community connections is presented as a moral force that places a check on individualism but at the same time has a more voluntary and authentic character than state-sponsored schemes are adjudged to have. Critics of communitarianism's vision argue that it is rooted in old-fashioned notions of community solidarity that embody conventional assumptions about gender roles and class relationships. These are criticised for locking women and poorer members of communities into sets of obligations over which they have little choice or control. Community traditions are for these reasons seen as problematic by communitarianisms's critics who regard them as unviable as bases of collective endeavour in contemporary circumstances.

Solidarity has the potential to be expressed in diverse forms and contexts but it is often unstable. A good example of this is the Polish *Solidarity* movement which played a crucial role in the transition to post-communism in Poland. It proved impossible to sustain the unity of its heterogeneous constituents once their common opponent (the communist state) was removed in 1989, and the movement declined almost as rapidly as it had arisen. The mercurial character of social solidarity is apparent in the speed with which many other social movements have come into and passed out of existence. A similar point can be made about the tendency of more mundane community and family solidarities to wax and wane over time. This temporal dimension has led to renewed interest in Durkheim's notion of group members needing periodically to share moments of collective effervescence in order to re-charge their mutual identification. Arguably, the phenomenon of solidarity becomes more rather than less important in the context of unsettled societies in which fixed roles and identities are increasingly hard for individuals to sustain.

Further reading

Crow, Graham (2002) *Social Solidarities: Theories, Identities and Social Change*. Buckingham: Open University Press.

Graham Crow

STATE

The state is one of the most central and elusive of sociological concepts. It is central because states perform so many functions and regulate almost every aspect of people's lives. This centrality also makes the state elusive, for it is hard to pin down precisely which institutions constitute it and how far it extends. Most would agree to include central and local government, the civil service, the courts, the police and the armed forces. Whether schools, trade unions, the church, the mass media or the family should be included is more contentious, though these have arguably acted as state agencies. The range of functions performed by states is also debatable, for most would agree that maintaining order and managing a society's external relationships are typical state functions but whether and to what extent states should provide welfare or manage the economy is hotly contested.

For Weber, a state 'claims the monopoly of the legitimate use of physical force within a given territory'. While control of the use of force was essential, its use could only be effective if it was considered justified by those being controlled. Legitimacy could be derived from tradition or charismatic leadership but increasingly came from the 'rational-legal' authority exercised by bureaucrats whose duties and responsibilities were specified by laws. The payment of salaries to bureaucrats made them obedient and honest servants of the state. The discipline and expertise of the bureaucratic official became a highly efficient means of organising and controlling industrial nation-states.

Weber's work raised the much-debated issue of the relationship between democracy and **bureaucracy**. Bureaucrats should, in principle, obey government instructions but they have their own interests, and their expertise and authority can make it difficult for politicians to impose their will upon them. Indeed, it has often been argued that politicians seeking to implement radical change are captured by conservatively inclined ministries with established policies – hence the increasing introduction of political advisers to monitor and steer the work of British civil servants. In other societies the role of bureaucrats in formulating policy has been viewed more positively, as in Japan, where economic growth has been ascribed to the expert management of the economy by bureaucrats rather than politicians.

While a state was to Weber an instrument of the ruler, to Marx it was an instrument of the ruling class. In the *Communist Manifesto*, Marx and Engels declared that 'the executive of the modern state is but a committee for managing the affairs of the whole bourgeoisie'. Nineteenth-century parliaments merely masked the power of the capitalist bourgeoisie and it was only through a revolution that the working class could take control of the state. Social Democratic theorists argued, however, that workers could force through democratic reforms and then use their numerical superiority to elect socialist governments, take control of the state, and through legislation construct a socialist society, without having recourse to revolution.

Later Marxist theorising was much more sceptical, arguing that capitalism is maintained by the state. According to Antonio Gramsci, the capitalist ruling class controlled labour through the ideological domination of society. Louis Althusser took this idea further with his concept of the 'ideological state apparatus', which operated through religion, education, the trade unions and the mass media. Ralph Miliband has more accessibly examined the multiple processes and agencies through which 'conservative indoctrination' takes place, the greatly superior resources that business, as compared with labour, organisations can devote to this task, and the networks through which business influences the state.

Some neo-Marxists and also Weberian critics of the Marxist approach, such as Theda Skocpol, have held that it does not allow states sufficient autonomy. The neo-Marxist Nicos Poulantzas argued that a state required some autonomy from capital if it was to maintain the capitalist system, for it could only act in the *long-term* interests of capital *as a whole* if it had some detachment from the immediate concerns of particular capitalist interests. Skocpol argued that states do not, anyway, simply act on behalf of classes, for the requirements of maintaining order, and managing national affairs in an international context, give those who control states some autonomy from the demands of domestic interest groups.

Since the 1980s the British state has been transformed as governments pursued neo-liberal policies promoting greater freedom of choice, the revival of market forces, and increased competition. It was claimed that these involved a 'rolling back' of the state. There has certainly been an extensive privatisation of state-owned companies, public sector housing and public services, as well as considerable de-regulation of the financial sector. But state regulation also increased, with the creation of bodies to police privatised monopolies, the greater regulation of trade unions, the centralising reform of education and health-care, and new kinds of financial regulation. This transformation provides some support for the Marxist perspective, since these policies maintained capitalism by restoring the profitability of a failing capitalist economy and by weakening a labour movement which had previously been growing in strength and power.

It must also be placed in the context of **globalisation**. The growing transnational mobility of capital has forced nation-states to compete for it, and adopt pro-capital and anti-labour policies. The weakening of organised labour in the old industrial societies resulted partly from the movement of capital to exploit cheaper labour elsewhere, and also from the mobility of unorganised, often illegal, labour between countries. Writers, such as Martin Albrow and Zygmunt Bauman, have, indeed, claimed that nation-states themselves are in terminal decline as a global society emerges. This might suggest that the Weberian conception of states as territorially based units is now out-of-date.

Counter-arguments claim there is plenty of life left in the nation-state. While transnational corporations can move money and employment across borders, they are still also national companies, with a base and much of their labour located in a particular nation-state, that depend on that state's resources and support. World politics are still dominated by nation-states and the most global of political organisations, the United Nations, is composed of national units and controlled by their representatives. In a world where international inequalities of wealth and power have been increasing, national units and the states that control them have hardly been superseded.

Further reading

Hall, John A. and Ikenberry, G. John (1989) *The State*. Milton Keynes: Open University Press.

Hay, Colin (1996) *Re-stating Social and Political Change*. Milton Keynes: Open University Press.

Miliband, Ralph (1969) *The State in Capitalist Society*. London: Weidenfeld and Nicolson.

Sorensen, Georg (2004) *Transformation of the State: Beyond the Myth of Retreat?* Houndmills: Palgrave.

James Fulcher

STATUS

Weber's sociology distinguished status from **class** as the two principal bases of social stratification. Where class referred to social differences based on economic divisions and inequalities, status designated the differentiation of groups in the 'communal' sphere in terms of their social honour and social standing. Weber related both of these to the third source of differentiation that he found in the distribution of authority and the production of **elites**.

Status relations can be seen in terms of the particular status situations that individuals occupy. The explicit parallels that Weber drew between class situation and status situation make it very clear that he intended the latter to designate a specific causal component in life chances that is distinct from the economic component involved in the possession and acquisition of property. He argued that 'we wish to designate as *status situation* every typical component of the life chances of people that is determined by a specific, positive or negative, social estimation of *honor*'. Status situations result from the communal relations through which the social honour attributed to a style of life becomes the basis of life chances. Where economic action involves an interest in the preservation or enhancement of utilities, status-oriented actions involve interests in the preservation or enhancement of social honour.

The actual social groups that can be formed on the basis of status situations are 'social estates' (*Stände*), a term sometimes loosely translated as 'status group'. These are social strata, divided by their social honour or social standing and that follow a particular style of life. Identification with specific social groups becomes the basis of exclusive networks of interaction within which social actions are geared to stressing the distinctiveness of a style of life. These actions involve attitudes of acceptance and rejection, recognition and denial, or approval and disapproval of others in terms of their conformity to the preferred style of life. In its purest form, this social estimation of honour expresses a conception of the prestige associated with the style of life.

The concept of social honour involves the communal ideas of prestige that Durkheim saw as defining the 'sacred' aspects of social life, and it is the 'religious' organisation of communities that must be looked to for the sources of status divisions. It is through such sacred conceptions that judgements of moral superiority and inferiority are made and that status situations arise. **Religion** here must be understood as the whole moral and symbolic order that provides the cultural framework in which people live. Thus, traditional religious world views and ideologies, along with the hereditary charisma of patrimonial kinship groups, are the most frequent sources of those social meanings that define one particular style of life as highly valued and that derogates others.

Weber saw class and status as factors that operate alongside each other in all actual societies. Thus, particular forms of social stratification will show elements of each. Nevertheless, he recognised that societies can be distinguished by the relative importance of class and status and that it is possible to identify a broad transition in European societies from traditional 'status societies' to the 'class societies' of modernity. In modern societies, status is a secondary factor that tends to reflect class divisions, with differences of social honour reinforcing differences of class.

Much American sociology all but ignored the economic aspects of 'class'. While the *word* 'class' was retained to describe the social strata of contemporary American society, structural functionalist sociologists re-defined this in normative terms and collapsed it into the concept of 'status'. For Talcott Parsons and the mainstream of American sociology, social stratification was a matter of social ranking in relation to shared cultural values, and it was these normative relations that gave rise to 'class' relations.

Parsons set out the idea that 'differential ranking' is one of the funda-mental analytical dimensions of the organisation of **social systems**. Individuals evaluate each other's **roles** in relation to their shared social values, and this is the basis of their ranking as superior or inferior with respect to each other. The shared values define a normative pattern, an institutionalised *scale* of stratification, while the actual evaluations that individuals make in relation to this scale generates the actual *system* of stratification. Parsons held that individuals are oriented towards the values that they share with the other members of their society and, therefore, to the particular scale of stratification institutionalised in their society. He concluded that systems of stratification will vary according to the particular values that underpin scales of stratification. There will, in any society, be a 'paramount value system', and it is this that shapes its scale of stratification. Some societies, for example, will stress personal qualities such as age, sex or intelligence, while others may stress 'achievements' or 'possessions'. These variations in the attributes of roles that are regarded as socially significant are the sources of the observable variation in systems of stratification – differences, for example, between a 'caste' system and a modern system of 'class' relations. In the contemporary United States, for example, the achieve-ments attached to occupational roles are the principal objects of evaluation, and it is the ranking of occupations that forms the backbone of the stratification system. Parsons agreed, therefore, that modern status differentiation reflects and reinforces the occupational divisions of the economy.

In the United States – which Parsons regarded as proto-typical of all modern 'industrial' societies – there is a strong cultural emphasis on **role** 'performance' in relation to standards of 'universalism' and 'achievement'. As a result, productive or 'adaptive' activities are seen as having a crucial significance, and it is occupational roles that are the principal sources of status. This ranking of occupations occurs within a framework of values that stress 'equality of opportunity', and the actual system of stratification, therefore, has a certain degree of 'openness' and 'mobility' by comparison with those found in traditional societies. Indeed, this gives it a particular 'classless' character, in so far as status and rewards are not sharply fixed or immutable and in so far as individuals are able to move relatively freely from one role to another.

Parsons sees differentiation by **ethnicity** as being one way in which actual systems of stratification may depart from the institutionalised scale: while the paramount value system may stress occupational achievement, subordinate value systems may stress racial or ethnic qualities and establish lines of division that cut across the relatively 'open' class system. Parsons further explored these issues through considering Marshall's work on **citizenship** and equality.

In his later work, Parsons came to see the paramount values of societies as defining the particular 'functional' activities regarded as being of critical importance to their survival. It is through the ranking of roles in relation to their functional significance that effective mechanisms of recruitment and commitment to roles can be built up: individuals are motivated to enter and to perform in those roles that are especially important in terms of the paramount value system.

Further reading

Scott, John (1996) *Stratification and Power.* Cambridge: Polity Press.
Turner, Bryan (1989) *Status.* Buckingham: Open University Press.

John Scott

SUBCULTURE

Although the term subculture was initially coined by anthropologists, it has been extensively used by sociologists on a range of topics, including delinquency in the 1950s, education in the 1960s and style in the 1970s. The initial sociological definitions regarded subcultures as subdivisions of a national **culture**. This emphasis on the difference between a particular social group and a larger collectivity continues in later developments of the concept. In this sense culture is understood as a 'whole way of life' and includes the 'maps of meaning' that give shape to how the world is experienced and understood. The prefix 'sub' highlights the ways that the groups studied tend to be subordinate, subversive or subterranean and are thereby viewed as beneath, but still within, a dominant or mainstream culture. Consequently, sociologists have not simply studied how the majority censures subcultures, but they have also examined the ways subculture members perceive their difference and can challenge the status quo by developing alternative lifestyles in opposition to the wider culture.

The origins of the concept are diverse, but the American sociology of deviance has been especially influential. In particular, the sociology of **urbanism**, developed at the University of Chicago in the early twentieth century, established many of the focal concerns developed in later scholarship. The Chicago sociologists understood the city as an ordered mosaic of distinctive regions, including industrial districts, ethnic enclaves and criminal areas. These so-called natural areas evolved in relation to one another to form an urban ecology. Their research on juvenile delinquency revealed how certain parts of the city are more crime-prone, irrespective of which ethnic group lives there and that as these groups move to other areas their crime rates decrease. This important finding challenged the then dominant psychological explanations of deviance, which held that crime resulted from individual pathologies and personality defects. Instead, they concluded that slums had their own social structures and cultural norms that gave deviant lifestyles validity and normalised criminal activity in gangs.

By the 1950s, the difficulties of sociologically defining gangs were addressed through the concept of subculture. Again American developments are significant as sociologists turned to issues that had been ignored by the Chicagoans: namely how to explain social problems in relation to class inequalities. The gang came to be defined as a subculture with a value system at odds with mainstream culture, distinguished by specialised vocabulary, shared beliefs and distinctive fashions. Subcultures were then regarded as collective solutions to the structural problems posed by **class** location and the experience of **anomie**. The argument was that working-class youth join gangs in reaction to dominant middle-class values that discriminate against them. Thus status is achieved through deviant means and the inversion of middle-class values (like respect for property and delayed pleasures). However, the sharp distinction drawn between delinquent and conventional values was soon criticised with researchers pointing out how juveniles drift in to and out of delinquency.

When this subcultural theory was applied in Britain in the 1960s, little evidence was found to support the claim that working-class boys suffered from 'status frustration'. Instead they dissociated themselves from the middle-class dominated worlds of school and work. In doing so, attention was drawn not only to class inequality, but also to the meaninglessness of education for working-class youth. A number of studies emphasised how leisure provided a collective solution to their problems and an alternative to achievement at school. The dual emphasis on class and leisure was later developed by the Centre for Contemporary Cultural Studies at Birmingham University in a series of seminal publications in the 1970s.

Strongly influenced by both the latest theoretical work in European Marxism and the new criminology emerging in Britain, this more cultural approach sought to situate subcultural styles in relation to class, culture and **ideology**. An early account by Phil Cohen studied the emergence of 'mods' and 'skinheads' in the East End of London through a subtle analysis of the destruction of working-class community and the erosion of its traditional culture wrought by economic decline and urban change. Youth subcultures do not solve the crises in class relations. Instead, they are symbolic attempts at resolving hidden problems. This study established many central themes in the Birmingham approach. The various postwar working-class youth subcultures were then understood as symbolic representations of social contradictions in the British class structure. Crucially, they were viewed as oppositional rather than simply deviant. However, this resistance is played out in the fields of leisure and consumption so that it ultimately fails to challenge broader structures of power and may, tragically, reinforce them.

The Birmingham scholarship has left a lasting legacy. Yet critics soon disputed the political significance attached to subcultures in this tradition. Others found fault with the tendency to romantically read youth style as internal to the group, with commercialisation only coming later, which underestimates the way changes in youth culture are manufactured by culture industries. Concerns were also raised over the preoccupation with white, male and working-class subcultures. The celebration of the spectacular ignored the racism and sexism in these youth cultures. However, it is important to recognise that feminists at the Birmingham Centre contested the Marxist emphasis on class while the relative neglect of ethnicity has been addressed in subsequent scholarship.

Contemporary critics have complained that subcultural theory relies on problematic binaries, such as authentic-manufactured; resistance-incorporation; subordinate and dominant, all of which simplify the complexities of social practice. For instance, there are conflicts within subcultures and the differences are best understood as taste distinctions rather than forms of resistance. Some now argue that society has fragmented to the extent that we live in 'post-subculture' times, implying that the concept has outlived its usefulness and is unable to grasp contemporary cultural formations. Few deny that the existing concept has limits, yet it is too soon to conclude that the idea has run its course.

Further reading

Cohen, Phil (1972) 'Subcultural conflict and working class community', *CCCS Working Papers*. Reprinted in Gelder and Thornton, 1997.

Gelder, Ken and Thornton, Sarah (eds) (1997) *The Subcultures Reader*. London: Routledge.

Hebdige, Dick (1979) *Subculture: The Meaning of Style*. London: Methuen.

Jenks, Chris (2005) *Subculture: The Fragmentation of the Social*. London: Sage.

Muggleton, David and Weizierl, Rupert (eds) (2003) *The Post-Subcultures Reader*. Oxford: Berg.

Eamonn Carrabine

SURVEILLANCE

The literal definition of surveillance, to 'watch over', conveys the way the process both enables and constrains the activities of the monitored. Yet surveillance also has more sinister overtones, not least since it is a crucial element in totalitarian rule and has inspired a series of literary works, such as Orwell's *1984* and Kafka's *The Trial*, that provide nightmare visions of what it is to experience such domination.

Until the 1970s, the sociology of surveillance did not exist. It was the French philosopher Michel Foucault's influential historical studies that have provoked the surge of interest in the topic. Since then, the classical tradition has been revisited to establish the field and yield a variety of sociological positions: Marx's analysis of political economy is examined to situate surveillance in workplace struggles between labour and capital, while Weber's characterisation of an 'iron cage' of rationality and **bureaucracy** offers an analysis that goes beyond class relations. Yet the crucial point that Foucault makes is that modernity is above all else defined by surveillance. From the early nineteenth century a range of institutions emerged that were organised on the basis of order through surveillance: prisons, barracks, asylums, schools, factories and hospitals. By the early twenty-first century surveillance techniques operate in so many spheres of daily life that they are impossible to avoid. Paying supermarket bills, making phone calls and using the internet will each trigger some surveillance device.

Central to Foucault's argument is that the Panopticon (a model prison design created by Jeremy Bentham in 1778) is the prime archetype of the disciplining society. One irony is that, at the very moment in the 1970s when Foucault's analysis of the 'Great Incarcerations' of the nineteenth century was published, many Western societies seemed to be radically reversing this pattern through decarceration of the confined. Community correction came to be regarded as a more humane way of dealing with offenders, while treating mental illness in the community was generally seen as preferable to the asylum. However, many authors were sceptical and argued that treatment in the community amounted to malign neglect, with the mentally ill left to fend for themselves in uncaring environments. Others maintained that the development of community corrections marks both a continuation and an intensification of the social control patterns identified by Foucault.

Developments since the 1990s include the rapid expansion of electronic, information and visual technologies, all of which greatly enhance the surveillance capacities of the state and commercial enterprises. Likewise urban fortress living has become a reality, so that contemporary surveillance is both inclusionary (offering a sense of safety, security and order) for some city dwellers and exclusionary for others: prohibiting certain teenagers from entering panoptic shopping centres while planners develop sadistic street environments to displace the homeless from particular localities. For instance, one analysis of video surveillance in an American city revealed how it is a rapidly developing control strategy focused on the young black male. Clearly, such findings are a disturbing instance of the totalitarian undercurrents in late modern democracies.

Further reading

Cohen, Stanley (1985) *Visions of Social Control.* Cambridge: Polity Press.
Fiske, John (1998) 'Surveilling the city: whiteness, the black man and democratic totalitarianism', *Theory, Culture and Society*, 15, 2: 67–88.
Foucault, Michel (1977) *Discipline and Punish: The Birth of the Prison.* London: Allen Lane.
Lyon, David (2001) *Surveillance Society.* Buckingham: Open University Press.

Eamonn Carrabine

TIME AND SPACE

Time has been a long-term concern for sociological theory, varying conceptualisations deriving from differing overall theoretical perspectives. Marx's analysis of commodity exchange and exploitation assumed an 'abstract labour time'. For Weber, processes of routinisation and bureaucratisation, integral to the transition to modern rational-legal society, owed much to the abstract chronometric time associated with the institutionalisation of the Protestant ethic. Durkheim, by contrast, emphasised the integrative and social synchronising function of time. For the French school of anthropology with which he was associated, time was a collective phenomenon derived from social life. Time has been central also to Anthony Giddens's theories of structuration, and the allied concepts of sedimentation, 'time-space distanciation', the recursiveness of knowledge and commodified time. In his approach, time is constituted through the replication of social practices: order and stability are no more timeless than change and revolution. In addition to these approaches are functionalist, symbolic interactionist, phenomenological, social constructionist and numerous other theories of time, each stressing different dimensions of temporality and differing in fairly predictable ways.

In many of these theories, however, time often appears simply as an epiphenomenon of the overall framework, with little attention given, until recent decades, to its actual nature or to the substantive temporal dimensions of social and historical process. Pierre Bourdieu's work on the Kabyle of Algeria, and Eviatar Zerubavel's work on hospitals and the calendar, represent notable exceptions to the latter and the work of Norbert Elias to the former.

Elias conceptualises time as a symbol which clarifies one sequence of events by reference to another, a human tool that permits events to be compared indirectly when it is impossible to do so directly. Because 'positions and sequences which have their places successively in the unending flow of events cannot be juxtaposed', a second sequence of recurrent patterns is needed to serve as standardised reference points. Time thus refers to the 'relating together of positions or segments within two or more continuously moving series of events'. As such, time instruments themselves do not structure events, no more than does a map create the rivers and seas that it charts.

Parallel considerations apply to sociological conceptualisation of space, though this has been a less dominant theme of classical than of late twentieth-century theory and has usually been more substantively approached. Since the opening-out of geography as a discipline from the 1980s, spatial concepts of mapping, boundary, location, inscription and sedimentation have been widely adopted in sociology as both real and metaphorical means of characterising the links or causal connections between social relations and processes.

Henri Lefebvre's position that spatial organisation makes a difference to how society works has formed the basis for later approaches to the intersection of spatial and social relations. Doreen Massey conceives of the spatial form of the social as having 'causal effectivity'. As 'a moment in the intersection of configured social relations', space is constructed out of the complex interlocking of networks of relations across all scales from the most global to the most local. This suggests a relational conception of 'place' as a differentially located node in a network of relations, unbounded and unstable.

Most approaches today conceptualise time and space as inseparable aspects of each other (as 'time/space'). Temporality and spatiality are understood as being mutually constructed with social process in such a way that the organisation and sorting of social relations also structures time and space. There is no pre-given context of space and time into which people and things are fitted. Rather, it is the arrangement of things in space and time, their spatial linkage and temporal sorting, that constitute place and time. When viewed like this, space cannot be conceived as static, any more than time can be conceived as spaceless.

In the wake of ongoing global transformations, time and space are both high on the agenda of contemporary sociology, generating considerable research activity and the emergence of new perspectives and methodologies for capturing the specificity of socio-temporal-spatial relations. Changing places and times of work disrupt previous synchronies and divisions of home and work, providing a basis for the study of time-budgets and of temporalities that are not clock-based. Time/space 'compression' and 'distanciation', 'glocalisation', time-pressure, the gendering and experience of time and space, convenience and virtuality are some amongst many topical themes in the analysis of the impact of new electronic technologies and global relations.

Further reading

Adam, Barbara (1990) *Time and Social Theory*. Cambridge: Polity.
Elias, Norbert (1992) *Time: An Essay*, tran. E. Jephcott. Oxford: Blackwell.
Gershuny, Jonathan (2000) *Changing Times. Work and Leisure in Postindustrial Society*. Oxford: Oxford University Press.
Gregory, Derek and Urry, John (eds) (1985) *Social Relations and Spatial Structures*. London: Macmillan.
Hassard, John (ed.) (1990) *The Sociology of Time*. London: Macmillan.
Massey, Doreen (1994) *Space, Place and Gender*. Oxford: Blackwell.

Miriam Glucksmann

TRADITION AND TRADITIONALISM

A tradition is a cultural object – a system of meanings or ideas – that is transmitted from the past and handed on to successive generations. Traditions exist as the meanings sustained by the members of a particular society and communicated from one to another in the chains of meaning that comprise collective or shared memories, collective representations and customary ways of doing things. The contents of a tradition may change imperceptibly over time, but they are experienced by the individuals who acquire them through their **socialisation** as things that have persisted, largely without change, for considerable periods of time. Such customs are built up unreflectively, as social **institutions** that influence people's behaviour by instilling habits of action that they follow without conscious intent or rational deliberation. Customary institutions grounded in tradition are often referred to as the folkways of a society.

Customary ways of acting tend to be received authoritatively, as matters not to be challenged, by the individuals who encounter them as given social facts. When this authority becomes a conscious act of reflection and people seek to justify their customs and folkways as 'the way we have always done things', they are according their traditions a legitimacy by constructing reasons for people to conform to them. The idea of tradition as any practice handed down from the past is sometimes distinguished from the legitimation of such practices in terms of their long standing character by referring to the latter as traditionalism. According to Weber, traditionalism is one of the principal types of authority found in the large-scale **state**.

The idea of traditionalism has been taken up in debates on **modernity**, where a contrast has been drawn between traditional and modern societies. **Modernisation** is typically seen as involving a transition from traditional to modern societies as a result of a continuing **rationalisation** of social activities. Rationalisation is a process in which the value standards that define people's orientations towards each other are marked by an ever greater degree of formal rationality and all matters are subjected to the criteria of calculation, technique and effectiveness. This was seen by Weber as a progressive 'disenchantment' of the world as religion, superstition and traditionalism lose their spiritual force. Anthony Giddens has seen this as producing 'detraditionalised' societies in which all issues are a matter of secular consideration and discussion. This argument has tended to change the meaning of 'tradition' by giving it a substantive content. Traditional ideas come to be seen not as *any* set of ideas handed down from the past but as those specific ideas that are counterposed to modern, rational ways of acting.

Sociology itself was a product of this detraditionalisation and the theorists of the formative period attempted to grasp this transition in their theories. Best known is the contrast made by Ferdinand Tönnies between *Gemeinschaft* and *Gesellschaft*, between the recurrent and harmonious relations of **community** and the rational and impersonal relations of modern **civil society**. Traditional Gemeinschaft societies are organised around custom and established norms as the folkways that shape people's actions, and they are typically seen as homogeneous societies characterised by high levels of consensus and mechanical **solidarity**. Modern Gesellschaft societies are organised around the rational action of individuals and their instrumental orientation towards each other, and they are typically seen as heterogeneous societies characterised by high levels of conflict and impersonality.

The most influential attempt to unpack this contrast in societal forms is that of Talcott Parsons, whose 'pattern variables' were intended to describe the ways in which cultural value patterns vary from one society to another. Individuals face 'dilemmas of choice' that are resolved by the value patterns provided by their **culture**. The traditional cultures associated with Gemeinschaft are organised around ascriptive, affective, diffuse and particularistic value standards, while the modern cultures responsible for Gesellschaft are organised around achievement, neutral, specific and universalistic ones. Rationalisation involves a change in one or more of these pattern variables.

Changes along the ascriptive-achievement dimension mean that people come to define each other in terms of their effectiveness or success in attaining their goals rather than by their personal qualities. People are judged on the basis of what they have actually achieved or what they may achieve in future acts. The affectivity-neutrality variable describes alterations in the emotional content of social relations from impulsive and emotionally engaged participation that allows people an immediate satisfaction of their wants and wishes to impersonal and disciplined relations that require a calculative and pragmatic orientation towards the satisfaction of desires. The diffuse-specific dimension of change in value patterns involves a move away from judgements of the overall character of a person as a whole and towards relations in which participants restrict their expectations and interests to narrow and limited aspects of their actions, seeing them as functionally specialised in relation to specific purposes. Finally, the particularistic-universalistic variable describes changes from concerns about the unique significance of others and their actions to considerations of what it is they share with others in the same class or category.

The different usages of tradition have been brought together in the argument of Jürgen Habermas that modernisation has involved the progressive elimination of all inherited cultural orientations. Custom and habit cannot be given a rational justification and so rational actors cannot rely on them as guides for action. In the modern world, he argues, the rise of science and technology has undermined spiritual legitimation and has compelled people to make their own choices and decisions with purely formal and instrumental criteria and without invoking moral considerations or referring to how things have been done in the past. This argument has been enlarged by post-modernist theorists, who point to the eroding of all foundations for knowledge and morality, including those of science and technology itself. The post-modern condition is the social condition in which all social activities have become disenchanted and detraditionalised and are now without ultimate meaning or significance.

Tradition, then, has a complex range of meanings, but this has allowed it to figure as one of the central concepts in recent debates over the nature of modernity.

Further reading

Eisenstadt, Shmuel N. (1973) *Tradition, Change, and Modernity*. New York: Wiley.

Giddens, Anthony (1991) *Modernity and Self-Identity*. Cambridge: Polity Press.

Misztal, Barbara (2003) *Theories of Social Remembering*. Maidenhead: Open University Press.

Shils, Edward (1981) *Tradition*. Chicago: University of Chicago Press.

John Scott

UNDERCLASS

This term refers to a group in society which operates outside its traditional norms and practices. Such norms and practices include traditional morality, traditional family forms, in particular the nuclear family, engagement with the labour market and independence from state or charitable financial support. The underclass is also seen as being able to reproduce itself by transmitting its particular morality and practices to the next generation. The notion of the underclass provides a way of locating society's perceived ills or potentially perplexing changes in society, such as the rise of unemployment or the increase in lone parenthood, in a discrete group of individuals and their lifestyles.

This makes problems of **poverty**, economic transition and social change appear containable, and a solution that will not impact on the continuation of traditional patterns of work and life seem achievable. The construction of a 'problem class' with the potential to disrupt or destabilise the foundations of a society also offers a reassuring opportunity to allocate blame for unwelcome social or economic changes. The threatening nature of those outside of mainstream society, encapsulated in the Victorian era in the term 'dangerous classes', continues to be a key aspect of the concept of the underclass.

The term reached a particular prominence in the 1980s with the work of Charles Murray. Here, the concept was heavily racialised and linked particularly with 'welfare mothers', that is, lone mothers in receipt of the main non-insurance benefit, then called Aid for Families with Dependent Children (AFDC). However, the concept of an excluded or self-excluding group can be seen to have had a much longer heritage, with the age-old distinction between the deserving and the undeserving poor that was, and, arguably, continues to be, a primary tenet of poor relief or social security provision in Britain. Key elements of the underclass concept can also be found in the concern over 'problem families' and the attention paid to 'cycles of deprivation' in 1960s Britain, the stigmatising treatment of the unemployed in the 1980s and in the current concern with social exclusion, discussed further below.

Charles Murray's formulation of the underclass stemmed in part from the publication of the Moynihan Report in 1965, which highlighted the particular disadvantage of Black Americans and made a link with the prevalence of lone-parent families. William Julius Wilson also used the Moynihan Report as a starting point, but developed his argument in a rather different direction from Murray's. Though recognising that certain, highly deprived areas were characterised by high rates of lone parenthood, high concentrations of Black Americans and high levels of 'welfare' (AFDC) receipt, Wilson was concerned to identify their structural causes rather than seeing them, as Murray did, as representing the moral failure of individuals.

Both ways of conceiving an underclass – morally deficient and distinct from the worthy poor, or forced into an extreme, and extremely disadvantaged, situation by economic and state processes (in particular, changes in industrialisation and location of industry) – have fed into the contemporary British focus on social exclusion. Social exclusion is identified as both a process which affects individuals as a result of failings in the state and by society, and also as a property of individuals, who fail the rest of society by bringing up children on their own, preferring benefits to work and not seizing educational opportunities. As Ruth Levitas has pointed out, though, the underclass is only one of a number of strands in the multifaceted concept of social exclusion. What has, by and large, not been absorbed in the British discussion is the **racialisation** associated with the US version of the underclass concept. However, the ongoing concern with transmission of characteristics across generations that is common to both underclass and social exclusion concepts has shown a recent tendency to be associated with anxiety that 'fatherless families' may produce criminal young men, particularly in the case of young black men.

Further reading

Levitas, Ruth (1998) *The Inclusive Society? Social Exclusion and New Labour*. Basingstoke: Macmillan.

Lister, Ruth (ed.) (1996) *Charles Murray and the Underclass: The Developing Debate*. London: IEA Health and Welfare Unit in association with The Sunday Times.

Morris, Lydia (1994) *Dangerous Classes: The Underclass and Social Citizenship*. London: Routledge.

Welshman, John (2005) *Underclass: A History of the Excluded, 1880–2000*. London: Hambledon & London.

Wilson, W. Julius (1987) *The Truly Disadvantaged: The Inner City, The Underclass, and Public Policy*. Chicago: University of Chicago Press.

Lucinda Platt

URBANISM

The clearest distinction is between urbanisation, the process of growth of the urban population in a society, and urbanism, the way of life of urban dwellers. We look at both in turn. Outside sociology urbanism may be used to mean the planned creation of particular environments with the aim of creating particular lifestyles, as in the 'new urbanism'.

Nearly half (47.8 per cent in 2001) of the world's population now lives in urban areas; the figures vary from 31.2% to 52.8% and 77.8% in low-, middle- and high-income countries. In Europe and North America, after an early phase of small-scale rural industrialisation, capitalist industrialisation (see **industrialism**) and urbanisation have typically gone hand in hand. Towns and cities became the places in which capital and hence labour were concentrated and Marx rightly foresaw that this would encourage workers to combine. Later in the twentieth century the economics of location changed and de-urbanisation emerged in many advanced capitalist societies. This was partly driven by employer preferences as motorway networks lessened the locational advantages of cities, and semi-rural areas offered access to space and non-unionised labour, and partly due to households' residential preferences. As manufacturing goods are increasingly imported and the demand for services has risen, the 'post-industrial city' has emerged, and writers have distinguished between cities based on their economic functions: from the 'world city' (which houses the multinational and financial headquarters which control production trade and finance) to resort and retirement towns. Recently Patrick Le Galès has suggested a contrast between the (Western) 'European city' and the US city based on their different histories and traditions of state intervention.

By contrast, in Third World countries urbanisation is not so closely linked with industrialisation and the term 'overurbanisation' was introduced by Kingsley Davis and H. H. Golden. Based on the assumption that the West offered the model for successful 'modernisation', the term referred to the fact that Third World cities typically had larger urban populations than was 'warranted' by their level of industrial employment. At first seen as a problem, the Third World combination of low state social spending, an unregulated informal economic sector and shanty towns became accepted as a solution, thus establishing a new urban pattern.

Further recognition of diversity came from studies of state socialist societies which led Ivan Szelenyi to introduce the term 'under-urbanisation' to refer to the policy of channelling resources into industrialisation while restricting investment in urban housing. Living in cities became a privilege and was policed by controlling residence; many workers in urban industries had to commute from rural areas. Today the former state socialist societies have abandoned this investment strategy and ending all controls on residence, thus allowing the expansion of their urban populations to restart.

Weber, who emphasised the autonomy of medieval Western cities, was equally aware of their local interdependence with feudal lords and their linkages with international trading networks. Ever since, the key issue for sociologists studying the city has been to capture both the dependence of what happens in cities on wider social relations and to acknowledge that what happens in particular places cannot be read off from these wider processes. Rather, places have distinctive histories. Wider processes combine in distinctive ways in them, and they occupy differentiated places within wider systems. In brief, place matters.

The study of urbanism, the alleged way of life of city dwellers illustrates this tension. It has two focal questions: is there a way of life characteristic of cities, and if so what shapes it?

The earliest writers on the subject, Georg Simmel, Robert Park and Louis Wirth all agreed that settlements of different sizes had different ways of life, and introduced the idea of the contrast between rural and urban ways of life. This had links with Durkheim's mechanical and organic solidarity and Tönnies's community and society. For Simmel the city dweller had a distinctive personality (intellectual, blasé and free from constraints) which he attributed to the dominance of economic rationality, and the sheer nervous stimulation of living in a large population. Park and Wirth added to this focus on personality an interest in social relations. For them urbanism involved impersonal, transitory and segmental relations, and the rise of the 'secondary' relations of associations at the expense of the 'primary' relations of the family. They attributed urbanism to the demographic features of population size, density and heterogeneity. This followed from their adherence to the human ecology school of thought which sought parallels between the ways that human, and other animal and plant populations adapted to their environments. Economic competition for land among humans was equivalent to the competition for light and food, and the movement of social groups between areas was described by such ecological terms as 'invasion', 'zone in transition' and 'succession'. Finally the drive to generalise led Wirth to give culture a secondary explanatory role. Cities in poor non-industrial countries were ignored: his thinking was based on the cities he knew in Germany and the USA.

Wirth's critics argued that he was both inaccurate descriptively and mistaken theoretically. Herbert Gans claimed that there was no single urban way of life but that in the US the 'city' (in the UK, the inner city) and 'suburb' had contrasting ways of life. Moreover the 'city' itself showed great diversity as it housed both the 'deprived' and 'trapped' households (who could not afford to move away) and well-off young professionals attracted by cultural facilities. He argued that these groups' lifestyles were shaped not by the population density of the inner city but by their income levels and lifecycle positions. Lastly ethnic villages showed their independence of their location by constructing communal lifestyles quite unlike Wirth's model. Gans acknowledged that isolated individuals could be found displaying Wirth's urbanism but argued that this was due to their socio-economic deprivation. On the other hand the suburbs showed quasi-primary lifestyles based on homogeneity of income and lifestyle, and residential mobility. Hence Gans's conclusion was that lifestyles depend not on ecological factors but on people's class and lifecycle position and degree of residential mobility. In this way he was trying to bring the wider society into the picture as Weber had advocated.

Finally Manuel Castells took Gans's critique of Wirth one step further by arguing that it left the influence of capitalism implicit. Instead Castells claimed that what Wirth described as urbanism was the cultural translation of advanced capitalism. This was part of his more general argument that explanations which attributed social processes to their urban location demonstrated the 'urban ideology', namely a refusal to look beyond place to fundamental social structures. For his part Castells denied the importance of studying urban lifestyles and in successive works proposed new ways of looking at the city. In *The Urban Question* the urban referred to a unit of society in which all the basic structures were present but which specialised in 'collective consumption' (state intervention in consumption) and where the conflicts around this could open up a second 'urban' front of conflict which when joined to industrial conflict and party politics had great transformative potential. In *The City and the Grassroots* Castells argues that groups of citizens can shape the development of cities through organisations based on identity and community but that there are severe limits to the effects they can create. Lastly in *The Information Age* Castells focuses directly on the networks and flows which constitute the wider processes which provide the links between places, but says little about actors and groups.

Besides urbanisation and urbanism, other themes in writing on the city range from the built environment and the spatial structure of urban activities; housing, land and labour markets; social order in public spaces and inequalities of access to schools and healthcare facilities; to urban politics and policy-making, and city promotion.

Further reading

Bridge, Gary and Watson, Sophie (eds) (2000) *A Companion to the City*. Oxford: Blackwell.

Eade, John and Mele, Christopher (eds) (2002) *Understanding the City: Contemporary and Future Perspectives*. Oxford: Blackwell.

Le Galès, Patrick (2002) *European Cities*. Oxford: Oxford University Press.

Saunders, Peter (1986) *Social Theory and the Urban Question*, 2nd edn. London: Hutchinson.

Savage, Mike, Warde, Alan and Ward, Kevin (2003) *Urban Sociology, Capitalism and Modernity*, 2nd edn. London: Palgrave.

Chris Pickvance

WORLD SYSTEMS

This concept is associated with Immanuel Wallerstein, who developed it in his 1974 book *The Modern World System*. Scholars in a variety of disciplines have found that Wallerstein's approach provides them with a useful framework and examples of their work can be found in *The Journal of World Systems Research*. Similar ideas were developed by André Gunder Frank in his research into underdevelopment in Latin America, though in the 1990s he came to reject what he saw as the eurocentrism in Wallerstein's approach.

According to Wallerstein, a **social system** is a self-contained unit within which there is a complete division of labour. World systems are social systems that stretch across many different **cultures**. They may not cover the whole world but to their inhabitants they are complete worlds because they include many different peoples and contain a range of activities that meet all the needs of those that live there.

Two types of world system can be found: *world empires* and *world economies*. The civilisations of China, Egypt and ancient Rome were world empires. This kind of world system was held together by a single political centre that controlled the distribution of the world's resources. *World economies* in contrast had multiple political centres and were economically integrated by market relationships. A world economy came into existence with the emergence of **capitalism** in sixteenth-century Europe. After the decline of Rome, no world empire had been able to establish itself in Europe, which had fragmented into competing national states. By the sixteenth century the capitalist merchants of north-west Europe had created a network of relationships that stretched across these states and was soon extended across much of the rest of the globe. It was at this time that the first European overseas empires were constructed but these were not, according to Wallerstein's terminology, world empires, for they were not self-sufficient units.

Wallerstein sees the capitalist world economy as structured into three distinct zones: core, periphery and semi-periphery. These perform different functions and have different modes of production, each with its own distinctive means of controlling labour. The core consists of economically advanced industrial countries with wage labour. The labour intensive periphery produces raw materials and food, exporting these to the core areas and importing their manufactured goods. Labour in the periphery is controlled by force, either by slavery or 'coerced cash-crop labour'. Between these two is the semi-periphery, character-ised by an intermediate capital intensiveness and the extraction of the agricultural surplus through sharecropping. The core is economically dominant and exploits the periphery, with the assistance of the semi-periphery. The use of **state** power is crucial to this and the strongest states are to be found in the core, the weakest in the periphery. While the capitalist world economy always has the same structure, the position of countries may change and particular countries have risen and fallen within it.

Wallerstein's approach owes much to Marxism, but he rejected what he called the 'official Marxism' of state socialist societies. These did not, as they claimed, present an alternative to **capitalism**, since their economies were integrated with the capitalist world economy and could not stand apart from it. This did not mean that Wallerstein thought that capitalism would continue for ever. He believed that the capitalist world economy was doomed by its contradictions. First, the reduction of labour costs to make greater profits would destroy the mass demand necessary to keep profitable production going, and this would lead to greater and greater crises. Second, each time that an opposition movement was bought off by concessions, these became a platform for the demands of the next opposition movement, and it would eventually become impossible to buy off the opposition. The capitalist world system would meet its demise. A 'socialist world-system' could then be created, though he did not expect this to happen in the near future.

André Gunder Frank found in Wallerstein a kindred spirit with the same 'world-systemic historical interests'. Like Wallerstein, Frank rejected the **modernisation** theory that had become something of an orthodoxy in the 1960s. The explanation of the lack of development in Latin America was not the persistence of traditional societies that had not yet been modernised by being drawn into the world economy. It was in fact their position in the world economy and their exploitation by economically developed countries that kept them undeveloped. In his famous phrase 'the development of underdevelopment', Frank argued that the industrial societies had actually reduced the level of development elsewhere by, for example, destroying local crafts that could not compete with imported industrial goods.

By the end of the 1980s Frank was, however, becoming increasingly critical of Wallerstein's approach. In his 1998 book *ReORIENT: Global Economy in the Asian Age*, he claimed that Wallerstein, and indeed Marx, Durkheim, Weber and many others, have provided a Eurocentric version of world history. Wallerstein had shown how a capitalist world economy had first emerged in Europe in the sixteenth century and then spread to incorporate most of the rest of the world. Frank argued that this ignores the earlier development of a world economy centred on Asian countries. He claimed that until 1800 Asia was indeed ahead of Europe in economic development. Europe did not rise on its own but climbed up 'on the shoulders of the Asian economies'. It was only in the nineteenth century that the West overtook Asia. The later rise of Asian economies in the second half of the twentieth century, and their future dominance of the world economy, should not be seen as something new but rather as a return to the Asian economic dominance of earlier times. This is a contentious but undoubtedly refreshing view of world history.

Frank also rejected the notion that a distinctively capitalist mode of production originated in early modern Europe. The much-debated question of why capitalism emerged in Europe was a non-issue to Frank. He rejected the whole Marxian idea of a sequence of modes of production, a series of stages that all countries pass through, and argues that many different relations of production can coexist and have in fact always done so. There is an echo here of Wallerstein's position that different modes of production have coexisted within the capitalist world economy.

Frank did not reject Wallerstein's concept of a world system but rather argued that he was trapped by his eurocentrism and did not become global enough in his analysis. At the end of his book Frank launched into an attack on those who are preoccupied with the distinctiveness of civilisations and fail to see that they have 'the same essential *functional* structure and process'. Where there are genuine differences these are, he argues, actually generated by interactions within the world system and are not the result of some original cultural diversity. He was particularly scathing about Samuel Huntington's fashionable notion that world history is characterised by an eternal clash of civilisations.

Does this call for a truly global analysis mean that the world-system approach and globalisation theory have merged? World system theorists are often critical of those who write about globalisation because of their focus on recent change, as though it is only in recent years that the world has become a single unit. They also consider much of the globalisation literature to be uncritical of the process and unconcerned with the relationship between capital and labour. Those writing from a **globalisation** perspective find the world systems approach too Marxist and unable to deal with cultural change. In its insistence on the continued existence of a world system that emerged centuries ago, it arguably fails to appreciate the recent emergence of a distinctively global age. There is, however, so much diversity within both camps that the two approaches overlap considerably.

The world systems approach has demonstrated the weaknesses of the modernisation approach that advocates integration in the world economy as the route to development. It has effectively demolished theories of social development (see **change and development**) that see all societies as passing through the same stages. It shows a critical awareness of the persistence of global inequalities, of the relationships of exploitation between developed and undeveloped countries and their maintenance by global structures. It links the relations of production in particular societies to their position in the world economy. It has given historical depth to the analysis of contemporary global relationships. The problem with some world system writings is, however, a static 'nothing really changes' approach, a tendency to economic reductionism, and, as Frank claimed, a eurocentric focus on the achievements of the West.

Further reading

Frank, André G. (1998) *ReORIENT: Global Economy in the Asian Age*. Berkeley: University of California Press.
Hopkins, Terence K. and Wallerstein, Immanuel (1996) *The Age of Transition: Trajectory of the World-System 1945–2025*. London: Zed Books.
Wallerstein, Immanuel (1974–89) *The Modern World System*, 3 volumes. New York: Academic Press.

James Fulcher

GLOSSARY OF THEORETICAL APPROACHES

Chicago School

Developed at the University of Chicago through the inspiration of Albion Small and under the academic leadership of Robert Park, its heyday lasted through the 1920s and 1930s. The approach stressed the importance of group conflict and the struggle over resources. Chicago sociologists applied these ideas to the struggle for control over space in urban contexts and their 'ecological' model depicted the city as formed into a series of concentric zones, each characterised by a different form of land use and social organisation. Leading members of the School included William Thomas, Nels Anderson, Paul Cressey, Clifford Shaw and Harvey Zorbaugh, and their studies covered such topics as ethnic divisions, crime and leisure. This work was closely allied with the symbolic interactionism of George Mead. Later Chicago sociologists such as Everett Hughes and Howard Becker combined these two elements into a powerful 'labelling' theory of deviance.

Conflict theory

Early conflict theorists included Ludwig Gumplowicz, Gaetano Mosca and Karl Marx, who produced theories of ethnic conflict, the conflicts between elites and masses, and revolutionary class struggles. These ideas influenced the work of the Chicago School and the later development of pluralist political theory. The works of Ralf Dahrendorf, John Rex and, perhaps, Lewis Coser have often been described as examples of conflict theory because of their criticisms of structural functionalism for its static focus on social order. Dahrendorf looked at the conflict of power-based classes and the interest groups that represent them, while John Rex looked at ethnic and class conflicts in the property, employment and housing markets. Randall Collins has recently proposed a version of conflict theory that begins from micro-level individual conflict.

Conversation analysis

An offshoot of ethnomethodology, conversation analysis developed as a way of analysing natural conversations and the social organisation of talk. Leading theorists include Harvey Sacks, Emmanuel Schegloff and Gail Jefferson, who have shown the ways in which people draw on interactional competences and skills to organise their talk and to make it socially intelligible. A particular concern has been to highlight the taken-for-granted rules embodied in these competences, such as the rules governing turn-taking in everyday discussions. See **conversation**.

Critical realism

Realist philosophy has a long and diverse history, but the term critical realism is generally applied to work inspired by the philosophy of science produced by Rom Harré and by his student Roy Bhaskar. The position holds that an objective external world of causal mechanisms can be grasped conceptually through scientific investigation, but that the models produced by science can never be seen as direct reflections of that reality. The causal mechanisms at work in the social world are seen as social structures. Substantively, critical realism shares a great deal with the Marxist analysis of class structure and modes of production and with Durkheim's analysis of the autonomy of social facts. A leading social theorist in the critical realist tradition is Margaret Archer.

Critical theory

Critical theory is often equated with the work of the theorists of the Frankfurt School and, in particular, with the ideas of Jürgen Habermas. Critical theorists see all social theory as oriented by distinct human interests that shape the perspectives adopted. They see critical theory itself as oriented by an interest in emancipation from power and domination in the spheres of work and interaction. The knowledge produced by critical theory is contrasted with that produced by positivism and hermeneutics, where knowledge is oriented by conservative interests in the maintenance of tradition and social order.

Ethnomethodology

This approach originated in the attempt by Harold Garfinkel to reconstruct the ways in which the structural functionalism of Talcott Parsons conceptualised the everyday basis of social order. Garfinkel rejected Parsons's reliance on socialisation and argued that agents actively draw on taken-for-granted knowledge and methods in order to make sense of their social encounters and to account for their actions. His focus was on the *sense* of social structure rather than any external social structures themselves. Ethnomethodologists such as Aaron Cicourel, Egon Bittner, Melvin Pollner and David Sudnow have investigated a range of topics including police encounters with juveniles and the homeless, jury decision-making, the medical organisation of death and the art of walking. An important offshoot of ethnomethodology is conversation analysis.

Evolutionism

Many nineteenth-century social theorists, inspired by advances in biology, argued that societies and cultural traits could be understood as developing over time through adaptation to their physical environments. From this point of view, societies exhibit long-term processes of structured social change. Charles Darwin's evolutionary biology highlighted the method of 'natural selection' through which biological traits are brought into line with environmental conditions. Social evolutionists such as Herbert Spencer, William Sumner and James Frazer saw a similar process at work in the social sphere, though they also saw social evolution as 'progress' in the direction of moral improvement. Evolutionary theory was eclipsed by the emergence of functionalist approaches, but it was taken up again in the 1960s as an integral part of Talcott Parsons's formulation of a system theory.

Feminist theory

A diverse set of feminist social theories are united by a common commitment to the aims of the women's movement and liberation from male-dominated social structures and practices. Current strands of feminist social theory have their roots in the so-called second-wave feminism of the 1960s and 1970s. Pioneering work by Kate Millett, Betty Friedan and Shulamith Firestone was taken up in liberal and radical versions of feminism and also in forms of socialist or Marxist feminism. These theorists explored the ways in which women were subordinated by male power – through structures of patriarchy – in such areas as reproductive technology, socialisation, family relations, domestic violence, employment practices and cultural representations. Established social theory was criticised for its 'malestream' characteristics. Most recently, post-structuralist and post-colonial approaches have influenced feminist theory, leading to the claim that women are diverse and pluralistic and that there is no single 'essence' to the feminine.

Frankfurt School

This is a school of thought within Marxism that began at the University of Frankfurt in the 1920s. Under the leadership of Max Horkheimer, its members at one time included Theodor Adorno, Erich Fromm and Herbert Marcuse. They aimed to develop an approach to Marxism that owed a great deal to Hegel and that gave greater emphasis to politics and culture than was the case in orthodox Marxism. Leading members worked in the United States during the Second World War, but many returned to Frankfurt in the 1950s. In this postwar period, when the theoretical approach came to be called critical theory, Jürgen Habermas had become the dominant thinker. His work draws heavily on both structural functionalism and hermeneutics and is a self-consciously synthetic theory that some argue now has little connection with Marxism.

Hermeneutics

Hermeneutic philosophy is rooted in the ideas of Ernst Schleiermacher and Wilhelm Dilthey, who extended the principles and practices of biblical interpretation to all other cultural products. The central idea is that the meaning of an item can be grasped only through a process of interpretation in which it is placed in the context of the worldview from which it has emerged. This argument had a great influence on Weber's view of the methodology of the cultural sciences. The most important recent philosopher in this tradition was Hans-Georg Gadamer, who showed that such ideas as 'truth' have a meaning only within particular cultural traditions. This claim has found its echo in post-modernist rejections of 'absolutism' and 'foundationalism' in knowledge.

Interpretative sociology

This is a general term for a diverse set of approaches that have in common the argument that sociology must begin from human action, rather than social structures, and that actions must be studied through interpreting their subjective meaning for the individual actor. Hermeneutic philosophy provides a basis for many of these theorists, though interpretative theorists have also drawn on phenomenology and pragmatism. Examples of interpretative sociologies include ethnomethodology, symbolic interactionism and some approaches that take Weber's analysis of action as their point of reference.

Marxism

Marx characterised his own work by its emphasis on the material factors of production and class relations, seeing these as forming the basis of any social structure. Following Marx's death, this was formed into a rigid orthodoxy in the hands of Friedrich Engels, Karl Kautsky and then Vladimir Lenin. In reaction to this rather deterministic approach, other Marxists sought to build more critical and reflexive theories that gave more attention to the relative autonomy of political and cultural phenomena. Particularly important figures outside the orthodoxy were Georg Lukács, Antonio Gramsci and the members of the Frankfurt School. In the second half of the twentieth century, a more 'scientific' approach was reassessed by writers such as Louis Althusser and Nicos Poulantzas, who drew on structuralism for their methodology and intellectual orientation.

Neofunctionalism

This form of structural functionalism developed during the 1980s following the criticisms that had been levelled against Parsons and symbolic interactionists. Neofunctionalists such as Jeffrey Alexander, together with radical 'old' functionalists such as Bernard Barber and Neil Smelser, constructed models of social systems in which system processes were seen as resulting from group conflict as well as from socialisation into a common culture. Neofunctionalism, therefore, took power and conflict more seriously than had the original structural functionalism.

Phenomenology

Phenomenology developed as a philosophical position from the work of Edmund Husserl and was popularised within social science by Alfred Schütz. This held that social analysis must begin from the analysis of the contents of individual consciousness – the 'phenomena' of which people are aware – and must treat these as socially shared stocks of knowledge. This approach has found its most important expression in ethnomethodology and in the works of Peter Berger and Thomas Luckmann. The existentialism of Jean-Paul Sartre owes a great deal to phenomenology, which has also influenced the 'anti-psychiatry' of Ronald Laing.

Positivism

This is one of the most over-used terms in sociology. It is most often used as a term of abuse for any quantitative or empiricist approach to social life that is held to ignore the part played by individual action and subjective meanings. 'Positivism', therefore, is often contrasted with interpretative sociology. Strictly, however, the term describes the methodological approach of Auguste Comte, especially as this was developed by Durkheim in his *Rules of the Sociological Method*. It involves an emphasis on the search for objectivity through rigorous and disciplined empirical methods and an eschewing of all preconceived ideas and ideological forms. This method is not, in itself, opposed to the study of individual actions, though Durkheim himself emphasised the importance of recognising the autonomy of social facts.

Post-colonialism

Post-colonialism originated in studies of Indian history undertaken by the Subaltern Studies Group, who rejected history that was written from the standpoint of the colonial authorities and sought to invoke the voice of the colonised subjects – the subalterns. Related ideas were developed in the work of Franz Fanon, Edward Said and black nationalists in the United States. The post-colonial viewpoint proposes that knowledge is shaped by the perspectives of the social groups that produce it and that in a colonial context the power positions of colonisers and colonised shape their knowledge and consciousness. These relativist conclusions are shared with feminist theory and both post-modernism and post-structuralism, as is apparent in the recent works of Giyatri Spivak and Homi Bhaba.

Post-modernism

The term relates to a very diverse set of approaches that often seem to have very little in common with each other. The idea of the post-modern arose in art criticism to describe artistic trends opposed to the artistic modernism of the early twentieth century. A number of philosophers and social theorists held that similar considerations should apply to the 'modernist' theories of the classical sociologists and that contemporary social theory should have a distinctively post-modern character. For other writers, the post-modern is linked to the ideas of 'post-industrialism', 'post-capitalism' and the knowledge society – these are held to be the social changes responsible for the emergence of post-modern art and ideas. These arguments are connected in the otherwise dissimilar views of Jean-François Lyotard and Jean Baudrillard, who see the contemporary post-modern condition as involving plurality, diversity and relativity in knowledge. See **modernity**.

Post-structuralism

A reaction to the structuralism of Lévi-Strauss, post-structuralism emphasises that cultural codes and social structures are diverse and fragmentary. The approach developed in a number of intellectual fields, finding various forms of expression in Jacques Derrida, Jacques Lacan and Michel Foucault. These writers argue that texts and modes of discourse must be 'deconstructed' in order to uncover the contradictions and absences that structure them as cultural products. They hold that there is no reality independent of the textual and cultural constructions through which we come to know it. Foucault's work has had the greatest impact on sociology through his work on the development of prisons and penal regimes, of hospitals and medical regimes, and of sexuality and intimacy.

Psychoanalysis

This is an approach to socialisation that originated in the work of Sigmund Freud. His argument was that human behaviour is driven by unconscious drives and impulses – and, in particular, by sexual impulses. Normal human development, he argued, involves the building of psychological structures (the ego and the superego) that allow people to cope with their unconscious drives and to interact normally with others. Where these drives are repressed, they may make themselves felt, in disguised form, in dreams, jokes, slips of the tongue and hysterical symptoms. Freud's ideas were elaborated by orthodox Freudians, such as his daughter Anna, and by 'object relations' theorists influenced by Melanie Klein. Psychoanalysis remains an important basis for counselling and therapy, with significant divisions existing between Freudians and those influenced by Carl Jung. The work of Juliet Mitchell and Nancy Chodorow has integrated these concerns with feminist theory. Many have criticised Freud's reliance on biological models of human impulses, and psychoanalysts such as Erich Fromm and Karen Horney developed a stronger cultural orientation that brought them close to the socialisation theories of Parsons and structural functionalism.

Queer theory

Queer theory rejects the assumptions of heterosexuality and of the male/female gender divide that are seen as having dominated social theory until recently. It arose in response to the development of lesbian and gay studies, which it saw as in need of radicalisation through ideas taken from post-structuralism. Although Foucault's work is a major influence, the first statements of queer theory were Eve Sedgwick's *The Epistemology of the Closet* and Judith Butler's *Gender Trouble*. Butler argues that gender is 'performative', not fixed, and this leads her to see all sexual categories and identities as open, fluid and fractured.

Rational choice theory

This is an approach that draws on models from economics to understand all other forms of social action, which it sees as instrumentally rational and calculative. It can be found in the work of Gary Becker and James Coleman and in the 'exchange theory' of George Homans. See **rational action**.

Semiotics/semiology

The study of signs and symbols was given different labels by its founders – Charles Peirce called it semiotics and Ferdinand de Saussure called it semiology. This has emerged as one of the most important contemporary approaches to social theory. It achieved popularity with the rise of structuralism and found its most influential formulation in the work of Roland Barthes. Semiology approaches the study of social life from its cultural organisation through the use of signs that can be combined only according to certain rules or codes. Social activity is, therefore, 'encoded' and social theory, as much as social interaction, involves a 'decoding' of the cultural significance of observed actions. Social theory, therefore, is a process of interpretation in which the meanings of cultural signs are inferred from their use in power relations. Semiology prepared the way for the later arguments of post-structuralism.

Social Darwinism

Social Darwinism draws on the biological work of Charles Darwin to construct theories of social evolution. In some approaches this work is highly individualistic and seeks to explain social behaviour in terms of inherited 'instincts' and genetic responses. In contemporary theory this approach is represented by the biological reductionism found in sociobiology and evolutionary psychology. Other approaches have taken Darwin's emphasis on struggle and conflict to build a form of conflict theory in which the ethnic struggles of populations are the driving force in history. Many such theories have seen ethnic conflict in racial terms, arguing that ethnic groups are defined by their particular genetic inheritance and that social conflict is, therefore, a mechanism of genetic selection. While conflict theory itself remains important, its racial forms have now been discredited by advances in biological knowledge.

Structural functionalism

Structural functionalism is often seen as rooted in the work of Herbert Spencer and other theorists who took the organismic metaphor as the basis for social understanding. Arguing that societies could be seen as having 'organic' properties through which their constituent parts are bound together into a larger whole, these theorists sought to identify the function or contribution made by each part to the perpetuation of the whole. Alfred Radcliffe-Brown, who owed a great deal to the arguments of Durkheim, stressed the need to identify the key structures of a society and to investigate their interdependence. Bronislaw Malinowski placed more emphasis on the interdependence of traits within cultural wholes. Talcott Parsons was the leading figure in bringing these ideas to the centre of sociological attention, and structural functionalism was, through the middle years of the twentieth century, the mainstream approach to sociology in the United States. Parsons's later work presented system theory as the contemporary development of structural functionalism.

Structuralism

This was associated with the work of Claude Lévi-Strauss, which achieved great popularity in the 1960s and 1970s. Structuralism is an approach that seeks to uncover the structures that underlie and are responsible for the more immediately observable features of social interaction and social relations. It is structures such as modes of production, kinship systems and mythologies that explain the observable economic activities, marriage patterns and narrative accounts produced in a society. Lévi-Strauss argued that comparative investigation was essential if the common underlying structures were to be found. When Lévi-Strauss turned to the analysis of cultural structures, his argument came close to that of semiology.

Symbolic interactionism

This approach has its origins in the pragmatist philosophy and psychology of William James and its foundations were established by Charles Cooley and by George Mead. The name, however, was invented by Herbert Blumer in his commentaries on and interpretations of Mead's work. The key concern is with the interaction of individuals and the ways in which they construct meanings that define situations for them and so allow them to act in particular ways. These meanings and definitions are acquired through socialisation but are also actively created by the socialised individuals. Thus, interaction is a dynamic process of the creation, communication and elaboration of meaning. Contemporary work in symbolic interactionism includes that of Howard Becker and Erving Goffman, though each writer has also drawn on related theoretical approaches.

System theory

A development from structural functionalism that also drew on work in computing and cybernetics, where theorists were developing models of information systems. System theory highlights the structuring of societies into distinct and specialised subsystems – economies, polities, kinship systems, etc. – with varying degrees of autonomy. The focus of sociological attention is the interdependence and degree of equilibrium attained in the overall social system. Talcott Parsons depicted a flow or circulation of energy and information through subsystems and saw this as the means through which systems are able to adapt to their environments. Drawing on similar ideas to those that inspired neofunctionalism, Niklas Luhmann has developed a form of system theory in which ideas of self-regulation or 'autopoiesis' play a key part.

John Scott

The leading social theorists who figure in these and other theoretical traditions are discussed at greater length in two further volumes in the Routledge Key Guides Series, both edited by John Scott: *50 Key Sociologists: The Formative Theorists* and *50 Key Sociologists: The Contemporary Theorists.*

INDEX

Items in **bold** indicate main entries in the text or the glossary.